Early Praise for *Exploring Graphs with Elixir*

This book opens up and makes accessible a technology which few developers have used so far in creating cutting-edge products, especially in the Elixir world. It will help Elixir software developers understand better why graph technology is great, and how easy it is to use to build applications in ways they had never thought of before.

➤ **Dmitry Russ**
Lead Engineer, Appian Corporation

In Exploring Graphs with Elixir, Tony takes the reader through a hands-on journey with several major graph databases. While I had worked with a few already, the hands-on comparison across several provided a refreshing perspective. Enrich yourself by joining Tony on this journey and confidently tackle your next graph problem with ease.

➤ **David Swafford**
VP, Product Engineering, LynkState

I really like that this book gives such a full overview of contemporary ways of working with graphs. I have never read anything that brings all the different types of graphs together so comprehensively, and I feel that for this reason the book gives valuable insights even to people like myself who are not working with Elixir.

➤ **Tony Seale**
Developer, UBS

This book presents cutting-edge topics that will be of interest to developers working in the field and utilizing graph databases, and it is certain to be a very valuable resource.

➤ **Eoghan O'Donnell**
Senior Staff Engineer

Exploring Graphs with Elixir

Connect Data with Native Graph Libraries and Graph Databases

Tony Hammond

The Pragmatic Bookshelf

Raleigh, North Carolina

Many of the designations used by manufacturers and sellers to distinguish their products are claimed as trademarks. Where those designations appear in this book, and The Pragmatic Programmers, LLC was aware of a trademark claim, the designations have been printed in initial capital letters or in all capitals. The Pragmatic Starter Kit, The Pragmatic Programmer, Pragmatic Programming, Pragmatic Bookshelf, PragProg and the linking *g* device are trademarks of The Pragmatic Programmers, LLC.

Every precaution was taken in the preparation of this book. However, the publisher assumes no responsibility for errors or omissions, or for damages that may result from the use of information (including program listings) contained herein.

For our complete catalog of hands-on, practical, and Pragmatic content for software developers, please visit *https://pragprog.com*.

The team that produced this book includes:

CEO: Dave Rankin
COO: Janet Furlow
Managing Editor: Tammy Coron
Series Editor: Bruce A. Tate
Development Editor: Jacquelyn Carter
Copy Editor: Corina Lebegioara
Indexing: Potomac Indexing, LLC
Layout: Gilson Graphics
Founders: Andy Hunt and Dave Thomas

For sales, volume licensing, and support, please contact *support@pragprog.com*.

For international rights, please contact *rights@pragprog.com*.

ISBN-13: 978-1-68050-840-6
Book version: P1.0—November 2022

Contents

Part III — Graph to Graph

Acknowledgments

My beginning with this book, I suppose, was almost 30 years ago, in the sunshine, in Italy. I had just discovered the web and the graph of documents. Since then, I have been hooked. I don't think I had ever really focused on graphs much before that.

Then after a handful and more years, I got hooked again a second time with the semantic web. I had the good fortune to work on a number of linked data projects in my day job in science publishing over the next twenty years. And then when that run eventually came to an end, I was lucky enough to find the time to do some new learning, explore Elixir, and start working on this book.

For the last couple of years, I've been working for a new outfit to build out a knowledge graph. I've continued to learn still more with a whole new group of incredible colleagues while having competing demands on my time to finish this book. But now it's done.

My first callout is to Marcel Otto. When I was learning Elixir, I also wanted to see if I could apply it to any domain with which I was familiar. Was there any support in Elixir for graphs, especially RDF graphs? Marcel was there and had the whole thing covered with his wonderful set of Elixir packages (rdf, sparql, sparql_client, and json_ld). He has also been especially helpful to me both at the beginning of this trek and several times since in answering questions I have had.

I'd also like to thank the developers of the other Elixir packages I've used in this book. They all have taken the time to answer my questions: Paul Schoenfelder (libgraph), Florin Pătrașcu (bolt_sips), Barak Karavani (gremlex), and Dmitry Russ (dlex).

I didn't shop around for a publisher. I didn't have to. I only had The Pragmatic Bookshelf in my sights ever since they published the PickAxe Book. That book was such a joy to read. That publisher was the one for me.

As series editor, Bruce Tate has been really supportive in helping this book become a reality, believing in it, and helping me turn a bunch of blog posts into a more coherent package.

And then also my development editor Jackie Carter—what can I say? Maybe I should have listened to her from the outset. But then I had to learn for myself. She has kept me focused and helped me find a simpler, more direct voice. She has helped me turn my various writings into a book. She has stayed with me throughout this long haul.

And to all the other folks at The Pragmatic Bookshelf who have worked on this book. I can only mention a few names here: Michael Swaine who did an early review, Margaret Eldridge and Erica Sadun in publicity, Janet Furlow in operations, and Brian MacDonald as my acquisitions editor.

I especially need to thank all those who took the time to review the book and to provide heaps of feedback and constructive comments: Jesús Barrasa, Bob DuCharme, Victor Felder, Carlo Gilmar, Amos King, Carlos Krauss, Eoghan O'Donnell, Marcel Otto, Dmitry Russ, Tony Seale, Kim Shrier, Jason Stewart, Jo Stichbury, Alvise Susmel, David Swafford, and Dominique Vassard. You have all made this book so much better.

Other folks took time to answer questions I had along the way, in particular Bradley Fidler on ARPANET topology.

I'd also like to call out a couple of my former colleagues who acted as helpful sounding boards when I first started to work on the book: Azhar Jassal and Evangelos Theodoridis. Thank you, both. Your support was very much appreciated. And a special shoutout to Ilya Venger who hired me into my current gig on building an enterprise knowledge graph and who got to be such a graph enthusiast on the project.

Finally, I would like to thank my family who had to bear the burden of me talking about this book. I would especially like to thank my parents Peter and Elinor who started me out on my journey in life. I owe them so much.

And the very last words of thanks for being there go to my daughter Elsa, my son Ollie, and my grandchildren Corin and Juliet. You mean the world to me.

Introduction

This is a book about connections and disconnections. It's about graph data structures and Elixir. It's about distributed data and distributed compute. It's about the graph.

Graphs as an organizational pattern operate at all levels, from the smallest static structures—for example, chemical compounds such as a water molecule—to large-scale dynamic structures—for example, web-based social networks such as Facebook or Twitter. They allow us to link data points together with a minimum of fuss or overhead. As often noted, graphs lend themselves well to a schema-less style of data connection.

What kinds of graph models are there and how can we access them from our preferred language, Elixir? This is what we'll look to answer in this book. How easy is it to get started with graphs? How can we build native graph structures in Elixir? How can we query graph databases with Cypher, Gremlin, and GraphQL? How can we query linked open data with SPARQL?

We'll see how.

Graph structures are great at helping us connect data, but in practice, graphs tend to be disconnected from each other both physically in terms of location and conceptually in terms of a data model. We want to be able to move our graph data between graph models and graph databases. We want to straddle across different implementations.

We'll aim to get a better understanding of graph models and of Elixir packages that can be used to build graphs and query graph databases. We'll also see how we can use Elixir's support for concurrency in managing connected and distributed data.

Who This Book Is For

This book is directed primarily at the practicing Elixir programmer who wants to get a better understanding of the graph-processing landscape and see both what support already exists within Elixir and also what can be readily accessed from Elixir.

We'll be mainly interested in using graphs for creating and supporting information networks. The aim is more to move data around and work with, and across, different types of graph models rather than to explore graph algorithms per se. There are other resources for that. Here we want to focus on the graph models themselves and how we might bridge from one model to another.

The book works its way through developing a complete application and as such can be used as an Elixir learning aid. Some basic knowledge of Elixir is assumed, although the book proceeds at a gentle pace and will explain new concepts as they are encountered. The book will use a number of standard Elixir technologies:

- umbrella apps
- behaviours
- macros
- protocols
- OTP

The book may also be of interest to those who don't know Elixir but have some acquaintance with graphs and are curious to learn more about how the two main graph paradigms—property graphs and RDF graphs—intersect and the tooling to make them interoperate. In this case, the use of Elixir code examples throughout the book may be read as a kind of pseudocode.

How to Read This Book

The book is organized into three parts:

- Part I—Graphs Everywhere
- Part II—Getting to Grips with Graphs
- Part III—Graph to Graph

Part I will give a simple introduction to graphs and networks and then go on to set up the project that we will develop together. This entails creating an umbrella app and a common library app that will be used by the apps developed later.

We'll also spend a little time setting up project storage areas for graphs and queries for the various graph types and data structures for managing access to those areas. The goal of this exercise is to make it much simpler to reuse these components so that we can focus on graph manipulations rather than file operations.

Part II will be a hands-on investigation of a number of Elixir packages for working with graphs:

- libgraph
- bolt_sips
- rdf, sparql, sparql_query
- gremlex
- dlex

We'll first look at developing native graph models within Elixir and then look at applied graph models and interacting with graph databases. In this area, we'll look at the two main paradigms for modeling information networks: property graphs and RDF graphs.

We'll work with various graph types and their associated graph query languages and will introduce shorthand query forms to make querying simpler.

Part III will then look at moving between graphs, how we can transform graph models from one standard form to another, and how we can use Elixir's concurrent processing capabilities to manage distributed graphs and distributed compute.

That at least is the plan.

About the Code

The following conventions are followed in this book.

If something needs to be invoked on the command-line terminal, you'll see a $ sign preceding it in the text:

```
$ iex
Erlang/OTP 24 [erts-12.3.1] ...

Interactive Elixir (1.13.4) - press Ctrl+C to exit (type h() ENTER for help)
iex>
```

If something needs to be invoked from within the Elixir interactive shell IEx, you'll see a iex> sign preceding it in the text:

```
iex> g = Graph.new |> Graph.add_vertices([:a, :b])
```

Otherwise, if it's a source file listing, you'll usually see a file name banner:

```
apps/native_graph/lib/native_graph/builder.ex
def random_graph(limit) do
  for(n <- 1..limit, m <- (n + 1)..limit, do: do_evaluate(n, m))
  |> Enum.reject(&is_nil/1)
  |> Enum.reduce(
    Graph.new(),
```

```
    fn [rs, re], g ->
      Graph.add_edge(g, rs, re)
    end
  )
end
```

Some other conventions are also used.

While we follow the general convention to use pipes only for functions with multiple arguments, we do make an exception for query strings. Given the length of some of the query strings we will encounter, it seems more natural to pipe the query string into the query function instead of adding it as an argument:

```
iex> "MATCH p = ()-[*]->() RETURN DISTINCT length(p)" |> cypher!
[%{"length(p)" => 1}, %{"length(p)" => 2}, %{"length(p)" => 3}]
```

This also allows us to focus on the query itself and not the query function:

```
iex> """
...> {
...>   q(func: has(EX)) {
...>     uid
...>     EX { uid }
...>   }
...> }
...> """ |> dgraph!
  %{"q" => [%{"EX" => [%{"uid" => "0x4ebb"}], "uid" => "0x4eba"}]}
```

The emphasis in this book will mostly be on interactive exploration using IEx so certain practices are followed to simplify data entry and the number of keystrokes. For example, importing functions will be common so that we can reuse the same functions for different graph models, such as query_graph, read_graph, and others.

About the Software

To follow along with the book, you should have Elixir 1.10+ installed. The book will guide you through setting up an umbrella application for a graph test bed using a variety of graph databases. Instructions for installing the graph databases are given in an appendix.

This book was written in 2022, and the versions of the various software packages used in this book's development are listed in the table shown on page xv.

Software	Version Tested
Languages	
Elixir	1.13.4
Databases	
Dgraph	21.12.0
GraphDB Free	9.11.1
Gremlin Server	3.6.0
Neo4j Community Edition	4.4.5

Online Resources

The sample code for this book is available from the book page on the Pragmatic Programmers website.[1] You'll also find the errata-submission form there, where you can report problems with the text or make suggestions for future versions.

Tony Hammond
November 2022

---

1.   https://pragprog.com/titles/thgraphs

Part I

Graphs Everywhere

Graphs are simple data abstractions that lie behind networks of all stripes.

The graph provides the basic connection matrix, while the network maps the graph to a given subject domain and uses the wiring plan for its specific business goals.

Networks are found wherever distributed processes and systems occur and are used for all kinds of purposes. Yes, graphs are everywhere.

## CHAPTER 1

Engaging with Graphs

Graphs and graph databases are everywhere. This is no big surprise given that graphs can address the two main concerns we have in dealing with the huge volumes of data all around us—organization and scale. Differently from the more usual "buckets of data" or relational data approaches, graphs can bring both order and growth to data as data goes large. And they can do this both organically and holistically. This is what makes graphs such a fascinating field to work with.

As an organizational pattern, graphs operate at all levels from the smallest static structures, such as chemical compounds—think of a water molecule—to large-scale dynamic structures, such as web-based social networks—think Facebook or Twitter.

Graphs are especially useful in dealing with messy and irregular datasets and hard-to-fit data. They cope particularly well with sparse datasets. Unlike the relational model, with fixed tables optimized for transactional database requests, graphs tend to turn things on their head. Instead of dealing with objects as sets of relations and then attempting joins over these sets, it is the relationships between objects that become the chief organizing principle. It's all about the connections rather than the records. Schemas take a backseat—still incredibly useful but not overly restrictive. We have a much more fluid way to relate our data items.

With graphs, we are typically working with an open-world assumption and thus with partial knowledge. We can't conclude anything definite from missing data. Any missing data may arrive at any future time. This is in contrast to more familiar data models which commonly use a closed-world assumption where everything is known ahead of time and locked down. Those data models are predictable and provide solid guarantees about data integrity. The downside is that they are regimented.

More simply said, graphs are great at gluing pieces of data together.

Although graph data structures can connect data items, in practice graphs themselves tend to be disconnected from each other both physically in separate graph databases and conceptually in terms of data models. To move data between graphs, it helps to understand their respective data models and how we can transform data from one graph model to another.

In later chapters, we'll work with the different graph models and also look at graph transformations. The graph-to-graph problem is almost as challenging as the structured-data-to-graph (table or document to graph) problem.

So what's this book about then? Maybe this concept map (and yes, it's a graph) can assist in indicating some of the things we'll explore.

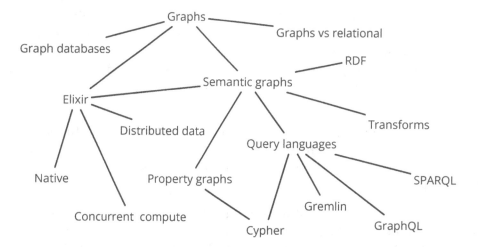

We'll deal with graphs as structures for organizing data at large. We'll see how we can use Elixir to process both database graphs and distributed graphs. We'll focus on the so-called "semantic" graphs—that is, graphs with an information-bearing capacity. We'll need to consider different graph models, what they provide, and how they can be related, and we'll need to work with different query languages. We'll cover all of these in this book.

First, let's look into what graphs actually are and also some common paradigms for graph models. In later chapters, we'll work with different graph packages in Elixir, but until then we can try our hand at building a graph with a library that ships with Elixir. To compare the different graph packages with their respective graph models, we'll need a reference graph model. We'll define one here so we can see how these graph models variously deal with this reference model.

First Contact

Before going further, let's establish some of the terms we'll be using in this book. First of all, when we talk about graphs, we obviously mean networks—not charts. Traditionally the term "graph" has referred to a diagram or plot of one quantity against another. This is the more widely understood sense of the term. But that's not our concern here. We'll use the term "graph" in its other sense of a data structure used to model relationships between things. That is, we have one set of things and another set of relationships between those things. Those two sets together constitute a graph. In its most general sense, a graph is a data model for relating a collection of things.

Network vs. Graph

We mentioned the word "network" before. This is the term used by network science as opposed to "graph," which is the preferred term used in graph theory, a branch of mathematics. A network is an engineering implementation of a graph. There are other differences too. A network is typically a dynamic system concerned with flows through a structure. A graph, on the other hand, is typically understood holistically as a static construct.

Vertex/Edge—What?

As noted, there are two components in a graph: things and relationships. In practice, you'll find many different terms for these graph building blocks:

vertex/edge
    terms used by graph theory, a formal theory in math

node/link
    terms used in network science theory

node/relationship
    terms used by the Neo4j graph database

node/arc
    terms used by the RDF graph data model

dot/line
    terms sometimes used in graph diagrams

object/arrow
    terms used by category theory, a foundational theory in math (a category is a graph with additional structure)

But it doesn't matter which terms we use. It's probably best to keep the *vertex/edge* pairing when dealing with graph theory topics and use the *node/link* pairing when talking about networks. In this book, however, we're going to use the terms *node* and *edge*, although we'll sometimes also use the term *vertex* for *node*.

Graph Models

Of course, there is more to all this than just nodes and edges. There are code libraries for modeling graphs and running graph algorithms. There are graph databases that implement particular graph models. It's important to establish now that there are two main graph models which are supported by graph databases: the property graph model, sometimes referred to as the labeled property graph, and the RDF model. The following table shows a direct feature comparison between these two graph models:

	Property Graph	RDF
sponsor	industry	W3C
standards	no	yes
field of origin	database	documents (web)
published	2007?	1999
strength	graph exploration	data integration
query language	Cypher, Gremlin	SPARQL
names	system	global (IRI)
annotations		
nodes	attributes	edges (with string nodes)
edges	attributes	—

This is obviously an oversimplification of the current position. For example, although property graphs are not standards-based, there is work ongoing to surface aspects of the model within various standards bodies. At the same time, there is the new development of RDF* (with SPARQL*), which seeks to close the gap between property graphs and RDF graphs by addressing the edge annotation problem.

But this is all getting ahead of ourselves. We'll look more closely at the different graph models as we explore the actual graph packages. And we haven't even seen a graph yet. So let's remedy that now.

Coding a Hello World Graph

As Elixir programmers, it's only natural to wonder what kind of support Elixir has for working with graph technologies. Quite a bit as it turns out. A growing number of Elixir graph packages have been in active development for some time now, and they are addressing all of the major graph types.

In this book, we're going to develop a project that will allow us to explore some of the main graph databases, graph query languages, and graph models. We'll also look at interchanging between graph types and transforming data from one to another.

But first, let's try something out of the box—no setup required.

Elixir comes with built-in graph support. We can use the Erlang library :digraph that ships with the Elixir distribution. Let's use this to string a couple of words together. Just fire up Elixir's interactive shell IEx from the command line:

```
$ iex
Erlang/OTP 24 [erts-12.3.1] ...

Interactive Elixir (1.13.4) - press Ctrl+C to exit (type h() ENTER for help)
iex>
```

Now that we're in IEx, import the :digraph library:

```
iex> import :digraph
:digraph

iex> g = new
{:digraph, #Reference<0.148244651.2766536707.134565>, ..., true}

iex> v1 = add_vertex(g, "Hello")
"Hello"

iex> v2 = add_vertex(g, "World")
"World"

iex> get_path(g, v1, v2)
false
```

So, here we created a couple of vertices and tried to get the path between them and, of course, we failed because we haven't yet defined any edges in our graph. Let's fix that and try again:

```
iex> add_edge(g, v1, v2)
[:"$e" | 0]

iex> get_path(g, v1, v2)
["Hello", "World"]
```

Ah, that's better. Our very first graph—a "Hello World" graph.

Modeling a Book Graph

We're going to explore different graph models in this book, so it might be handy to have a reference graph that we can use to gauge how each model behaves. Let's do that by creating a simple graph for a book catalog.

We'll start by populating our book graph with one book:

- *Adopting Elixir [Tat18]* by Ben Marx, José Valim, and Bruce Tate.

This simple exercise is meant to familiarize you with some basic semantic elements and later show you how these elements can be represented in the different graph models we'll encounter.

We can visualize our book graph in the following figure.

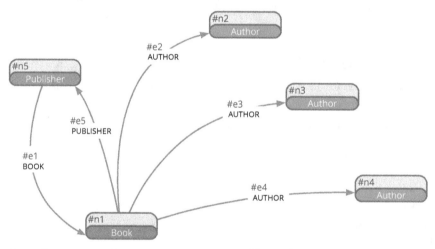

This is a diagrammatic representation. We'll see later how to represent this in the various graph models and how to query it.

This simple graph shows a small set of things and how they are related. The labels on the nodes (Author, Book, and Publisher) and edges (AUTHOR, BOOK, and PUB-LISHER) tell us what kinds of things are being related and how they are related. We've also added IDs for the nodes (such as #n1) and edges (such as #e1).

But this doesn't tell us much. There aren't any details.

What we'd like to do is to attach properties to the nodes and edges to better describe which book, author, and publisher they are relating to. Let's do that now. Let's add some properties to our book graph as shown in the figure on page 9.

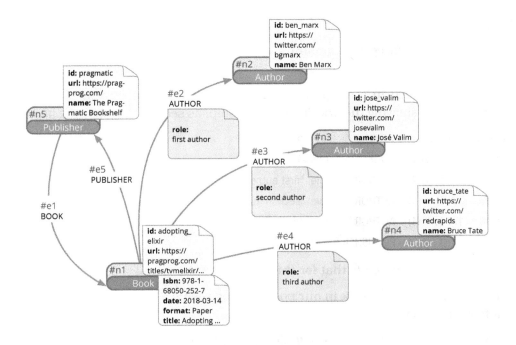

We've annotated our graph by adding some properties on the nodes to specify more precisely the things we're describing here. We've also added a property on some of the edges to qualify the relationships between those things.

Our book graph is now a semantic graph and carries information about the things it relates and the relationships between those things.

Let's dig in a little more.

Nodes

This simple graph relates five things: a Book node, three Author nodes, and a Publisher node. We've also added a minimal set of properties for each node, as shown in the following table.

Node	Type	Properties
#n1	Book	id: "adopting_elixir", url: "https://pragprog.com/titles/tvmelixir/adopting-elixir/", isbn: "978-1-68050-252-7", date: "2018-03-14", format: "Paper", title: "Adopting Elixir"
#n2	Author	id: "ben_marx", url: "https://twitter.com/bgmarx", name: "Ben Marx"
#n3	Author	id: "jose_valim", url: "https://twitter.com/josevalim", name: "José Valim"
#n4	Author	id: "bruce_tate", url: "https://twitter.com/redrapids", name: "Bruce Tate"
#n5	Publisher	id: "pragmatic", url: "https://pragprog.com/", name: "The Pragmatic Bookshelf"

Edges

We've created three relationships to relate the nodes: AUTHOR, BOOK, and PUBLISHER.

We've also added in a role property on the AUTHOR relationship with simple string values showing the priority of authorship, as seen in the following table.

Edge	Nodes	Type	Properties
#e1	(#n5, #n1)	BOOK	(none)
#e2	(#n1, #n2)	AUTHOR	role: "first author"
#e3	(#n1, #n3)	AUTHOR	role: "second author"
#e4	(#n1, #n4)	AUTHOR	role: "third author"
#e5	(#n1, #n5)	PUBLISHER	(none)

And that pretty much is that for this simple graph.

But having only one book in our book catalog seems a little stingy. Let's add a few more books:

- *Designing Elixir Systems with OTP [IT19]* by James Edward Gray, II and Bruce A. Tate.

- *Craft GraphQL APIs in Elixir with Absinthe [WW18]* by Bruce Williams and Ben Wilson.

- *Graph Algorithms [HN19]* by Amy Hodler and Mark Needham.

Now we have a fuller book graph as shown in the figure on page 11.

To make it easier this time to see the nodes and edges, we don't show the properties but label each node with its id property value.

Our Plan of Action

We have some options for how we might go about reviewing the various Elixir graph packages. We could treat them as separate things and talk about each of their idiosyncrasies. We could also focus on some real-world problems and see how each package might be able to support each particular use case. But that's not what we're going to do in this book.

We want to focus on the similarities—not the differences—between the various graph data models. We would like to have some of the following:

- an easy means to store graph queries and graph data
- an easy way to switch between different graph models
- an easy way to access different graph databases

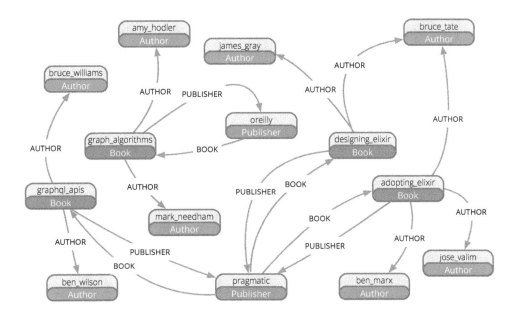

To do this, we're going to create a graph test bed application—a small laboratory—for testing and comparing graphs. In Elixir terms, this will be an umbrella app that is nothing more than a loose federation of related apps.

We'll describe how we build this app. In some places, we might go a little deep for an Elixir beginner. In other places, we'll belabor points that are probably well understood by more seasoned Elixir developers. Somewhere in the middle, we hope to offer something for everybody.

Wrapping Up

In this chapter, we've looked at graphs as a basic data structuring principle and considered how they compare to more familiar means of organizing data. Their open-data model and general flexibility are capabilities that are especially well suited to meeting the challenges posed by large and dispersed datasets.

We've introduced some common terms that we'll use in the book. We've contrasted the main graph models we'll be working with—property graphs and RDF graphs.

We've also used a built-in library to create our first graph—"Hello World." We then defined a simple book graph as a reference graph that we'll use later.

We're almost ready to start some coding. So let's set up an Elixir project and a common library that we'll use to build out our graph laboratory. We'll explore different graph models with this graph laboratory. We'll also use our book graph to see how that can be implemented with the different graph models we'll encounter.

## CHAPTER 2

Getting Started

In this book, we'll explore some of the graph packages that currently exist in the Elixir ecosystem, and we'll develop a set of applications to drill down into the various graph models. We'll build native Elixir graph models with the libgraph package, and we'll query remote graph databases of different flavors—property graphs with bolt_sips, RDF graphs with sparql_client, TinkerPop graphs with gremlex, and Dgraph graphs with dlex.

The overall plan is to get into some in-depth exploration of the individual graph models in Part II and then to see how they can interoperate in Part III. We'd like to make it super easy for you to work with different graph types, compare and contrast their data models, and see how they can be queried. Ideally, what we want is something like a graph playground that we can run from within an IEx session and that allows us to interact directly with the graphs.

We're going to build such a graph playground.

But we're going to need some organization first. We'll have to manage the code in our applications and the access to the data we're going to be working with.

In this chapter, you're going to create an Elixir umbrella app, which is a set of apps managed under a single container app. We'll use this as our code foundation for the book. We're going to be dealing with half a dozen or so separately managed apps.

The figure on page 14 shows the apps and data organizations and how they are related. The top half of the figure shows how the various apps are organized under the umbrella app and how they are introduced within the book. The bottom half of the figure shows how our graph data is managed and accessed both from a local graph store and via remote graph services. The graph stores are also shown in relation to their specific graph apps.

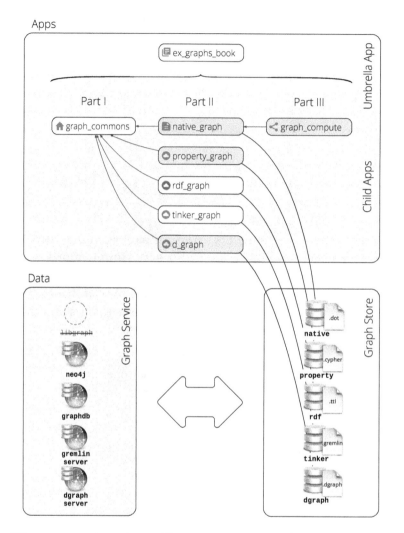

To simplify our experiments, we'll want to save graphs and queries for later reuse. We're going to build a graph store for managing these artifacts for the different graph types we'll be looking at. You'll first build some common data structures for saving graph queries and for serializing graphs. You'll also employ the use/__using__ macro pair to inject a set of generic read/write functions into the specific graph modules.

We'll also want to query the different graph types. But this means interacting with graph databases and graph libraries of different stripes. To make this simpler, we'll build up a set of graph services with a common interface. You'll be using the OTP behaviour pattern. You'll also learn how to install and run some common graph databases. Details for this will be given in the appendices.

General Project Outline

The project that we'll develop in this book falls into three main pieces: general setup, graph-specific apps, and graph applications.

In Part I of this book, we'll build a common library module graph_commons.

In Part II, we'll take an in-depth look at five separate Elixir graph packages (libgraph, bolt_sips, sparql_client, gremlex, and dlex), which we'll explore with a set of dedicated apps.

And then in Part III, we'll build a couple of graph applications that either reuse the existing apps or introduce new apps.

Essentially, we're dealing with two sets of apps plus a common library app. That's a lot of apps that we'll manage under a single umbrella app.

So let's set up our umbrella app and the common library app. We'll gradually introduce the other apps in the chapters to come.

Creating the Umbrella and Child Projects

We're going to start with some general project setups for organizing our code and data. For managing the code we'll use an umbrella app as this provides a simple but effective compromise when working with diverse packages within a single framework. On the data side, we'll separate out graph storage from graph services and use common interfaces for each of the graph models we'll consider.

We're going to do the following main project setups in this chapter, although we'll deal with specific service implementations in upcoming chapters:

Umbrella app
> We'll set up a modular app framework so that each of the separate graph projects we are going to create can be managed and related. We'll also add our first app—a library for common data structures.

Graph store
> We'll set up a common storage area for our graphs. This is for both storing example instances and queries for each separate graph type, as well as for imports and exports from other graph types.

Graph service
> We'll set up a common interface for graph services. These services will be provided by external databases. The one exception is for native Elixir graphs which have no service implementation.

So, let's get to it.

ExGraphsBook Umbrella

We're going to structure our code as an Elixir umbrella app. Let's call this umbrella project ExGraphsBook, which seems about right for an Elixir book on graphs. In Elixir, an umbrella app refers to a close-knit family of related apps which can be sourced together in a single repo, aka the "monorepo"[1] pattern. In essence, what we have is something like an app collective where apps loosely cooperate. This will allow us to follow a simple modular development as we initially progress through the early chapters and then move on to work across multiple apps in later chapters. We can consider the umbrella app as a parent app that manages a set of child apps.

At this point, we can set out the road map for this book. If you take another look at the previous diagram, you'll see the apps panel at the top with the umbrella app above and the child apps and their dependencies below. The diagram also shows the order of introducing the apps into the umbrella, that is in the left-to-right and top-to-bottom order, and how this order corresponds to the overall book organization. The shaded apps are supervised apps and have application callback modules. We'll discuss this more when we get to adding those apps.

For now, let's kick things off by creating the umbrella app itself.

ExGraphsBook Project Setup

See Appendix 1, Project Setups, on page 245, for details on retrieving a working project with code and data.

Switch to your Elixir projects directory and use Elixir's build tool Mix to create an umbrella app by using the mix new command with an --umbrella flag:

```
$ mix new ex_graphs_book --umbrella
```

You've just created a new ExGraphsBook project in the ex_graphs_book directory:

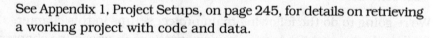

```
.
├── ex_graphs_book
```

Let's cd into the ex_graphs_book directory. You should have a project top-level directory structure that looks like this:

---

1. https://en.wikipedia.org/wiki/Monorepo

```
.
├── README.md
├── apps
├── config
│   └── config.exs
└── mix.exs
```

In an umbrella app, the project file mix.exs is largely empty and acts more as an organizer. It only contains a pointer apps_path to the apps directory:

mix.exs
```
def project do
  [
    apps_path: "apps",
    version: "0.1.0",
    start_permanent: Mix.env() == :prod,
    deps: deps()
  ]
end
```

We're ready now to begin adding apps to our umbrella.

GraphCommons Library

We want to build out a common storage area for saving graph experiments and define a common services API for querying test graphs. This is our rationale for developing a GraphCommons project.

You'll need to cd down into the apps directory. This is where we're going to create our first app—graph_commons.

So, without more ado, create a new project GraphCommons:

```
$ mix new graph_commons
```

Now we have our first app in the umbrella:

```
.
├── apps
│   └── graph_commons
```

Next, cd down into the graph_commons directory. Here we have the GraphCommons project top-level directory structure:

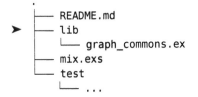

```
.
├── README.md
├── lib
│   └── graph_commons.ex
├── mix.exs
└── test
    └── ...
```

For the sake of brevity, we won't show any dependencies for documentation and testing in the projects we'll be creating in this book.

We're going to create a storage area in Creating a Storage Area, on page 25. For that, we are going to set up a priv directory in the GraphCommons project as our common holding area.

We'll need to somehow reference that location. Add this to the project config file config.exs in the config directory at the project top level:

```
config/config.exs
config :graph_commons, root_dir: File.cwd!
```

When we run IEx from the project directory, this will give us the current working directory and associate it with the graph_commons app which is where we will create our priv directory.

We can now read that location back in our GraphCommons module:

```
apps/graph_commons/lib/graph_commons.ex
@root_dir Application.fetch_env!(:graph_commons, :root_dir)
```

Let's also define a couple of functions for getting the locations of our apps and priv directories:

```
apps/graph_commons/lib/graph_commons.ex
def apps_dir(), do: @root_dir <> "/apps"
def priv_dir(), do: @root_dir <> "/apps/graph_commons/priv"
```

We'll use the priv_dir/0 function later.

We also want to add a space for tools. Create a new GraphCommons.Utils module, and then open up a new utils.ex file and place it under a lib/graph_commons directory:

```
lib
├── graph_commons
│   └── utils.ex
└── graph_commons.ex
```

Add the new module GraphCommons.Utils here:

```
defmodule GraphCommons.Utils do

  # ...

end
```

Now fetch and compile the dependencies with the following Mix calls:

```
$ mix deps.get; mix deps.compile
```

You'll need to run IEx with the project loaded as:

```
$ iex -S mix
Erlang/OTP 24 [erts-12.3.1] ...

Interactive Elixir (1.13.4) - press Ctrl+C to exit (type h() ENTER for help)
iex>
```

And now we're ready to start building out some structures to contain our graphs and graph queries.

Packaging Graphs and Queries

We're going to save our graph serializations and database queries in the graph store, and we'll need some data access properties to describe them. To keep things simple, let's say we're going to work with text-based formats only.

We'll want to encapsulate those graph and query serializations, along with the properties for accessing them, into data packages for transporting to and from the graph store. Essentially, we're building containers for the graphs and queries. We'll use structs for those data packages—one for graphs and one for queries.

So let's extend our module structure to add in a new module for a %GraphCommons.Graph{} struct to capture a graph serialization. We'll also add a module for a %GraphCommons.Query{} struct to capture a graph database query.

You'll need to cd back to the apps/graph_commons directory and create a file for each of the structs in the graph_commons directory under lib:

```
lib
├── graph_commons
➤   │   ├── graph.ex
➤   │   ├── query.ex
│   └── utils.ex
└── graph_commons.ex
```

Now we need to build the structs.

Graph Struct

Let's start with the graph struct %GraphCommons.Graph{} and define a new module GraphCommons.Graph:

```
defmodule GraphCommons.Graph do

  # ...

end
```

Then we add a @storage_dir attribute:

apps/graph_commons/lib/graph_commons/graph.ex
```
@storage_dir GraphCommons.storage_dir()
```

Note that we haven't defined the GraphCommons.storage_dir/0 function. That's coming up in Creating a Storage Area, on page 25.

Now add the following fields:

- :data—graph serialization
- :file—name of graph_file (within the graphs_dir)
- :type—graph type

For the actual storage we'll need an absolute path location on the filesystem, as well as an absolute URI for network access:

- :path—absolute path of graph_file
- :uri—absolute URI of graph_file

So we define this simply enough as:

apps/graph_commons/lib/graph_commons/graph.ex
```
@enforce_keys ~w[data file type]a
defstruct ~w[data file path type uri]a
```

We're using the sigil syntax ~w for bare words, and the modifier a marks these out as atoms.

We only enforce the user-supplied keys (:data, :file, and :type). The other two keys (:path and :uri) will be derived from the :file name and :type.

We'll also want a constructor—and note the guard which we'll need to define first:

apps/graph_commons/lib/graph_commons/graph.ex
```
def new(graph_data, graph_file, graph_type)
    when is_graph_type(graph_type) do
  graph_path = "#{@storage_dir}/#{graph_type}/graphs/#{graph_file}"

  %__MODULE__{
    # user
    data: graph_data,
    file: graph_file,
    type: graph_type,
    # system
    path: graph_path,
    uri: "file://" <> graph_path
  }
end
```

Here we've put the is_graph_type/1 guard in place to check the graph_type:

```
apps/graph_commons/lib/graph_commons/graph.ex
defguard is_graph_type(graph_type)
        when graph_type in [ :dgraph, :native, :property, :rdf, :tinker ]
```

We'll use the graph_type and graph_file args to build a graph_path and use that to populate the :path and :uri fields.

We haven't said anything yet about types for our struct. So let's define a type t for the struct as shown here:

```
apps/graph_commons/lib/graph_commons/graph.ex
@type graph_data :: String.t()
@type graph_file :: String.t()
@type graph_path :: String.t()
@type graph_type :: GraphCommons.graph_type()
@type graph_uri :: String.t()

@type t :: %__MODULE__{
        # user
        data: graph_data,
        file: graph_file,
        type: graph_type,
        # system
        path: graph_path,
        uri: graph_uri
      }
```

We've set the various fields as strings apart from the graph_type which is restricted to the GraphCommons.graph_type() types (:dgraph, :native, :property, :rdf, and :tinker). We need to add these types too:

```
apps/graph_commons/lib/graph_commons.ex
@type base_type :: :dgraph | :native | :property | :rdf | :tinker
@type graph_type :: base_type()
@type query_type :: base_type()

@type file_test :: :dir? | :regular? | :exists?
```

To check the graph_type we can use the IEx helper t/1:

```
iex> t GraphCommons.graph_type
@type graph_type() :: base_type()
```

```
iex> t GraphCommons.base_type
@type base_type() :: :dgraph | :native |:property | :rdf | :tinker
```

```
Types for graph storage.
```

Query Struct

Next, let's turn to our query struct %GraphCommons.Query{}. This will be a direct analog to the %GraphCommons.Graph{} struct in its own module GraphCommons.Query:

```
defmodule GraphCommons.Query do

  # ...

end
```

Since there is no real difference between the two modules other than replacing the term "query" for "graph" everywhere, we won't go through this here, but you can always check the code listings—see Appendix 1, Project Setups, on page 245.

By the way, we're using a separate struct for queries because some graph models maintain a clear distinction between serialization and query language. For example, RDF has many serializations—we're using Turtle (or .ttl) here—while SPARQL has its own representations for query (.rq) and update (.ru). By contrast, property graphs may use the same Cypher representation for both serialization and query.

Inspecting the Structs

So, let's try out the %GraphCommons.Graph{} struct by creating a new graph. We'll use a property graph model example here which generates a minimal graph with two nodes and one edge between them. (We'll look at querying property graphs in more detail in Chapter 5, Navigating Graphs with Neo4j, on page 71.)

The simple example shown in the figure will serve as our default graph.

We can create this simple graph with the Cypher string:

```
CREATE (a)-[:EX]->(b)
```

If we use the new/3 constructor, we'll get a presentation for the struct that looks something like this (but here the :path and :uri fields are truncated for legibility):

```
iex> "CREATE (a)-[:EX]->(b)" |>
...> GraphCommons.Graph.new("test.cypher", :property)
%GraphCommons.Graph{
```

```
    data: "CREATE (a)-[:EX]->(b)",
    file: "test.cypher",
    path: ".../graph_commons/priv/storage/property/graphs/test.cypher",
    type: :property,
    uri: "file:///.../graph_commons/priv/storage/property/graphs/test.cypher"
}
```

Frankly, that's not too smart because now we're exposing the :path and :uri fields which are implementation-dependent, that is they depend on where our project is installed and on which Mix environment we are using.

We could hide the :path and :uri fields by deriving the Inspect protocol and hiding those fields:

apps/graph_commons/lib/graph_commons/graph.ex
```
@derive {Inspect, except: [:path, :uri]}
```

This yields the following presentation:

```
iex> "CREATE (a)-[:EX]->(b)" |>
...> GraphCommons.Graph.new("test.cypher", :property)
#GraphCommons.Graph<
  data: "CREATE (a)-[:EX]->(b)",
  file: "test.cypher",
  type: :property,
  ...
>
```

It's better, but we still have a problem. We're going to be showing the full graph serialization, which may be rather large, in the :data field. Ideally, we want to see a snippet of the graph serialization.

Let's define a more user-friendly view for use with inspect:

apps/graph_commons/lib/graph_commons/graph.ex
```
Line 1  defimpl Inspect, for: __MODULE__ do
   -      @slice 16
   -      @quote <<?">>
   -
   5    def inspect(%GraphCommons.Graph{} = graph, _opts) do
   -        type = graph.type
   -        file = @quote <> graph.file <> @quote
   -
   -        str =
  10          graph.data
   -          |> String.replace("\n", "\\n")
   -          |> String.replace(@quote, "\\" <> @quote)
   -          |> String.slice(0, @slice)
   -
  15        data =
   -          case String.length(str) < @slice do
```

```
   -           true -> @quote <> str <> @quote
   -           false -> @quote <> str <> "..." <> @quote
   -         end
20
   -       "#GraphCommons.Graph<type: #{type}, file: #{file}, data: #{data}>"
   -     end
 - end
```

We'll restrict our view to the :type, :file, and :data fields with an Inspect protocol implementation. We'll also truncate the graph serialization to a small number of chars (16 here, but we could also make this configurable) so that a string representation of the whole struct can be shown on a single line. For that, we'll need to escape any newlines and quote chars. And we'll also show an ellipsis for any truncation.

We've done several interesting things here. On line 2 we've set @slice as our string truncation length, and on line 3 we've set @quote as <<?">>, or the bit-string for a double quote (") char. We escape newlines at line 11 and double quotes at line 12 before the actual truncation at line 13. We test at line 16 whether to add an ellipsis. Our struct representation for display with inspect is shown at line 21.

So let's try this:

```
iex> "CREATE (a)-[:EX]->(b)" |>
...> GraphCommons.Graph.new("test.cypher", :property)
#GraphCommons.Graph<type: property, file: "...", data: "CREATE (a)-[:EX]...">
```

That's much better. We only have an overview and no system-related info.

The code listings in this book will always use an ellipsis for the :file field value so the presentation fits the book's display width. The code will still display the filename.

One thing to mention in passing is that the order of the fields is inverted in the new/3 constructor and the inspect display. This is because we want to be able to pipe the :data field to the constructor although it seems more logical in the display to present it last.

Building a Graph Store

It's time to look at persistence.

We're going to work with graphs of various types. We'll want a place to store the graphs that we create and another place to source example graphs. We'll also want to save the selected queries for the various graph types, each of which has its own query language.

In short, we'll want a graph store. Let's build one.

Creating a Storage Area

You're going to set up a storage area in the usual place we use for bundling a project's static files—the priv directory. First, create a new directory priv:

```
.
├── README.md
├── lib
│   └── ...
├── mix.exs
➤ ├── priv
└── test
    └── ...
```

Here's the file organization we'll create under priv:

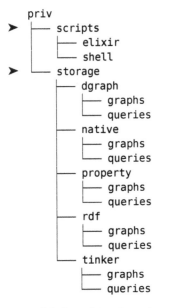

```
priv
➤ ├── scripts
│   ├── elixir
│   └── shell
➤ └── storage
    ├── dgraph
    │   ├── graphs
    │   └── queries
    ├── native
    │   ├── graphs
    │   └── queries
    ├── property
    │   ├── graphs
    │   └── queries
    ├── rdf
    │   ├── graphs
    │   └── queries
    └── tinker
        ├── graphs
        └── queries
```

Add that directory tree now:

```
$ mkdir -p \
> priv/scripts/{elixir,shell} \
> priv/storage/{dgraph,native,property,rdf,tinker}/{graphs,queries}
```

We're going to use the priv directory of this project as our common holding area. Under the priv directory, we'll partition two trees (scripts and storage) and define a couple of functions for key access points (scripts_dir/0 and storage_dir/0).

Now add some definitions to lib/graph_commons.ex:

```
apps/graph_commons/lib/graph_commons.ex
def scripts_dir(), do: priv_dir() <> "/scripts"
def storage_dir(), do: priv_dir() <> "/storage"
```

And import the GraphCommons module in our IEx startup file .iex.exs:

```
$ cat .iex.exs
import GraphCommons
```

If you don't already have a .iex.exs file, you may want to create one now as this is read in when IEx is started and is useful to set defaults.

Good. We've created a storage area—somewhere to save our graphs and queries. All we need now is to define a mechanism for reading and writing to this area.

Storing Graphs and Queries

So far, we've created data structs for transporting graphs and queries and carved out a directory tree for storing graphs and queries. We'll want to define a simple API for reading and writing from the structs to the graph store.

The following figure diagrams out a couple of data flows to and from the graph store.

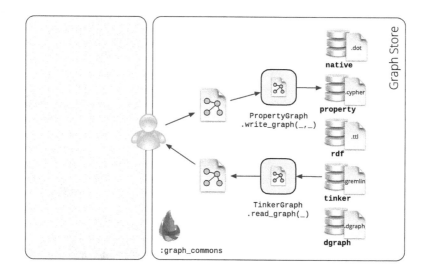

Here you can see two specific calls to the graph store—write_graph/2 and read_graph/1 for the PropertyGraph and TnkerGraph modules, respectively.

Reading and Writing

We've already defined our %GraphCommon.Graph{} struct for graph serializations. We only need some read/write functions to create new instances of the struct and to read/write a file.

So, add now a simple read_graph/2 function for reading a graph_file of graph_type:

apps/graph_commons/lib/graph_commons/graph.ex
```
def read_graph(graph_file, graph_type)
    when graph_file != "" and is_graph_type(graph_type) do
  graphs_dir = "#{@storage_dir}/#{graph_type}/graphs/"
  graph_data = File.read!(graphs_dir <> graph_file)

  new(graph_data, graph_file, graph_type)
end
```

Note that we have a guard clause which tests that the graph_file arg is non-empty and the graph_type is a valid graph type.

We'll add a corresponding write_graph/3 function for writing graph_data to a graph_file of graph_type:

apps/graph_commons/lib/graph_commons/graph.ex
```
def write_graph(graph_data, graph_file, graph_type)
    when graph_data != "" and
         graph_file != "" and is_graph_type(graph_type) do
  graphs_dir = "#{@storage_dir}/#{graph_type}/graphs/"
  File.write!(graphs_dir <> graph_file, graph_data)

  new(graph_data, graph_file, graph_type)
end
```

We have the same guard clause as before, but this time, we're also testing that the graph_data arg is non-empty.

In practice, we'll be calling these functions with lower-arity wrappers—the graph_type will be made implicit. We'll see examples later of how we'll define wrappers for these functions.

We'll also define a read_query/2 and a write_query/3 function pair.

Listing

We still need something more. We need to be able to get listings of the graphs and queries we're saving. And we'll also want to be able to access graphs and queries within any directories that we may add manually to our store.

Let's start with graphs—queries will be treated the same.

First, add a file_test type. We'll use this to select directories or regular file types:

apps/graph_commons/lib/graph_commons/graph.ex
```
@type file_test :: GraphCommons.file_test()
```

And we can check that with the IEx helper t/1:

```
iex> t GraphCommons.file_test
@type file_test() :: :dir? | :regular? | :exists?

Type for testing file types.
```

We're going to define the function pair list_graphs/2 and list_graphs_dir/3. As with the read/write functions, these will generally be accessed via lower-arity wrappers.

The list_graphs/2 function calls list_graphs_dir/3 with an empty graph_file arg:

apps/graph_commons/lib/graph_commons/graph.ex
```
def list_graphs(graph_type, file_test \\ :exists?) do
  list_graphs_dir("", graph_type, file_test)
end
```

The list_graphs_dir/3 function is our main listing function:

apps/graph_commons/lib/graph_commons/graph.ex
```
def list_graphs_dir(graph_file, graph_type, file_test \\ :exists?) do
  path = "#{@storage_dir}/#{graph_type}/graphs/"

  (path <> graph_file)
  |> File.ls!()
  |> do_filter(path, file_test)
  |> Enum.sort()
  |> Enum.map(fn f ->
    File.dir?(path <> f)
    |> case do
      true -> "#{String.upcase(f)}"
      false -> f
    end
  end)
end
```

This takes a graph_file arg in case we want to access directories or regular files only. The graph_type arg will be passed by the wrapper functions. The optional arg file_test allows for filtering.

After listing, filtering, and sorting, the file list is scanned, and directories are mapped in uppercase to better distinguish them from regular files.

The private do_filter/3 function filters the file list:

apps/graph_commons/lib/graph_commons/graph.ex
```
defp do_filter(files, path, file_test) do
  files
  |> Enum.filter(fn f ->
```

```
    case file_test do
      :dir? -> File.dir?(path <> f)
      :regular? -> File.regular?(path <> f)
      :exists? -> true
    end
  end)
end
```

File filtering is based on the file_test arg which takes values :dir? for directories and :regular? for regular files. Otherwise, the default :exists? keyword applies, and all files (both directories and regular files) will be returned.

This brings the graph store development to an end. We can turn now to the graph service component.

Defining a Graph Service API

Now let's look at querying graphs.

The graph databases we'll look at have web interfaces and support CRUD operations[2] on graphs in their own graph stores. They all have their own APIs and data representations, which can be a bit of a burden when switching between these services.

Let's define a common interface for these graph services. We can use the OTP behaviour pattern to define a set of callbacks which will be implemented by any module that adopts this behaviour. This allows us to define a graph service contract—an API.

We're looking to create a simple interface with the following operations:

- graph_create/1
- graph_read/0
- graph_update/1
- graph_delete/0

And to these we'll add an optional callback if supported by the service:

- graph_info/0

To be properly useful, graph databases also generally support a query interface so that subgraphs and individual data elements of the stored graphs can be returned. For that, we'll want to have a couple of query service callbacks for both simple and parametrized queries (queries plus parameters):

---

2. https://en.wikipedia.org/wiki/Create,_read,_update_and_delete

- query_graph/1
- query_graph/2

For interactive querying, it'll be handy to have a couple of bang-style callbacks which return a result value directly instead of being wrapped in a tuple:

- query_graph!/1
- query_graph!/2

The following figure diagrams out the data flows for a couple of graph API calls on the graph service.

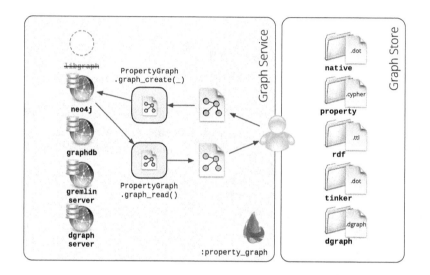

Here you can see graph_create/1 and graph_read/0 calls from the PropertyGraph module which implements the GraphCommons.Service behaviour.

By the way, the first graph type we'll explore in the next chapter uses the libgraph package which encodes graphs natively in Elixir. There is no corresponding graph database for this type, so we won't be able to create a graph service for it.

Let's create a new GraphCommons.Service module. Open up a new service.ex file and place it under the lib/graph_commons directory:

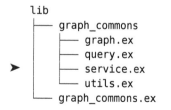

```
lib
├── graph_commons
│   ├── graph.ex
│   ├── query.ex
│   ├── service.ex
│   └── utils.ex
└── graph_commons.ex
```

We need to list out our service callbacks that take a function head with a typespec signature and no body:

```
apps/graph_commons/lib/graph_commons/service.ex
defmodule GraphCommons.Service do

  @optional_callbacks graph_info: 0
  @optional_callbacks query_graph: 2
  @optional_callbacks query_graph!: 2

  ## GRAPH
  @callback graph_create(GraphCommons.Graph.t()) :: any()
  @callback graph_delete() :: any()
  @callback graph_info() :: any()
  @callback graph_read() :: any()
  @callback graph_update(GraphCommons.Graph.t()) :: any()

  ## QUERY
  @callback query_graph(GraphCommons.Query.t()) :: any()
  @callback query_graph!(GraphCommons.Query.t()) :: any()
  @callback query_graph(GraphCommons.Query.t(), map()) :: any()
  @callback query_graph!(GraphCommons.Query.t(), map()) :: any()

end
```

The typespec attribute @optional_callbacks lists graph_info/0 graph_query/2 and graph_query!/2 as optional callbacks.

Note that we'll define callback modules for the specific graph types as we come to deal with each type in the chapters ahead.

One more thing. We'll define a GraphInfo struct for our service to return information about the graph held in the service, and we'll locate that under the GraphCommons.Service module. So create a new directory service under graph_commons and add a graph_info.ex file:

```
lib
├── graph_commons
│   ├── graph.ex
│   ├── query.ex
│   ├── service
│   │   └── graph_info.ex
│   ├── service.ex
│   └── utils.ex
└── graph_commons.ex
```

Now that we have that, add the GraphInfo struct:

```
apps/graph_commons/lib/graph_commons/service/graph_info.ex
defmodule GraphCommons.Service.GraphInfo do

  defstruct ~w[type file num_nodes num_edges labels]a

  @type t :: %__MODULE__{
```

```
      type: :dgraph | :native | :property | :rdf | :tinker,
      file: String.t(),
      num_nodes: integer,
      num_edges: integer,
      labels: list
    }
end
```

That's it. We've got our groundwork all set.

Wrapping Up

This chapter has all been about setting up a simple graph playground so that we can explore different graph types and pass easily between one type and another. Our focus in this book will be on accessing graphs and graph data irrespective of the underlying graph model.

We've organized our code by creating an umbrella project for this book, ExGraphsBook, and also created a first child project, the GraphCommons library.

We've organized our data by creating a graph store. We've built this with the following components: dedicated structs for annotating our graphs and queries, a file directory tree for storing the raw data structures, and functions for reading, writing, and listing them.

We've also created an Elixir behaviour for a graph service interface. We'll be implementing this service interface later for the various graph types we'll encounter.

We're ready to build some new projects to add to the umbrella, which we'll use for exploring the graph models themselves. This will be our focus in Part II, coming up.

Part II

Getting to Grips with Graphs

Elixir packages are on hand for dealing with native graph data structures, as well as for interacting with local and remote graph databases.

Graph databases also have their own graph models and organizations.

Let's dig into some of these packages now as we work our way through the various graph models.

## CHAPTER 3

Managing Graphs Natively with Elixir

We now have some structures in place for code and data organization, and we've set up an umbrella app. We also have some common infrastructure for storing graphs and queries and a common service interface for serving graphs. We're more than ready to begin exploring graphs.

Before we start experimenting with graph databases for property and RDF graphs in the chapters to come, we're first going to see how to represent graph data structures natively in Elixir using a native data model. With graph databases, we'll be more concerned with sending queries and retrieving result sets. Here, though, we'll have immediate access to the graphs themselves.

As we work with graph data structures natively in Elixir, we'll use the libgraph[1] package by Paul Schoenfelder[2]. We'll start with a quick introduction to the libgraph package by checking out some graph basics.

Next, we'll show how to extend our graph store API with the use/__using__ macro pair which will allow us to inject GraphCommons.Graph read/write functions into specific graph modules. And with that covered, we'll discuss a couple of routes to visualizing libgraph graphs and some issues regarding labeling.

But first, we'll create a new project specifically for managing our work with native graphs.

Creating the NativeGraph Project

To support working with the libgraph package, we're going to create the NativeGraph project which will provide us with an environment for running a dedicated graph store.

---

1. https://hex.pm/packages/libgraph
2. https://twitter.com/gotbones

NativeGraph Project Setup

See Appendix 1, Project Setups, on page 245, for details on retrieving a working project with code and data.

The libgraph project page[3] provides a rationale for why this package was developed. It addresses a number of shortcomings in the Erlang module digraph[4] (see Coding a Hello World Graph, on page 7) regarding performance and extensibility. Moreover, it provides an idiomatic Elixir API for manipulating graphs which allows functions to be pipelined by passing along a Graph struct as their first parameter.

Let's cd down into the apps directory of our ExGraphsBook project (see ExGraphsBook Umbrella, on page 16) and create a new project NativeGraph:

```
$ mix new native_graph
```

You should now have an apps directory that looks like this:

```
.
├── apps
│   ├── graph_commons
│   └── native_graph
```

Now let's cd into the native_graph directory:

```
.
├── lib
│   └── native_graph.ex
├── mix.exs
├── test
│   └── ...
```

And add some dependencies to mix.exs:

```elixir
apps/native_graph/mix.exs
defp deps do
  [
    # graph_commons
    {:graph_commons, in_umbrella: true},

    # native graphs
    {:libgraph, "~> 0.13"}
  ]
end
```

---

3.   https://github.com/bitwalker/libgraph
4.   http://erlang.org/doc/man/digraph.html

Besides the dependency on :libgraph, note that we also have a dependency on :graph_commons, which is one of our umbrella apps, so we use the :in_umbrella keyword and set it to true.

We'll fetch and compile the dependencies as usual:

```
$ mix deps.get; mix deps.compile
...
```

A quick word on graphs. We could risk creating some confusion here because we now have two Graph modules in play:

• Graph—a native graph data structure
• GraphCommons.Graph—a struct for serialized graph data access

We'll always make clear which kind of graph we're working with at any time, and we'll tend to use letters (for example, g) for Graph structs, and words (for example, graph) for GraphCommons.Graph structs.

Later we'll also encounter a couple more Graph modules. In Chapter 8, Querying RDF with SPARQL, on page 143, we'll introduce the RDF.Graph module which describes a set of RDF triples. In this case, though, RDF.Graph datasets will typically be invoked through wrapper functions. And in Chapter 9, Traversing Graphs with Gremlin, on page 163, we'll introduce the Gremlex.Graph module for traversing graphs.

Basic Workout

Let's first give the libgraph package a simple workout just to kick the tires.

As previously noted, the libgraph package uses the Graph module as its base namespace. This module defines a graph data structure, which supports directed and undirected graphs, in both acyclic and cyclic forms. It also defines the API for creating, manipulating, and querying that structure.

Directed Graph

Let's cd back to our ExGraphsBook root and open up IEx:

```
$ iex -S mix
```

Create a new directed graph:

```
iex> g = Graph.new
#Graph<type: directed, vertices: [], edges: []>
```

Note that this is of type directed by default.

We can inspect the graph with the info/1 function:

```
iex> Graph.info(g)
%{num_edges: 0, num_vertices: 0, size_in_bytes: 312, type: :directed}
```

It's empty, of course.

So add a couple of nodes, :a and :b, like this:

```
iex> g = Graph.add_vertex(g, :a)
#Graph<type: directed, vertices: [:a], edges: []>

iex> g = Graph.add_vertex(g, :b)
#Graph<type: directed, vertices: [:a, :b], edges: []>
```

Or do this in one line by piping:

```
iex> g = Graph.new |> Graph.add_vertices([:a, :b])
#Graph<type: directed, vertices: [:a, :b], edges: []>
```

What's in a Node?

The libgraph package allows any Elixir term to be used for vertices—simple or structured. Our initial experiments will use simple forms for nodes, although we'll see a case later in Using Maps for Nodes, on page 64, of using structured forms for nodes.

As we'll often be referring to nodes in query strings, it's generally going to be more straightforward to use atoms or integers in simple forms rather than using strings, which would need to be quoted.

Also, note that since libgraph requires nodes to be created with an Elixir term as a value, there is no notion of an empty node.

We add labels ("foo", "bar", and "baz") to the vertices again by piping:

```
iex> g = (g |> Graph.label_vertex(:a, ["foo"]) |>
...> Graph.label_vertex(:b, ["bar", "baz"]))
#Graph<type: directed, vertices: [:a, :b], edges: []>
```

Let's check those labels:

```
iex> Graph.vertex_labels(g, :a)
["foo"]

iex> Graph.vertex_labels(g, :b)
["bar", "baz"]
```

Note that vertex labels aren't shown in Graph string forms even if we can access them with the vertex_labels/2 function. But we can still see them if we want by inspecting the %Graph{} struct as a map:

```
iex> IO.inspect g, structs: false
%{
  __struct__: Graph,
  edges: %{},
  in_edges: %{},
  out_edges: %{},
  type: :directed,
  vertex_labels: %{97 => ["foo"], 98 => ["bar", "baz"]},
  vertices: %{97 => :a, 98 => :b}
}
#Graph<type: directed, vertices: [:a, :b], edges: []>
```

Now create a labeled edge (:EX) between those two nodes:

```
iex> g = Graph.add_edge(g, :a, :b, label: "EX")
#Graph<type: directed, vertices: [:a, :b], edges: [:a -[EX]-> :b]>
```

Use the info/1 function to inspect:

```
iex> Graph.info(g)
%{num_edges: 1, num_vertices: 2, size_in_bytes: 800, type: :directed}
```

Now let's look at that %Graph{} struct again:

```
iex> IO.inspect g, structs: false
%{
  __struct__: Graph,
  edges: %{{97, 98} => %{"EX" => 1}},
  in_edges: %{98 => %{__struct__: MapSet, map: %{97 => []}, version: 2}},
  out_edges: %{97 => %{__struct__: MapSet, map: %{98 => []}, version: 2}},
  type: :directed,
  vertex_labels: %{97 => ["foo"], 98 => ["bar", "baz"]},
  vertices: %{97 => :a, 98 => :b}
}
#Graph<type: directed, vertices: [:a, :b], edges: [:a -[EX]-> :b]>
```

We can get at both the vertices and the edges:

```
iex> Graph.vertices(g)
[:a, :b]

iex> Graph.edges(g)
[%Graph.Edge{label: :EX, v1: :a, v2: :b, weight: 1}]
```

We can also get counts of the vertices and edges:

```
iex> Graph.num_vertices(g)
2

iex> Graph.num_edges(g)
1
```

Note that we don't have to create nodes explicitly if they are connected by edges because the add_edge functions will create any nodes required. So we could create a one-edge graph (with two nodes) as:

```
iex> Graph.new |> Graph.add_edge(:a, :b, label: :EX)
#Graph<type: directed, vertices: [:a, :b], edges: [:a -[EX]-> :b]>
```

This is our default graph, which we saw before in Inspecting the Structs, on page 22.

Undirected Graph

For undirected graphs, we'll need to explicitly set the type as undirected like this:

```
iex> Graph.new(type: :undirected) |> Graph.add_edge(:a, :b, label: :EX)
#Graph<type: undirected, vertices: [:a, :b], edges: [:a <-[EX]-> :b]>
```

Note that this graph is of type undirected and that the edge arrows point both ways.

This graph (like the previous default graph) is unlabeled—that is, the nodes aren't labeled.

There's much more to the Graph module. For a quick overview, use the IEx auto-complete feature for listing module functions.[5] It's enough to enter the module name followed by a . char (for example, Graph.) and then press the Tab key:

```
iex> Graph.[TAB]
Directed                Edge                    EdgeSpecificationError
Pathfinding             Reducer                 Reducers
Serializer              Serializers             Utils
a_star/4                add_edge/2              add_edge/3
add_edge/4              add_edges/2             add_vertex/2
add_vertex/3            add_vertices/2          arborescence_root/1
...
```

You can then inspect any given function with the h/1 IEx helper:

```
iex> h Graph.is_acyclic?

  def is_acyclic?(g)

  @spec is_acyclic?(t()) :: boolean()

delegate_to: Graph.Directed.is_acyclic?/1

Returns true if and only if the graph g is acyclic.
```

Alternatively, you can always go to the libgraph API reference docs.[6]

---

5. https://hexdocs.pm/iex/IEx.html
6. https://hexdocs.pm/libgraph/Graph.html

Storing Graphs in the Graph Store

It's fine to enter the graph data interactively, but it can get a little tiresome after a while. We'd rather read our graphs back from a filestore, so we'll need to be able to write the graphs out to some text format—that is, to serialize the graph data structures—for disk-based storage.

The libgraph package includes two serialization functions in the Graph module: to_dot/1 and to_edgelist/1. The former renders the graph using the well-known DOT format from the Graphviz[7] distribution, while the latter is a plaintext rendering of graph edges suitable for using with graph libraries such as the igraph[8] library.

We'll work with the DOT format here as this is a common serialization used by many software packages for visualizing graphs. Essentially, the DOT format provides a text-based language specification for laying out graphs.

We've already defined the read_graph/2 and write_graph/3 functions in our GraphCommons.Graph module in Storing Graphs and Queries, on page 26. All we need to do here is provide simple wrappers, read_graph/1 and write_graph/2, in the NativeGraph module which will implicitly pass a :native atom for the graph_type field. That means that our generic read/write functions will be specific to this graph type (:native) so that we'll read/write to the correct bin in the storage area.

The read_graph/1 function takes a single argument—the graph_file to read:

```
def read_graph(graph_file), do:
    GraphCommons.Graph.read_graph(graph_file, :native)
```

And the write_graph/2 function works similarly:

```
def write_graph(graph_data, graph_file), do:
    GraphCommons.Graph.write_graph(graph_data, graph_file, :native)
```

Well, this isn't too bad.

At least it seems like that until we realize that we also need to add these functions for the other graph types. And we haven't added in the listing functions yet. We'll also want to do the same for queries and graphs. Let's not forget there are type @spec directives and doc strings we need to add in too. So, in all, a *lot* of duplication.

There must be a better way.

---

7. https://www.graphviz.org/
8. https://igraph.org/

There is. We can use macros to generate the functions for us on demand for a specific graph type and to pull those into the graph type module.

Here's how.

Using Macros

The idea is to build these wrapper functions in the common library and inject them into the particular graph type library. We'll use the _using_/1 macro for this, which will be called by the use/2 macro.

Let's outline this first for the common graph module GraphCommons.Graph. (We'll handle the common query module GraphCommons.Query in the same way.)

Here's our graph type library module, which has a use/2 macro for the common graph module GraphCommons.Graph:

```
defmodule NativeGraph do
  use GraphCommons.Graph, graph_type: :native, graph_module: __MODULE__

  # ...

end
```

This also passes the keyword pair graph_type: :native.

And here's the common graph module GraphCommons.Graph, which defines a _using_/1 macro and passes in the options using the opts keyword list:

```
defmodule GraphCommons.Graph do

  defmacro __using__(opts) do
    graph_type = Keyword.get(opts, :graph_type)
    graph_module = Keyword.get(opts, :graph_module)

    quote do

      # ...

    end

  end

end
```

From this, we can recover the :graph_type using Keyword.get/2. This is ready for use within the quote/2 block.

It's in the quote/2 block that the real magic happens. The quote/2 macro produces a quoted expression, in essence, something like an AST (abstract syntax tree) of the Elixir code. This allows us the opportunity to manipulate the code at the elemental, building block level. To escape this quoted expression, we use the unquote/1 macro. So here we can add in the graph_type keyword that we passed back from the calling module.

So, in our commons library we have this:

```
apps/graph_commons/lib/graph_commons/graph.ex
defmacro __using__(opts) do
  graph_type = Keyword.get(opts, :graph_type)
  graph_module = Keyword.get(opts, :graph_module)

  quote do

    ## TYPES

    @type graph_file_test :: GraphCommons.file_test()

    @type graph_data :: GraphCommons.Graph.graph_data()
    @type graph_file :: GraphCommons.Graph.graph_file()
    @type graph_path :: GraphCommons.Graph.graph_path()
    @type graph_type :: GraphCommons.Graph.graph_type()
    @type graph_uri :: GraphCommons.Graph.graph_uri()

    @type graph_t :: GraphCommons.Graph.t()

    ## FUNCTIONS

    def graph_context(), do: unquote(graph_module)

    def list_graphs(graph_file_test \\ :exists?),
      do: GraphCommons.Graph.list_graphs(
        unquote(graph_type), graph_file_test)

    def list_graphs_dir(dir, graph_file_test \\ :exists?),
      do: GraphCommons.Graph.list_graphs_dir(dir,
        unquote(graph_type), graph_file_test)

    def new_graph(graph_data), do: new_graph(graph_data, "")

    def new_graph(graph_data, graph_file),
      do: GraphCommons.Graph.new(graph_data, graph_file,
        unquote(graph_type))

    def read_graph(graph_file),
      do: GraphCommons.Graph.read_graph(graph_file,
        unquote(graph_type))

    def write_graph(graph_data, graph_file),
      do: GraphCommons.Graph.write_graph(graph_data, graph_file,
        unquote(graph_type))
  end
end
```

We also have an equivalent macro for queries in the GraphCommons.Query module with query substituted for graph everywhere.

apps/graph_commons/lib/graph_commons/query.ex

```elixir
defmacro __using__(opts) do
  query_type = Keyword.get(opts, :query_type)
  query_module = Keyword.get(opts, :query_module)

  quote do

    ## TYPES

    @type query_file_test :: GraphCommons.file_test()

    @type query_data :: GraphCommons.Query.query_data()
    @type query_file :: GraphCommons.Query.query_file()
    @type query_path :: GraphCommons.Query.query_path()
    @type query_type :: GraphCommons.Query.query_type()
    @type query_uri :: GraphCommons.Query.query_uri()

    @type query_t :: GraphCommons.Query.t()

    ## FUNCTIONS

    def query_context(), do: unquote(query_module)

    def list_queries(query_file_test \\ :exists?),
      do: GraphCommons.Query.list_queries(
        unquote(query_type), query_file_test)

    def list_queries_dir(dir, query_file_test \\ :exists?),
      do: GraphCommons.Query.list_queries_dir(dir,
        unquote(query_type), query_file_test)

    def new_query(query_data), do: new_query(query_data, "")

    def new_query(query_data, query_file),
      do: GraphCommons.Query.new(query_data, query_file,
        unquote(query_type))

    def read_query(query_file),
      do: GraphCommons.Query.read_query(query_file,
        unquote(query_type))

    def write_query(query_data, query_file),
      do: GraphCommons.Query.write_query(query_data, query_file,
        unquote(query_type))
  end
end
```

So in the graph type library module, we have these two use/2 macros:

apps/native_graph/lib/native_graph.ex

```elixir
use GraphCommons.Graph, graph_type: :native, graph_module: __MODULE__
use GraphCommons.Query, query_type: :native, query_module: __MODULE__
```

From those two macros alone, all these functions get added to the NativeGraph module. This includes the listings functions which we haven't seen here. You can see this with the IEx autocomplete feature:

```
iex> NativeGraph.[TAB]
...
list_graphs/0          list_graphs/1          list_graphs_dir/1
list_graphs_dir/2      list_queries/0         list_queries/1
list_queries_dir/1     list_queries_dir/2     new_graph/1
new_graph/2            new_query/1            new_query/2
read_graph/1          read_query/1            write_graph/2
write_query/2
```

Well, that's a handsome haul for a couple of simple use/2 macro calls. And that's just the graph functions shown here—we also have a parallel set of query functions.

Note that the type @spec directives and doc strings for the functions aren't shown here. Also, to keep things working smoothly in the receiving module, a lot of @type directives are added in the quote block.

The following figure shows roughly what's happening.

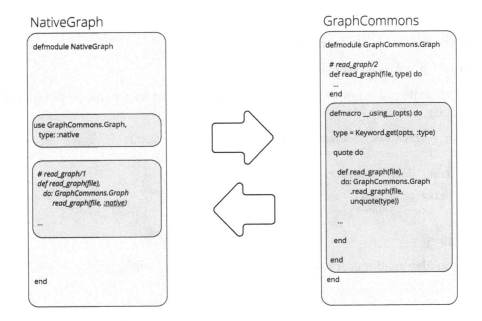

With the use/2 macro call, the NativeGraph module creates new functions defined by the __using__/1 macro in the GraphCommons.Graph module, and those functions are effectively customized for the NativeGraph module.

Writing

So, let's try this out now.

We'll import the functions we just added to the NativeGraph module so that we can drop the NativeGraph. prefix when calling these functions:

```
iex> import NativeGraph
```

If we want to persist this across IEx sessions, we can also add it to our IEx config file .iex.exs.

We already have our graphs folder, but let's say we want to create a couple of subfolders under that—for example, dot for DOT files, and images for PNG files.

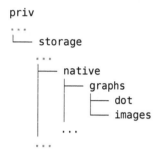

```
priv
...
└── storage
    ...
    ├── native
    │   ├── graphs
    │   │   ├── dot
    │   │   └── images
    │   ...
    ...
```

Let's create those directories now:

```
$ mkdir -p priv/storage/native/graphs/{dot,images}
```

We can write out a graph serialization in DOT format to a default.dot file in our dot folder:

```
iex> g = Graph.new |> Graph.add_edge(:a, :b, label: "EX")
#Graph<type: directed, vertices: [:a, :b], edges: [:a -[EX]-> :b]>

iex> {:ok, dot} = Graph.to_dot(g)

iex> write_graph(dot, "dot/default.dot")
#GraphCommons.Graph<type: native, file: "...", data: "strict digraph {...">
```

Reading

We can also read a graph serialization back in from a file:

```
iex> graph = read_graph("dot/default.dot")
#GraphCommons.Graph<type: native, file: "...", data: "strict digraph {...">
```

And we can print out the graph data:

```
iex> IO.puts graph.data
strict digraph {
    "a"
    "b"
    "a" -> "b" [label="EX"; weight=1]
}
:ok
```

And if we had a deserializer we could read that back into an Elixir Graph data structure. Unfortunately, the libgraph library stops short at this point—it allows us to serialize only. So, effectively, we can publish graphs but we can't consume graphs. Reader exercise, anyone?

One way around this impasse to reading graphs back in, at least for the purpose of this book, is to add a module to our NativeGraph library that provides some basic example graphs. Let's do that now:

```
defmodule NativeGraph.Examples do

  # ...

end
```

We can then extend this as required.

Listing

If we want to get a file listing, we can call the list_graphs/1 function where the file_test argument is optional:

```
iex> list_graphs
[..., "default.graph", "DOT", "IMAGES", ...]
```

This lists all files—both regular files and directories—and capitalizes the directory names. In this case, we've manually added an images/ directory.

To list regular files only, we can pass in the file_test argument :regular?:

```
iex> list_graphs(:regular?)
[..., "default.graph", ...]
```

To list directories only, we can pass in the file_test argument :dir?:

```
iex> list_graphs(:dir?)
[..., "DOT", "IMAGES", ...]
```

Visualizing Graphs

To render these DOT files, we can use either the Graphviz tools or a generic drawing package such as OmniGraffle for the Mac or the GraphVizio plugin for Visio on Windows. Let's look at rendering with Graphviz and also with OmniGraffle.

Rendering with Graphviz

Graphviz[9] is an open-source graph visualization software developed by AT&T Labs which is distributed with various layout programs. If you don't already have this installed, you can get a copy from the Graphviz download page.[10]

Graphviz ships with a number of tools for rendering DOT files. Typically, these are installed into /usr/local/bin on a Unix platform, but you need to check your own system for details of where they are located.

Now we can call the appropriate Graphviz tool from Elixir by using the System.cmd/3 function. Let's create a new module Format and put that under NativeGraph, and we'll add the function to_png/1 :

apps/native_graph/lib/native_graph/format.ex
```
@graph_images_dir GraphCommons.storage_dir() <> "/native/graphs/images/"
@dot_exe "/usr/local/bin/dot"

def to_png(%GraphCommons.Graph{} = graph) do
  dot_file = graph.path
  png_file = @graph_images_dir <> Path.basename(dot_file, ".dot") <> ".png"

  with {_, 0} <-
         System.cmd(@dot_exe, ["-T", "png", dot_file, "-o", png_file]) do
    {:ok, Path.basename(png_file)}
  else
    _ -> {:error, "! Error"}
  end
end
```

This function takes a %GraphCommons.Graph struct which wraps a DOT file.

The dot_file is read from the graph.path, and the png_file name is derived from this.

The System.cmd calls the installed Graphviz tool and passes command args as a list of strings as usual. For confirmation, the png_file name is returned.

To make this more accessible, we'll also add a delegate function to the Native-Graph module, so we can call Format.to_png/1 more simply as write_image/1:

apps/native_graph/lib/native_graph.ex
```
defdelegate write_image(arg), to: NativeGraph.Format, as: :to_png
```

Let's try it out. For better graph management, note that we've manually added the dot/ and images/ directories in our graph store:

```
iex> g = Graph.new |> Graph.add_edge(:a, :b, label: :EX)
#Graph<type: directed, vertices: [:a, :b], edges: [:a -[EX]-> :b]>
```

---

9. https://www.graphviz.org/
10. https://www.graphviz.org/download/

```
iex> {:ok, dot} = Graph.to_dot(g)
{:ok,
 "strict digraph {\n    \"a\"\n    \"b\"\n    \"a\" -> \"b\" [label=\"EX\";
weight=1]\n}\n"}
iex> write_graph(dot, "dot/default.dot")
#GraphCommons.Graph<type: native, file: "...", data: "strict digraph {...">

iex> write_image read_graph("dot/default.dot")
{:ok, "default.png"}

iex> list_graphs_dir("images")
[..., "default.png", ...]
```

And here's the image saved in default.png:

Now let's try another example graph, this time one with two edges. For this, we'll pick the chemical description for the water molecule—H_2O. This is an example of an undirected, labeled graph:

```
iex> g = Graph.new(type: :undirected) |>
...> Graph.add_vertex(:h1, "H") |>
...> Graph.add_vertex(:h2, "H") |>
...> Graph.add_vertex(:o, "O") |>
...> Graph.add_edge(:o, :h1) |>
...> Graph.add_edge(:o, :h2)
```

Let's generate a DOT file for this and save it to our graph store:

```
iex> {:ok, dot} = Graph.to_dot(g)

iex> write_graph(dot, "dot/h2o.dot")
#GraphCommons.Graph<type: native, file: "...", data: "strict graph {\n...">

iex> IO.puts read_graph("dot/h2o.dot").data
strict graph {
    "O"
    "H"
    "H"
    "H" -- "O" [weight=1]
    "H" -- "O" [weight=1]
}

:ok
```

We can check that this dot/h2o.dot file was indeed saved:

```
iex> list_graphs_dir("dot")
[..., "h2o.dot", ...]
```

Now we can read this DOT graph and pass it to the write_image/1 function:

```
iex> write_image read_graph("dot/h2o.dot")
{:ok, "h2o.png"}
```

This is the image that is saved in h2o.png:

What? Well, there's something clearly not right here. We have only two nodes instead of the three we were expecting to see. We were expecting a water molecule—H_2O—and ended up with a hydroxyl radical—OH—instead!

It turns out that the DOT serializer in libgraph uses the node label to name the node in the DOT serialization, instead of using the actual node term provided. But the label isn't guaranteed to be unique and here it is not unique. We have two nodes with labels "H". Compare this graph with the previous default graph where no node label properties were present.

Let's patch this for now in our project and push ahead. We've copied the Graph.Serializer[11] and Graph.Serializers.DOT[12] modules as NativeGraph.Serializer and NativeGraph.Serializers.DOT, respectively, and made some changes to preserve the node term, even if a label is present. Check the code listings for the changed versions in Appendix 1, Project Setups, on page 245.

Now we can provide our own version of to_dot/1 and to_dot!/1 under NativeGraph:

apps/native_graph/lib/native_graph.ex
```
defdelegate to_dot(arg), to: NativeGraph.Serializers.DOT, as: :serialize
defdelegate to_dot!(arg), to: NativeGraph.Serializers.DOT, as: :serialize!
```

So we can try this NativeGraph version of to_dot/1:

```
iex> {:ok, dot} = NativeGraph.to_dot(g)

iex> write_graph(dot, "dot/h2o.dot")
#GraphCommons.Graph<type: native, file: "...", data: "strict graph {\n...">

iex> IO.puts read_graph("dot/h2o.dot").data
strict graph {
    "o" [label="O"]
```

---

11. https://github.com/bitwalker/libgraph/blob/main/lib/graph/serializer.ex
12. https://github.com/bitwalker/libgraph/blob/main/lib/graph/serializers/dot.ex

```
    "h1" [label="H"]
    "h2" [label="H"]
    "h1" -- "o" [weight=1]
    "h2" -- "o" [weight=1]
}

:ok
```

That DOT description already looks better. We can now generate a PNG image from it as before:

Much better.

Rendering with OmniGraffle

A number of drawing tools can import DOT format files. OmniGraffle[13] for the Mac is one such package that allows for greater control over the presentation form. (Another tool is the GraphVizio[14] plugin for Visio on Windows, although I haven't yet tried that.)

In fact, OmniGraffle can open DOT files directly, which will bring up a Dot Import pop-up menu with some layout options—Hierarchical, Force-Directed, Circular, and Radial. Choose one and afterward visit the Canvas sidebar and scoot down to the Diagram Layout and Style panel. There you can uncheck the Auto layout button to allow the graph shape to be rearranged. You can also change the Layout option you selected on opening the file.

For a more interesting graph to render, let's anticipate an actual network graph we'll be querying later with Cypher in Recalling the ARPANET, on page 105—Arpanet (1969). We'll add a libgraph version of this as one of our example graphs.

First, we'll create a module for Arpanet examples:

```
defmodule NativeGraph.Examples.Arpa do

  # ...

end
```

Let's add in an arpa/0 function to define the graph:

---

13. https://www.omnigroup.com/omnigraffle/
14. http://www.calvert.ch/graphvizio/

apps/native_graph/lib/native_graph/examples/arpa.ex

```elixir
def arpa do
  ## GRAPH

  g = Graph.new(type: :undirected)

  ## SEGMENT 1 - Outer Circuit (Clockwise from UCLA to SRI)

  # Site: UCLA
  g =
    g
    |> Graph.add_vertex(:ucla, "UCLA")
    |> Graph.add_vertex(:ucla_h1, "SIGMA7")
    |> Graph.add_edge(:ucla_h1, :ucla)

  # Site: UCSB
  g =
    g
    |> Graph.add_vertex(:ucsb, "UCSB")
    |> Graph.add_vertex(:ucsb_h1, "360")
    |> Graph.add_edge(:ucsb_h1, :ucsb)

  # Site: SRI
  g =
    g
    |> Graph.add_vertex(:sri, "SRI")
    |> Graph.add_vertex(:sri_h1, "940")
    |> Graph.add_edge(:sri_h1, :sri)

  ##
  ## SEGMENT 2 - Inner Path (Right from SRI to UTAH)

  # Site: UTAH
  g =
    g
    |> Graph.add_vertex(:utah, "UTAH")
    |> Graph.add_vertex(:utah_h1, "PDP-10")
    |> Graph.add_edge(:utah_h1, :utah)

  ##
  ## NETWORK (3+1=4)

  g =
    g
    ## SEGMENT 1 - Outer Circuit (Clockwise from UCLA to SRI)
    |> Graph.add_edge(:ucla, :ucsb)
    |> Graph.add_edge(:ucsb, :sri)
    |> Graph.add_edge(:sri, :ucla)
    ## SEGMENT 2 - Inner Path (Right from SRI to UTAH)
    |> Graph.add_edge(:sri, :utah)

  # add reversed edges
  g =
    g
    |> Graph.edges()
```

```
    |> Enum.reduce(g, fn %{v1: v1, v2: v2, label: label} = _e, g ->
      Graph.add_edge(g, v2, v1, label: label)
    end)
  g
end
```

One thing to note in this example is that even though we've declared the graph to be of type :undirected we still need to explicitly add in reverse edges if we want to traverse the graph in either direction. That's what the last section here does.

We can use this example as follows:

```
iex> arpa = NativeGraph.Examples.Arpa.arpa
#Graph<type: undirected, vertices: [:sri, :ucla, :ucsb, :utah, :sri_h1,
  ...
 :utah_h1]>
iex> {:ok, dot} = Graph.to_dot(arpa)
{:ok,
 "strict graph {\n    \"SRI\"\n    \"UCLA\"\n    \"UCSB\"\n    \"UTAH\"\n
  ...
 [weight=1]\n    \"UTAH\" -- \"PDP-10\" [weight=1]\n}\n"}
iex> write_graph(dot, "dot/arpa.dot")
#GraphCommons.Graph<type: native, file: "...", data: "strict graph {\n...">
```

We can open this DOT file directly in OmniGraffle and edit it as shown in the following figure.

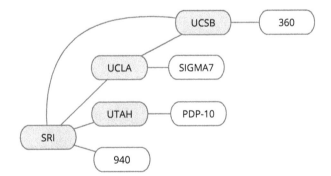

If you have problems importing the files—see the DOT Serialization warning here—you'll need to edit the DOT file for the ";" char. The NativeGraph patch for the to_dot/1 function already fixes this.

A DOT Serialization Gotcha

There is a small bug in the libgraph serializer for DOT. The serializer currently writes out a ";" char separator between edge attributes, whereas according to the published grammar for DOT (see Appendix D in the *Drawing graphs with dot*[15] guide) the separator should either be a "," char separator or be empty.

Apparently, this isn't problematic for the dot command-line tool but does cause OmniGraffle to complain, requiring a hand edit.

Wrapping Up

We've seen in this chapter how we can use Elixir to build native graph data structures using the libgraph package.

We started with some graph basics. Then we looked at how to serialize libgraph graphs and how we can use macros to simplify building wrapper functions to our GraphCommons functions for working with stored graphs and queries.

We next looked at how to visualize these graphs by using the DOT serializer and either converting them to PNG format for display or importing them into a drawing program for further elaboration.

We'll carry on with our native graph explorations in the next chapter using our book graph model.

---

15. https://graphviz.gitlab.io/_pages/pdf/dotguide.pdf

## CHAPTER 4

Exploring Graph Structures

In this chapter, we'll explore some graph structures with the libgraph package.

We'll work first with the book graph, an example graph that has been created in the libgraph format, and then see how to model our basic book graph building block using the libgraph library package.

We'll also build a simple graph generator to demonstrate using synthetic data.

So let's start by exploring a real example graph that is modeled using libgraph.

A Worked Example

It's time to get in some practice with an extended workout with a real graph to see what we can discover about it when using the libgraph package. This will give us a sense of the completeness of libgraph as a graph library.

As an initial worked example, we'll add the book graph to our library examples. This example will be helpful because of its small size and because we can get a simple visualization of the complete graph.

We'll start off by creating a module for the book example:

```
defmodule NativeGraph.Examples.Book do

  # ...

end
```

Next, we'll create the example graph. Because we'll want to retrieve either one book or all books, let's create two public entry points: book/1 (for one book) and books/1 (for all books), which both call the private function do_books/2. The public functions implicitly pass the first arg (all_books?) in do_books/2 which will select either one book or all books.

```
apps/native_graph/lib/native_graph/examples/book.ex
def book(use_id? \\ true), do: do_books(false, use_id?)
def books(use_id? \\ true), do: do_books(true, use_id?)
```

Here's the skeleton code for do_books/2:

```
defp do_books(all_books?, use_id?) do
  # function to select id/map based on use_id? setting
  val = fn map -> if use_id?, do: map.id, else: map end

  # book 1
  bk1 = val.(%{ id: :adopting_elixir, ... })
  ...

  # book 2
  bk2 = val.(%{ id: :graphql_apis, ... })
  ...

  # book 3
  bk3 = val.(%{ id: :designing_elixir, ... })
  ...

  # book 4
  bk4 = val.(%{ id: :graph_algorithms, ... })
  ...

  # build graph
  g =
    Graph.new(type: :directed)
    #
    |> Graph.add_vertex(bk1, "Book")
    ...

  g =
    if all_books? do
      g
      |> Graph.add_vertex(bk2, "Book")
      ...
      #
      |> Graph.add_vertex(bk3, "Book")
      ...
      #
      |> Graph.add_vertex(bk4, "Book")
      ...
    else
      g
    end

  g
end
```

The use_id? parameter which is passed to do_books/2 sets an anonymous function to return either the id element from a map or the map itself. This will be used for the vertex identifier.

Let's take this book node as an example:

```
bk1 =
  val.(%{
    id: :adopting_elixir,
    date: "2018-03-14",
    format: "Paper",
    isbn: "978-1-68050-252-7",
    title: "Adopting Elixir",
    url: "https://pragprog.com/titles/tvmelixir/adopting-elixir/"
  })
```

If we call book(true), for example, we'll get this for our book node:

```
bk1 = :adopting_elixir
```

If, on the other hand, we call book(false) we'll get this for our book node:

```
bk1 = %{
    id: :adopting_elixir,
    date: "2018-03-14",
    format: "Paper",
    isbn: "978-1-68050-252-7",
    title: "Adopting Elixir",
    url: "https://pragprog.com/titles/tvmelixir/adopting-elixir/"
  }
```

We'll look at what this all means in the next section, Modeling the Book Graph, on page 61, but for now, it's enough to know we have a graph with a number of nodes and that these nodes are by default identified simply by Elixir atoms, but can also be identified with Elixir maps.

The next section will give you enough code to build the do_books/2 function to support the book/1 function. You'll have to consult the code listings to get the full implementation of the books/1 function.

That said, let's now see the books/1 function in action:

```
iex> g = NativeGraph.Examples.Book.books
#Graph<type: directed, vertices: [:graph_algorithms, :graphql_apis,
 :mark_needham, :adopting_elixir, :amy_hodler, :oreilly, :ben_wilson,
 :bruce_williams, :pragmatic, :bruce_tate, :designing_elixir, :jose_valim,
 :ben_marx,
 :james_gray], edges: [:graph_algorithms -[AUTHOR]-> :mark_needham,
 :graph_algorithms -[AUTHOR]-> :amy_hodler, :graph_algorithms -[PUBLISHER]->
 :oreilly, :graphql_apis -[AUTHOR]-> :ben_wilson, :graphql_apis -[AUTHOR]->
 :bruce_williams, :graphql_apis -[PUBLISHER]-> :pragmatic, :adopting_elixir
 [PUBLISHER]-> :pragmatic, :adopting_elixir -[AUTHOR]-> :bruce_tate,
 :adopting_elixir -[AUTHOR]-> :jose_valim, :adopting_elixir -[AUTHOR]->
 :ben_marx, :oreilly -[BOOK]-> :graph_algorithms, :pragmatic -[BOOK]->
 :graphql_apis, :pragmatic -[BOOK]-> :adopting_elixir, :pragmatic -[BOOK]->
```

```
:designing_elixir, :designing_elixir -[PUBLISHER]-> :pragmatic,
:designing_elixir -[AUTHOR]-> :bruce_tate, :designing_elixir -[AUTHOR]
:james_gray]>
```

Now let's check that we have a valid graph model:

```
iex> Graph.vertices(g)
[:graph_algorithms, :graphql_apis, :mark_needham, :adopting_elixir,
 :amy_hodler, :oreilly, :ben_wilson, :bruce_williams, :pragmatic,
 :bruce_tate, :designing_elixir, :jose_valim, :ben_marx, :james_gray]
iex> Graph.edges(g)
[
  %Graph.Edge{
    label: "AUTHOR",
    v1: :graph_algorithms,
    v2: :mark_needham,
    weight: 1
  },
  ...
]
```

Before going further, let's serialize the graph as a DOT file, which we'll import into OmniGraffle and prettify:

```
iex> {:ok, dot} = Graph.to_dot(g)
iex> write_graph(dot, "dot/books.dot")
#GraphCommons.Graph<type: native, file: "...", data: "strict digraph {...">
```

The following figure shows what we can do with OmniGraffle.

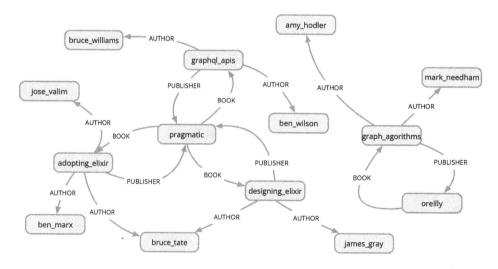

We can now begin exploring.

What are the neighbors of the node :pragmatic?

```
iex> Graph.neighbors(g, :pragmatic)
[:graphql_apis, :adopting_elixir, :designing_elixir]
```

What are the out-edges from the node :pragmatic?

```
iex> Graph.out_edges(g, :pragmatic)
[
  %Graph.Edge{
    label: "BOOK",
    v1: :pragmatic,
    v2: :graphql_apis,
    weight: 1
  },
  %Graph.Edge{
    label: "BOOK",
    v1: :pragmatic,
    v2: :adopting_elixir,
    weight: 1
  },
  %Graph.Edge{
    label: "BOOK",
    v1: :pragmatic,
    v2: :designing_elixir,
    weight: 1
  }
]
```

So, there are three as confirmed by the out-degree:

```
iex> Graph.out_degree(g, :pragmatic)
3
```

And what are the in-edges to the node :pragmatic, then?

```
iex> Graph.in_edges(g, :pragmatic)
[
  %Graph.Edge{
    label: "PUBLISHER",
    v1: :graphql_apis,
    v2: :pragmatic,
    weight: 1
  },
  %Graph.Edge{
    label: "PUBLISHER",
    v1: :adopting_elixir,
    v2: :pragmatic,
    weight: 1
  },
  %Graph.Edge{
    label: "PUBLISHER",
```

```
      v1: :designing_elixir,
      v2: :pragmatic,
      weight: 1
  }
]
```

Again, three. As confirmed by the in-degree:

```
iex> Graph.in_degree(g, :pragmatic)
3
```

Let's look at some paths. How many paths are between the node :pragmatic and the node :bruce_tate?

```
iex> Graph.get_paths(g, :pragmatic, :bruce_tate)
[
  [:pragmatic, :designing_elixir, :bruce_tate],
  [:pragmatic, :adopting_elixir, :bruce_tate]
]
```

Well, that's two.

Both paths are the same length. So if we aim to get the shortest path, we'll get one of these paths randomly:

```
iex> Graph.get_shortest_path(g, :pragmatic, :bruce_tate)
[:pragmatic, :adopting_elixir, :bruce_tate]
```

And there are no paths between the node :pragmatic and the node :bruce_tate with the edges reversed:

```
iex> g |> Graph.transpose |> Graph.get_paths(:pragmatic, :bruce_tate)
[]
```

But what about the overall structure?

```
iex> Graph.components(g)
[
  [:bruce_williams, :ben_wilson, :ben_marx, :jose_valim, :james_gray,
   :designing_elixir, :bruce_tate, :adopting_elixir, :pragmatic,
   :graphql_apis],
  [:amy_hodler, :mark_needham, :oreilly, :graph_algorithms]
]
```

So, libgraph clearly identifies the two islands we saw in the previous graph figure which correspond to different publishers.

We can extract one of those islands from graph g as subgraph g1:

```
iex> nodes = (g |> Graph.components |> List.first)
[:bruce_williams, :ben_wilson, :ben_marx, :jose_valim, :james_gray,
 :designing_elixir, :bruce_tate, :adopting_elixir, :pragmatic, :graphql_apis]
```

```
iex> g1 = Graph.subgraph(g, nodes)
#Graph<type: directed, vertices: [:graphql_apis, :adopting_elixir, ...]>
```

And we can compare the graph and subgraph:

```
iex> Graph.info(g)
%{num_edges: 17, num_vertices: 14, size_in_bytes: 7072, type: :directed}

iex> Graph.info(g1)
%{num_edges: 13, num_vertices: 10, size_in_bytes: 4608, type: :directed}
```

We can also ask some basic graph questions, such as:

```
iex> Graph.is_tree?(g)
false

iex> Graph.is_arborescence?(g)
false

iex> Graph.is_acyclic?(g)
false
```

There's more. But that should at least give some idea of what can be done.

Modeling the Book Graph

Recall the book graph we introduced in our first chapter. (You might want to refer back to Modeling a Book Graph, on page 8, for specific details.) This is a simple reference graph we created to test implementations under different graph models. We're defining a book catalog where each catalog entry has book, author, and publisher entities and a few basic properties.

We want to implement the book graph now using libgraph. Note that libgraph supports labels that we can use for the node and edge types. And while it allows for node properties, we have to exclude edge properties since libgraph doesn't natively support them. Of course, this is something of a requirement as far as implementing a property graph is concerned, but we'll see a way of managing edge properties for libgraph in Adding Edge Properties, on page 234.

So, here's one way of building the book graph. For this example, you'll want to copy the example that is provided in the NativeGraph.Examples.Book module in the sample code. Since libgraph creates nodes using Elixir terms, we can choose whether to use, for example, an atom or a map for the node value. We'll specify our node values as maps and use an anonymous function as a simple toggle to select either an atom from the map or the map itself.

We'll first define our anonymous function and bind this to a val variable:

```
apps/native_graph/lib/native_graph/examples/book.ex
# function to select id/map based on use_id? setting
val = fn map -> if use_id?, do: map.id, else: map end
```

Note that this is hardwired in the source graph file and is preset to select an atom value associated with the :id key. To select the full map as the value, simply set use_id? = false in the file.

Next, we'll define our nodes as maps filtered through the val.() function:

```
apps/native_graph/lib/native_graph/examples/book.ex
# book 1
bk1 =
  val.(%{
    id: :adopting_elixir,
    date: "2018-03-14",
    format: "Paper",
    isbn: "978-1-68050-252-7",
    title: "Adopting Elixir",
    url: "https://pragprog.com/titles/tvmelixir/adopting-elixir/"
  })

bk1_au1 =
  val.(%{
    id: :ben_marx,
    name: "Ben Marx",
    url: "https://twitter.com/bgmarx"
  })

bk1_au2 =
  val.(%{
    id: :jose_valim,
    name: "José Valim",
    url: "https://twitter.com/josevalim"
  })

bk1_au3 =
  val.(%{
    id: :bruce_tate,
    name: "Bruce Tate",
    url: "https://twitter.com/redrapids"
  })

bk1_pub =
  val.(%{
    id: :pragmatic,
    name: "The Pragmatic Bookshelf",
    url: "https://pragprog.com/"
  })
```

Note that for the id: key value we'll use an atom rather than a string.

And lastly, we'll build the graph:

```
apps/native_graph/lib/native_graph/examples/book.ex
# build graph
g =
  Graph.new(type: :directed)
  #
  |> Graph.add_vertex(bk1, "Book")
  |> Graph.add_vertex(bk1_au1, "Author")
  |> Graph.add_vertex(bk1_au2, "Author")
  |> Graph.add_vertex(bk1_au3, "Author")
  |> Graph.add_vertex(bk1_pub, "Publisher")
  |> Graph.add_edge(bk1_pub, bk1, label: "BOOK")
  |> Graph.add_edge(bk1, bk1_au1, label: "AUTHOR")
  |> Graph.add_edge(bk1, bk1_au2, label: "AUTHOR")
  |> Graph.add_edge(bk1, bk1_au3, label: "AUTHOR")
  |> Graph.add_edge(bk1, bk1_pub, label: "PUBLISHER")
```

Using Atoms for Nodes

The following figure shows how the book graph looks when using atoms for node values.

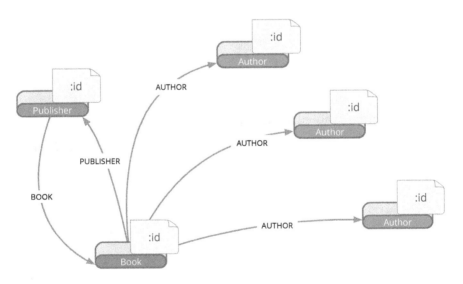

We can read our book graph selecting atoms for node values as:

```
iex> g = NativeGraph.Examples.Book.book(true)
#Graph<type: directed, vertices: [:adopting_elixir, :pragmatic, :bruce_tate,
 :jose_valim,
 :ben_marx], edges: [:adopting_elixir -[PUBLISHER]-> :pragmatic,
 :adopting_elixir -[AUTHOR]-> :bruce_tate, :adopting_elixir -[AUTHOR]
 :jose_valim, :adopting_elixir -[AUTHOR]-> :ben_marx, :pragmatic -[BOOK]
 :adopting_elixir]>
```

And now we can query this graph in the usual way. For example, to get the vertices, we do this:

```
iex> Graph.vertices(g)
[:adopting_elixir, :pragmatic, :bruce_tate, :jose_valim, :ben_marx]
```

Or let's say we want to find all edges (inbound and outbound) to the node with the property id: :pragmatic:

```
iex> Graph.in_edges(g, :pragmatic)
[
  %Graph.Edge{
    label: "PUBLISHER",
    v1: :adopting_elixir,
    v2: :pragmatic,
    weight: 1
  }
]
iex> Graph.out_edges(g, :pragmatic)
[
  %Graph.Edge{
    label: "BOOK",
    v1: :pragmatic,
    v2: :adopting_elixir,
    weight: 1
  }
]
```

Here we have one inbound edge and one outbound edge.

The book graph is a directed graph, and there should be a path from the Publisher node p to an Author node a. Let's test that:

```
iex> p = :pragmatic
iex> a = :ben_marx
```

Now is there a path between nodes p and a?

```
iex> Graph.get_paths(g, p, a)
[[:pragmatic, :adopting_elixir, :ben_marx]]
```

There is indeed a path, via the Book node :adopting_elixir.

Using Maps for Nodes

Alternately, we can use a map for node values, as shown in the figure on page 65.

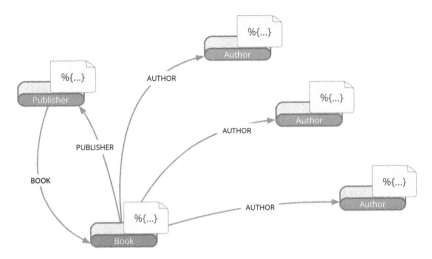

We can read our book graph selecting maps for node values as:

```
iex> g = NativeGraph.Examples.Book.book(false)
#Graph<type: directed, vertices: [
  %{id: :jose_valim, url: "https://twitter.com/josevalim", name: "José Valim"},
  %{id: :ben_marx, url: "https://twitter.com/bgmarx", name: "Ben Marx"},
  %{id: :bruce_tate, url: "https://twitter.com/redrapids", name: "Bruce Tate"},
  %{
    date: "2018-03-14",
    format: "Paper",
    id: :adopting_elixir,
    isbn: "978-1-68050-252-7",
    title: "Adopting Elixir",
    url: "https://pragprog.com/titles/tvmelixir/adopting-elixir/"
  },
  %{
    id: :pragmatic,
    name: "The Pragmatic Bookshelf",
    url: "https://pragprog.com/"
  }
], edges: [%{
  date: "2018-03-14",
  format: "Paper",
  id: :adopting_elixir,
  isbn: "978-1-68050-252-7",
  title: "Adopting Elixir"
  url: "https://pragprog.com/titles/tvmelixir/adopting-elixir/",
} -[AUTHOR]-> %{
  id: :jose_valim,
  name: "José Valim",
  url: "https://twitter.com/josevalim"
},
...
]>
```

And now we can query this graph in the usual way. For example, to get the vertices we can do this:

```
iex> Graph.vertices(g)
[
  %{
    id: :jose_valim,
    name: "José Valim",
    url: "https://twitter.com/josevalim"
  },
  %{
    id: :ben_marx,
    name: "Ben Marx",
    url: "https://twitter.com/bgmarx"
  },
  %{
    id: :bruce_tate,
    name: "Bruce Tate",
    url: "https://twitter.com/redrapids"
  },
  %{
    date: "2018-03-14",
    format: "Paper",
    id: :adopting_elixir,
    isbn: "978-1-68050-252-7",
    title: "Adopting Elixir",
    url: "https://pragprog.com/titles/tvmelixir/adopting-elixir/"
  },
  %{
    id: :pragmatic,
    name: "The Pragmatic Bookshelf",
    url: "https://pragprog.com/"
  }
]
```

Or, let's say we want to find all edges (inbound and outbound) to the node whose property id: is equal to :pragmatic:

```
iex> prag = g |> Graph.vertices |>
...> Enum.find(&(match?(%{id: :pragmatic}, &1)))
%{
  id: :pragmatic,
  url: "https://pragprog.com/",
  name: "The Pragmatic Bookshelf"
}

iex> Graph.in_edges(g, prag)
[
  %Graph.Edge{
    label: "PUBLISHER",
    v1: %{
```

```
      date: "2018-03-14",
      format: "Paper",
      id: :adopting_elixir,
      isbn: "978-1-68050-252-7",
      title: "Adopting Elixir",
      url: "https://pragprog.com/titles/tvmelixir/adopting-elixir/"
    },
    v2: %{
      id: :pragmatic,
      name: "The Pragmatic Bookshelf",
      url: "https://pragprog.com/"
    },
    weight: 1
  }
]
iex> Graph.out_edges(g, prag)
[
  %Graph.Edge{
    label: "BOOK",
    v1: %{
      id: :pragmatic,
      name: "The Pragmatic Bookshelf",
      url: "https://pragprog.com/"
    },
    v2: %{
      date: "2018-03-14",
      format: "Paper",
      id: :adopting_elixir,
      isbn: "978-1-68050-252-7",
      title: "Adopting Elixir",
      url: "https://pragprog.com/titles/tvmelixir/adopting-elixir/"
    },
    weight: 1
  }
]
```

Here we have one inbound edge and one outbound edge.

The book graph is a directed graph, and there should be a path from the Publisher node p to an Author node a.

Let's test that:

```
iex> nodes = Graph.vertices(g)
[
  %{id: :jose_valim,
    name: "José Valim",
    url: "https://twitter.com/josevalim"
  },
  ...
]
```

```
iex> p = (nodes |> Enum.find(&(match?(%{id: :pragmatic}, &1))))
%{
  id: :pragmatic,
  name: "The Pragmatic Bookshelf",
  url: "https://pragprog.com/"
}
iex> a = (nodes |> Enum.find(&(match?(%{id: :ben_marx}, &1))))
%{
  id: :ben_marx,
  name: "Ben Marx",
  url: "https://twitter.com/bgmarx"
}
```

Now is there a path between nodes p and a?

```
iex> Graph.get_paths(g, p, a)
[
  [
    %{
      id: :pragmatic,
      name: "The Pragmatic Bookshelf",
      url: "https://pragprog.com/"
    },
    %{
      date: "2018-03-14",
      format: "Paper",
      id: :adopting_elixir,
      isbn: "978-1-68050-252-7",
      title: "Adopting Elixir",
      url: "https://pragprog.com/titles/tvmelixir/adopting-elixir/"
    },
    %{
      id: :ben_marx,
      name: "Ben Marx",
      url: "https://twitter.com/bgmarx"
    }
  ]
]
```

There is indeed a path, via the Book node %{id: :adopting_elixir}.

Now that we've seen a real graph example, let's consider testing with synthetic graphs and see how we might generate those.

Generating Graphs

One of the challenges with testing data structures is to have a suitable number of test examples. We have two approaches to dealing with this: 1) include a library with a large number of instances, and 2) provide a set of generator functions. We'd ideally like to have both an atlas full of standard and example graphs and a library of graph generators.

We already have a few examples of graphs in our NativeGraph.Examples module. This library could be expanded.

As for graph generators, let's create a simple graph generator to get a taste of what can be done.

Create a new module NativeGraph.Builder and add this random_graph/1 function:

```
apps/native_graph/lib/native_graph/builder.ex
def random_graph(limit) do
  for(n <- 1..limit, m <- (n + 1)..limit, do: do_evaluate(n, m))
  |> Enum.reject(&is_nil/1)
  |> Enum.reduce(
    Graph.new(),
    fn [rs, re], g ->
      Graph.add_edge(g, rs, re)
    end
  )
end
```

Also add a delegate function to the NativeGraph module, so we can call Builder.random_graph/1 more simply as random_graph/1:

```
apps/native_graph/lib/native_graph.ex
defdelegate random_graph(arg), to: NativeGraph.Builder, as: :random_graph
```

This is a naive attempt to build a random connected graph. Since it's a connected graph, we'll only need to add edges—the vertices are implicit. We'll take one argument limit—the number of vertices—and use a comprehension to build up vertex pairs for the edges.

We'll drop some of the edges to make this an incomplete graph and use a crude test based on the system clock:

```
apps/native_graph/lib/native_graph/builder.ex
defp do_evaluate(n, m) do
  case Integer.is_even(Kernel.trunc(System.os_time() / 1000)) do
    true -> [n, m]
    false -> nil
  end
end
```

Note that we're using the Integer.is_even/1 macro here, so we'll first need to add a require Integer directive in our module.

Here's how we can generate such a random graph:

```
iex> g7 = random_graph(7)
#Graph<type: directed, vertices: [1, ...], edges: [1 -> 2, ...]>
iex> g7 |> Graph.to_dot |> elem(1) |>
...> write_graph("dot/g7.dot") |> write_image
{:ok, "g7.png"}
```

This is the image that is saved in g7.png:

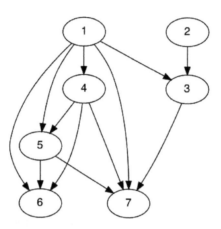

We've just shown here a simple example of a graph generator.

Wrapping Up

In this chapter, we explored querying some native graph structures built using the libgraph Elixir package.

We got in some initial practice with the example book graph and then implemented our reference book graph with libgraph. We noted that there is no native support in libgraph for edge properties, although we'll see in Chapter 11, Transforming Graph Models, on page 201, how we can enhance libgraph to work with edge properties.

We also touched on graph generators with a naive example.

Now let's move on to a full-blown implementation of the property graph model backed by a best-of-breed graph database.

## CHAPTER 5

Navigating Graphs with Neo4j

We are now going to turn our attention to property graphs. The property graph is perhaps the best-known data model for semantic graphs (graphs with an explicit information superstructure).

Property graphs—also known as labeled property graphs—are graphs in which both nodes and edges may be attributed properties and in which nodes may be labeled for grouping.

To study property graphs in a more controlled way, we'll benefit greatly by using a database to store our graphs so that we can requery them without having to rebuild them. And a true graph database—a database that deals with graphs as first-class data structures—would be even better. Unquestionably, one of the most popular graph databases is Neo4j,[1] which was one of the initial movers in this field. Neo4j has been a major player in driving forward the current interest in graph databases.

We should call out here a couple of key Neo4j technologies that we'll be using for connecting to the database and for querying over the graphs it manages:

- *Bolt*[2] is a high-performance network protocol that was introduced with the Neo4j 3.0 release in 2016 to speed up database connections. It uses binary encoding over TCP or web sockets and has built-in TLS support.

- *Cypher*[3] is the declarative graph query language developed by Neo4j and is now open-sourced to the openCypher[4] project. (See the Cypher Refcard[5] for a handy quick reference.)

---

1. https://neo4j.com/
2. https://boltprotocol.org/
3. https://neo4j.com/docs/cypher-manual/current/
4. http://www.opencypher.org/
5. https://neo4j.com/docs/cypher-refcard/current/

We're going to use the bolt_sips[6] package from Florin Pătraşcu[7] that implements a Neo4j driver for Elixir wrapped around the Bolt protocol. (The package integrates and continues work from boltex,[8] an independent implementation of the Bolt protocol in Elixir by Michael Schaefermeyer.[9])

But before we get to that, let's first review the property graph model. We'll then create a new PropertyGraph project and look at querying with Cypher, and we'll also try out the Bolt driver. And then we'll implement a graph service for the project using our common graph services API. Lastly, we'll see how to switch graph service contexts easily.

Property Graph Model

The distinguishing feature of a property graph is that graph vertices and edges may be decorated with attributes (or properties). In Neo4j parlance, we talk about *nodes* (for vertices) and *relationships* (for edges).

We'll discuss property graphs here from a Neo4j perspective.

The graph elements we'll talk about are nodes, relationships, and paths, along with their associated IDs, properties, labels, and types. See Graph Database Concepts[10] in the Neo4j documentation for more details.

The following diagram here shows some of these graph constructs:

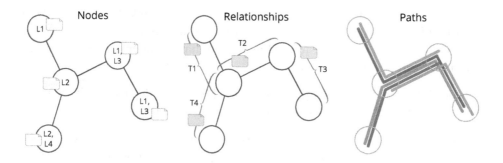

Nodes are shown with optional labels L1, L2, and so on, while the required single-value relationship types are shown as T1, T2, and so on. Property maps

---

6.   https://hex.pm/packages/bolt_sips
7.   https://hex.pm/users/florin
8.   https://hex.pm/packages/boltex
9.   https://about.me/mschae
10. https://neo4j.com/docs/getting-started/current/graphdb-concepts/

are shown with yellow document icons for nodes and green document icons for relationships. Some various paths are shown between node pairs.

Nodes

Nodes in Neo4j are graph vertices and are allocated a system ID. They may have zero or more user-defined labels associated with them. Labels are used for grouping nodes into sets.

Nodes may additionally have a map of property names and property values associated with them.

Relationships

Relationships in Neo4j are graph edges that relate two nodes and are allocated a system ID. They take a single user-defined relationship type.

Relationships may additionally have a map of property names and property values associated with them.

Note that relationships in Neo4j always have a direction that is defined at create time but may be omitted at query time.

Paths

Paths in Neo4j are sequences of relationships that join sequences of nodes and are used to answer traversal questions. The sequence of relationships in the path is always distinct, whereas the sequence of nodes may or may not be distinct.

One common traversal question is: "What is the shortest path between two given nodes?" This also brings up the notion of path length. Cypher includes many handy functions to answer such questions.

Creating the PropertyGraph Project

OK, enough of the theory. Let's try querying some property graphs for real. We're going to need a couple of things: a database and a database driver.

PropertyGraph Project/Database Setup

See Appendix 1, Project Setups, on page 245, for details on retrieving a working project with code and data.

And see Appendix 2, Database Setups, on page 247, for help on setting up a local copy of Neo4j.

For the database driver, we'll use the bolt_sips package. We'll want to create a new project under our umbrella app. Let's call this project PropertyGraph. (See the bolt_sips project for detailed installation instructions.[11])

Follow the usual drill for creating the new project, PropertyGraph. Go to the ExGraphsBook home project (see ExGraphsBook Umbrella, on page 16), cd down into the apps directory, and open up the new PropertyGraph project:

```
$ mix new property_graph --sup
```

This will generate an app with a supervision tree and an application callback. We'll use the PropertyGraph.Application module to set up the supervision tree.

You should now have an apps directory that looks like this:

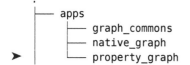

```
.
├── apps
    ├── graph_commons
    ├── native_graph
    └── property_graph
```

Now cd into the property_graph directory:

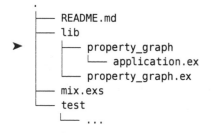

```
.
├── README.md
├── lib
    ├── property_graph
        └── application.ex
    └── property_graph.ex
├── mix.exs
└── test
    └── ...
```

Note that the --sup flag has generated an extra directory property_graph under lib with an application.ex file.

We can declare a dependency on bolt_sips by adding the :bolt_sips dependency to the mix.exs file:

```
apps/property_graph/mix.exs
defp deps do
  [
    # graph_commons
    {:graph_commons, in_umbrella: true},
    # property graphs
    {:bolt_sips, "~> 2.0"}
  ]
end
```

---

11. https://github.com/florinpatrascu/bolt_sips

As usual, use Mix to add in the dependency:

```
$ mix deps.get; mix deps.compile
```

We'll need to specify our connection details:

```
config :bolt_sips, Bolt,
  url: "bolt://localhost:7687",
  basic_auth: [username: "neo4j", password: "neo4jtest"]
```

Add these lines (with details updated as required) to the umbrella config.exs file in the main project directory or to an environment-specific import (for example, dev.exs). Note that the url: option uses an explicit bolt: URI scheme.

We'll also need to start up our PropertyGraph.Application module:

```
apps/property_graph/mix.exs
def application do
  [
    extra_applications: [:logger],
➤   mod: {PropertyGraph.Application, []}
  ]
end
```

The :mod option specifies the application callback module, followed by any arguments to be passed on application start. The application callback module is any module that implements the Application behaviour.

We update the start/2 function in lib/property_graph/application.ex as:

```
apps/property_graph/lib/property_graph/application.ex
defmodule PropertyGraph.Application do
  use Application

  def start(_type, _args) do
    children = [
➤     {Bolt.Sips, Application.get_env(:bolt_sips, Bolt)}
    ]

➤   opts = [strategy: :one_for_one, name: PropertyGraph.Service]
    Supervisor.start_link(children, opts)
  end

end
```

The application will now be started automatically and can be tested by calling the info/0 function in Bolt.Sips:

```
iex> Bolt.Sips.info()
%{
  default: %{
    connections: %{direct: %{"localhost:7687" => 0}, routing_query: nil},
    user_options: [
```

```
        socket: Bolt.Sips.Socket,
        basic_auth: [username: "neo4j", password: "neo4jtest"],
        port: 7687,
        routing_context: %{},
        schema: "bolt",
        hostname: "localhost",
        pool_size: 15,
        max_overflow: 0,
        timeout: 15000,
        ssl: false,
        with_etls: false,
        retry_linear_backoff: [delay: 150, factor: 2, tries: 3],
        prefix: :default,
        url: "bolt://neo4j:neo4jtest@localhost:7687"
    ]
  }
}
```

Let's get a database connection:

```
iex> Bolt.Sips.conn()
#PID<0.352.0>
```

In direct mode, which is our current configuration, all the operations—read/write and delete—are sent to the database using a common connection (from a connection pool). The conn/0 function returns the process ID for this pool connection.

Finally, let's wire our graph storage into the PropertyGraph module with these use/2 macros:

```
apps/property_graph/lib/property_graph.ex
use GraphCommons.Graph, graph_type: :property, graph_module: __MODULE__
use GraphCommons.Query, query_type: :property, query_module: __MODULE__
```

Well, that about covers the setup. But before we get into any real querying, which we'll cover in Chapter 6, Querying Neo4j with Cypher, on page 93, we'll spend the rest of this chapter looking at how to create queries and send them to the database.

Querying with Cypher and APOC

It's time to talk about how to query Neo4j, which will be our prime interface for interacting with the graph database.

The query language used by Neo4j is called Cypher (no points here for spotting the common name origin in *The Matrix*). Cypher supports the full range of CRUD operations to manage graph structures within the database. This query language has been augmented with a stored procedure library known as

APOC that provides hundreds of procedures and functions, adding a lot of new functionality.

Cypher

Cypher is a declarative graph query language that was developed in 2011 by Neo4j to query and manipulate graphs. It has subsequently been open-sourced, and the openCypher project is developing an open language specification and a reference implementation. It was inspired by the existing query languages SQL, XPath, and SPARQL.

As a declarative language, Cypher focuses on the "what" rather than the "how." It provides a specification for graph operations rather than an imperative procedure for implementation. This allows the user to focus on the business problem to be solved rather than any particular technical solution. It's the query engine that takes care of translating the business logic into the best execution plan for the current graph structure.

To give a flavor of the language, here's a query which looks for a friend of a friend (fof) of a given person (john):

```
MATCH (john:Person {name: 'John'})-[:friend]->()-[:friend]->(fof)
RETURN john.name, fof.name
```

This roughly looks like an upside-down SQL query, with the RETURN clause following the MATCH clause instead of leading the match as with SQL's SELECT clause.

We would send this query to the database using the query!/2 function in Bolt.Sips:

```
iex> query_string = """
...> MATCH (john:Person {name: 'John'})-[:friend]->()-[:friend]->(fof)
...> RETURN john.name, fof.name
...> """

iex> Bolt.Sips.query!(Bolt.Sips.conn(), query_string)
...
```

The main thing to note here is that Cypher uses an ASCII art style of writing down query match patterns, for example, ()-[]->() or ()<-[]-() for directed relationships and ()-[]-() for undirected relationships. Nodes are indicated with parentheses and relationships with brackets.

Nodes and relationships may be referenced with variable names (john, fof). Nodes may also be qualified with a label and relationships with a type. In this query, john has a Person label, and the two relationships have a type of friend.

Both nodes and relationships may be further constrained with a set of property key/value pairs. Here, the node referenced by john has a name property with the value John.

For more information on Cypher, see the Cypher Resources[12] page and the Neo4j Cypher Manual.[13]

APOC

On the Neo4j platform, Cypher may be extended via a library of stored procedures known as APOC, or Awesome Procedures on Cypher. This has now matured into a rather impressive collection of procedures and functions.

For a primer on APOC, see the Neo4j APOC Library manual.[14]

The APOC Core library is packaged as a jar file with the Neo4j distribution, although, if you want to use the APOC Full library, you'll have to download that jar file separately. Whichever library you choose, you'll need to copy it to the plugins/ folder. Instructions for installing APOC are provided on the Installation page.[15]

You may also need to review the security settings in the conf/neo4j.conf file. A server restart is required.

These procedures are invoked using the CALL clause in Cypher. So, for example, we could get a report on the contents of the database by calling the procedure apoc.meta.stats. Here is the JSON result we get for the book graph:

```
iex> Bolt.Sips.query!(Bolt.Sips.conn(), "CALL apoc.meta.stats")
%Bolt.Sips.Response{
  ...
  results: [
    %{
      ...
      "stats" => %{
        "labelCount" => 39,
        "labels" => %{"Author" => 9, "Book" => 4, "Publisher" => 4},
        "nodeCount" => 17,
        "propertyKeyCount" => 63,
        "relCount" => 17,
        "relTypeCount" => 24,
        "relTypes" => %{
```

---

12. https://neo4j.com/developer/cypher/resources/
13. https://neo4j.com/docs/cypher-manual/current/
14. https://neo4j.com/developer/neo4j-apoc/
15. https://neo4j.com/labs/apoc/4.4/installation/

```
           "()-[:AUTHOR]->()" => 9,
           "()-[:AUTHOR]->(:Author)" => 9,
           "()-[:BOOK]->()" => 4,
           "()-[:BOOK]->(:Book)" => 4,
           "()-[:PUBLISHER]->()" => 4,
           "()-[:PUBLISHER]->(:Publisher)" => 4,
           "(:Book)-[:AUTHOR]->()" => 9,
           "(:Book)-[:PUBLISHER]->()" => 4,
           "(:Publisher)-[:BOOK]->()" => 4
          }
        }
      }
  ],
  ...
}
```

We can also get a comprehensive list of all of the procedures:

```
iex> Bolt.Sips.query!(Bolt.Sips.conn(), "CALL apoc.help('apoc')")
%Bolt.Sips.Response{
  ...
  results: [
      %{
         "name" => "apoc.algo.aStar",
         ...
      },
      ...
  ],
  ...
}
```

We've seen briefly what Cypher queries look like and how Cypher can be used to run stored procedures using APOC. Next, we'll see how Cypher queries can be sent to the database using Bolt and how responses are received.

Trying Out the Bolt Driver

Before we get down to the nitty-gritty of querying graphs, let's look at some raw Bolt.Sips responses to gain some familiarity with how graph data is shipped across our comms channel—the Bolt connection.

Let's first take a quick peek at the %Bolt.Sips.Response{} struct to get a feel for how this is structured and what kinds of data fields are supported:

```
iex> %Bolt.Sips.Response{}
%Bolt.Sips.Response{
  bookmark: nil,
  fields: nil,
  notifications: [],
  plan: nil,
```

```
      profile: nil,
      records: [],
►     results: [],
►     stats: [],
      type: nil
    }
```

For now, we are going to be mainly looking at the results and stats fields, and later we'll use the type field as a means to select between the two.

We'll keep things simple here by importing the Bolt.Sips namespace:

```
iex> import Bolt.Sips
```

Now we can try out a minimal Cypher query with the query!/2 function:

```
iex> query!(conn(), "RETURN 1 AS n")
%Bolt.Sips.Response{
  bookmark: "FB:kcwQ0rvNq4LvQBm2WwphACLw5xmQ",
  fields: ["n"],
  notifications: [],
  plan: nil,
  profile: nil,
  records: [[1]],
  results: [%{"n" => 1}],
  stats: [],
  type: "r"
}
```

The query "RETURN 1 AS n" is sufficient to exercise the server without requiring any loaded data and to show the full %Bolt.Sips.Response{} struct.

Note that we use the bang form query!/2 rather than query/2 as this is more convenient for interactive use.

We can use simple pattern matching to pull out the results field from the struct:

```
iex> %Bolt.Sips.Response{results: results} = query!(conn(), "RETURN 1 AS n")
%Bolt.Sips.Response{
  ...
}
iex> results
[%{"n" => 1}]
```

By the end of this chapter, we'll find a better way to query with Bolt.Sips so that we can streamline our querying.

Types

The bolt_sips package defines types for a number of graph entities in the Bolt.Sips.Types module.[16] We have types for nodes, relationships, and paths. There is also a type for unbound relationships.

For details on how these entities are serialized in Bolt protocol messages, see Graph Type Structures on the Message Serialization page.[17]

The structs for node and relationship types have common id and properties fields, with nodes taking an additional labels field and relationships taking an additional type field along with start and end fields for the start and end node IDs of the relationship:

```
iex> t Bolt.Sips.Types.Node
@type t() :: %Bolt.Sips.Types.Node{
        id: integer(),
        labels: [String.t()],
        properties: map()
    }
iex> t Bolt.Sips.Types.Relationship
@type t() :: %Bolt.Sips.Types.Relationship{
        end: term(),
        id: integer(),
        properties: map(),
        start: term(),
        type: term()
    }
```

The unbound relationship type is the same as the relationship type:

```
iex> t Bolt.Sips.Types.UnboundRelationship
@type t() :: %Bolt.Sips.Types.UnboundRelationship{
        end: term(),
        id: integer(),
        properties: map(),
        start: term(),
        type: term()
    }
```

Lastly, the path type is a container type with node and relationship lists (nodes and relationships fields) and a sequence field for indexing into these lists:

```
iex> t Bolt.Sips.Types.Path
@type t() :: %Bolt.Sips.Types.Path{
```

---

16. https://hexdocs.pm/bolt_sips/Bolt.Sips.Types.html
17. https://github.com/boltprotocol/boltprotocol/blob/master/v1/_serialization.asciidoc

```
  nodes: list() | nil,
  relationships: list() | nil,
  sequence: list() | nil
}
```

Let's see what this looks like in practice.

Nodes

We're going to need some data to do real querying. Let's assume that you've loaded the demo movies graph in your Neo4j database.

This will depend on how you've installed Neo4j (see Installing Neo4j, on page 247). If you've installed Neo4j Desktop, you should already have the movies graph loaded. If you've installed a standalone server, for example, the Neo4j Community Edition, you'll need to download the movies graph—see Movies Graph Example[18] for instructions.

(More example graphs are available on the Guide: Example Datasets[19] page.)

Let's get one node with the query "MATCH (n) RETURN n LIMIT 1":

```
iex> %Bolt.Sips.Response{results: results} =
...> query!(conn(), "MATCH (n) RETURN n LIMIT 1")
%Bolt.Sips.Response{
  ...
}
iex> results
[
  %{
    "n" => %Bolt.Sips.Types.Node{
      id: 2634,
      labels: ["Movie"],
      properties: %{
        "released" => 1999,
        "tagline" => "Welcome to the Real World",
        "title" => "The Matrix"
      }
    }
  }
]
```

This is returned as a %Bolt.Sips.Types.Node{} struct with an integer id, a list of labels, and a map of properties.

---

18. https://github.com/neo4j-graph-examples/movies
19. https://neo4j.com/developer/example-data/

Relationships

Let's get one relationship with the query "MATCH ()-[r]-() RETURN r LIMIT 1":

```
iex> %Bolt.Sips.Response{results: results} =
...> query!(conn(), "MATCH ()-[r]-() RETURN r LIMIT 1")
%Bolt.Sips.Response{
  ...
}
iex> results
[
  %{
    "r" => %Bolt.Sips.Types.Relationship{
      end: 2634,
      id: 1034,
      properties: %{"roles" => ["Agent Smith"]},
      start: 2638,
      type: "ACTED_IN"
    }
  }
]
```

This is returned as a %Bolt.Sips.Types.Relationship{} struct with an integer id, a string type, a map of properties, and integer start and end fields.

Paths

Let's get one path with the query "MATCH p = ()--() RETURN p LIMIT 1":

```
iex> %Bolt.Sips.Response{results: results} =
...> query!(conn(), "MATCH p = ()--() RETURN p LIMIT 1")
%Bolt.Sips.Response{
  ...
}
iex> results
[
  %{
    "p" => %Bolt.Sips.Types.Path{
      nodes: [
        %Bolt.Sips.Types.Node{
          id: 2638,
          labels: ["Person"],
          properties: %{"born" => 1960, "name" => "Hugo Weaving"}
        },
        %Bolt.Sips.Types.Node{
          id: 2634,
          labels: ["Movie"],
          properties: %{
```

```
        "released" => 1999,
        "tagline" => "Welcome to the Real World",
        "title" => "The Matrix"
      }
    }
  ],
  relationships: [
    %Bolt.Sips.Types.UnboundRelationship{
      end: nil,
      id: 1034,
      properties: %{"roles" => ["Agent Smith"]},
      start: nil,
      type: "ACTED_IN"
    }
  ],
  sequence: [1, 1]
  }
 }
]
```

This is returned as a %Bolt.Sips.Types.Path{} struct, which is a more complicated affair with lists of nodes and (unbounded) relationships fields and a list of integers for the sequence field.

Setting Up a Graph Service

We can do graph management of our Neo4j instance using Cypher queries over Bolt.Sips to add and delete graphs. But we'd ideally like to bring this under our common graph services API so we can operate at a higher level of abstraction, which will make for less context switching when swapping between graph services.

Let's set up a graph service for our PropertyGraph project now:

```
defmodule PropertyGraph.Service do
  @behaviour GraphCommons.Service

  # ...

end
```

Note that this module is going to implement the GraphCommons.Service behaviour so we use the module attribute @behaviour.

Graph API

We'll first need to set up our Cypher queries for deleting all nodes and relationships and for reading them:

```
apps/property_graph/lib/property_graph/service.ex
@cypher_delete """
MATCH (n) OPTIONAL MATCH (n)-[r]-() DELETE n,r
"""

@cypher_read """
MATCH (n) OPTIONAL MATCH (n)-[r]-() RETURN DISTINCT n, r
"""
```

Both of these queries match all nodes, and then they optionally add any edges attached to those nodes. This means that we can be sure of discovering the complete graph, whether it's connected or not.

By the way, a more idiomatic Cypher query for deleting nodes is:

```
@cypher_delete """
MATCH (n) DETACH DELETE n
"""
```

We can now simply define our graph services API as follows:

```
apps/property_graph/lib/property_graph/service.ex
def graph_create(graph) do
  graph_delete()
  graph_update(graph)
end

def graph_delete(), do: Bolt.Sips.query!(Bolt.Sips.conn(), @cypher_delete)

def graph_read(), do: Bolt.Sips.query!(Bolt.Sips.conn(), @cypher_read)

def graph_update(%GraphCommons.Graph{} = graph),
  do: Bolt.Sips.query!(Bolt.Sips.conn(), graph.data)
```

This defines the API for CRUD operations, although we can expand the API further with an optional reporting function graph_info/0.

Graph Info

For our optional graph_info/0 function, we can use the APOC procedure apoc.meta.stats() and pull out the fields we need:

```
apps/property_graph/lib/property_graph/service.ex
@cypher_info """
CALL apoc.meta.stats()
YIELD labels, labelCount, nodeCount, relCount, relTypeCount
"""
```

We then send that query, and from the result set we can parse out the fields we're interested in and use them to populate the %GraphCommons.Service.GraphInfo{} struct:

```
apps/property_graph/lib/property_graph/service.ex
def graph_info() do
  {:ok, [stats]} =
    @cypher_info
    |> PropertyGraph.new_query()
    |> query_graph

  %GraphCommons.Service.GraphInfo{
    type: :property,
    file: "",
    num_nodes: stats["nodeCount"],
    num_edges: stats["relCount"],
    labels: Map.keys(stats["labels"])
  }
end
```

Query API

Now it's time to look at the query API.

The query API is different from the graph API, which is used only for graph management. Here we'd like to query *within* the current graph. To make this separation between the two APIs clearer, we'll use the differently named query_graph/1 function instead of the graph_*/1 and graph_*/0 naming:

```
apps/property_graph/lib/property_graph/service.ex
def query_graph(%GraphCommons.Query{} = query), do: query_graph(query, %{})

def query_graph(%GraphCommons.Query{} = query, params) do
  :property = query.type

  Bolt.Sips.query(Bolt.Sips.conn(), query.data, params)
  |> case do
    {:ok, response} -> parse_response(response, false)
    {:error, error} -> {:error, error}
  end
end
```

We'll also define a parallel query_graph!/1 function to simplify using this interactively:

```
apps/property_graph/lib/property_graph/service.ex
def query_graph!(%GraphCommons.Query{} = query), do: query_graph!(query, %{})

def query_graph!(%GraphCommons.Query{} = query, params) do
  :property = query.type

  Bolt.Sips.query(Bolt.Sips.conn(), query.data, params)
  |> case do
    {:ok, response} -> parse_response(response, true)
    {:error, error} -> raise "! #{inspect error}"
  end
end
```

In both cases, we'll pass in a %GraphCommons.Query{} struct with the actual query string contained in the :data field. If successful, we'll call the private function parse_response/2 with the %Bolt.Sips.Response{} struct and a boolean bang as true for query_graph!/1 and false for query_graph/1:

```
apps/property_graph/lib/property_graph/service.ex
defp parse_response(%Bolt.Sips.Response{} = response, bang) do
  %Bolt.Sips.Response{type: type} = response

  case type do
    r when r in ["r", "rw"] ->
      %Bolt.Sips.Response{results: results} = response
      unless bang, do: {:ok, results}, else: results
    s when s in ["s"] ->
      %Bolt.Sips.Response{results: results} = response
      unless bang, do: {:ok, results}, else: results
    w when w in ["w"] ->
      %Bolt.Sips.Response{stats: stats} = response
      unless bang, do: {:ok, stats}, else: stats
  end
end
```

We use simple pattern matching to pull out the results or stats fields, depending on whether the type field in the %Bolt.Sips.Response{} struct is r or w, respectively.

API Demo

As a demo, let's add our default graph to the Neo4j database. But first, let's import the PropertyGraph functions to save on typing:

```
iex> import PropertyGraph
PropertyGraph
```

We defined the default graph in Inspecting the Structs, on page 22. Let's now save that down into our graph storage with the write_graph/2 function:

```
iex> "CREATE (a)-[:EX]->(b)" |> write_graph("default.cypher")
#GraphCommons.Graph<type: property, file: "...", data: "CREATE (a)-[:EX]...">
```

We'll use the read_graph/1 function to read the default graph back from the graph store:

```
iex> default_graph = read_graph("default.cypher")
#GraphCommons.Graph<type: property, file: "...", data: "CREATE (a)-[:EX]...">
```

We can then simply pipe this into the graph_create/1 function to create our default graph in the graph service:

```
iex> graph_create default_graph
%Bolt.Sips.Response{
  ...
```

```
  stats: %{"nodes-created" => 2, "relationships-created" => 1},
  type: "w"
}
```

We can use the graph_info/0 function to confirm the service graph:

```
iex> graph_info
%GraphCommons.Service.GraphInfo{
  labels: [],
  num_edges: 1,
  num_nodes: 2,
  type: :property
}
```

And we can query this as before:

```
iex> %Bolt.Sips.Response{results: results} =
...> query!(conn(), "MATCH (n) RETURN n"), do: results
%Bolt.Sips.Response{
  ...
}

iex> results
[
  %{"n" => %Bolt.Sips.Types.Node{id: 2814, labels: [], properties: %{}}},
  %{"n" => %Bolt.Sips.Types.Node{id: 2815, labels: [], properties: %{}}}
]
```

Now let's see how we can simplify that without all the boilerplate so we can focus more clearly on the query itself. It's time to introduce some shorthand techniques.

Query Helper

For interactive use in IEx, we can define a helper function cypher!/1 in GraphCommons.Utils:

apps/graph_commons/lib/graph_commons/utils.ex
```
def cypher!(query_string), do: to_query_graph!(PropertyGraph, query_string)
```

This function takes a query string and calls the private function to_query_graph!/1 also in GraphCommons.Utils to convert the query string into a %GraphCommons.Query struct:

apps/graph_commons/lib/graph_commons/utils.ex
```
defp to_query_graph!(graph_module, query_string)
    when is_module(graph_module) do
  query_string
  |> graph_module.new_query()
  |> graph_module.query_graph!()
end
```

We are using the is_module/1 guard to ensure that the graph_module argument is a valid graph module. The guard definition itself is defined with the defguard/1 macro:

```
apps/graph_commons/lib/graph_commons/utils.ex
defguard is_module(graph_module)
  when graph_module in [DGraph, NativeGraph, PropertyGraph, RDFGraph,
  TinkerGraph]
```

And to simplify access to this helper function, let's import the GraphCommons.Utils module in our IEx startup file .iex.exs:

```
import GraphCommons
➤ import GraphCommons.Utils ; alias GraphCommons.Utils
```

Let's try this now:

```
iex> "MATCH (n) RETURN n" |> cypher!
[
  %{"n" => %Bolt.Sips.Types.Node{id: 2814, labels: [], properties: %{}}},
  %{"n" => %Bolt.Sips.Types.Node{id: 2815, labels: [], properties: %{}}}
]
```

This is much better. It eliminates the need to pass in the database connection, manage namespaces, and extract the results field from the %Bolt.Sips.Response{} struct. We can simply focus on the query string and the result types.

We'll use this form for querying from now on.

Graph Contexts

We've talked here about importing the PropertyGraph module to allow simplified access to the module functions without using the module namespace. And in the previous chapter, we also talked about importing the NativeGraph module.

If we import a second graph module, we'll run into a conflict in our function names:

```
iex> import NativeGraph
NativeGraph

iex> import PropertyGraph
PropertyGraph

iex> list_graphs
** (CompileError) iex:10: function list_graphs/0 imported from both
PropertyGraph and NativeGraph, call is ambiguous
    (elixir) src/elixir_dispatch.erl:111: :elixir_dispatch.expand_import/6
    (elixir) src/elixir_dispatch.erl:81: :elixir_dispatch.dispatch_import/5
```

This won't do.

We need to be able to delete any previous graph module import before attempting a new import.

There is a way, although I haven't seen it documented. If you do an import, restricting it to an empty set of functions will clear out the module from the environment.

Let's try this out. If we inspect the environment after the two previous imports of NativeGraph and PropertyGraph, we can see that we have list_graphs/0 imported under both modules:

```
iex> __ENV__.functions()
[
  ...
  {PropertyGraph,
   [
     ...
     list_graphs: 0,
     ...
   ]},
  {NativeGraph,
   [
     ...
     list_graphs: 0,
     ...
   ]},
  ...
]}
]
```

Try now to import an empty list of NativeGraph functions:

```
iex> import NativeGraph, only: []
PropertyGraph
```

And now inspect the environment again:

```
iex> __ENV__.functions()
[
  ...
  {PropertyGraph,
   [
     ...
     list_graphs: 0,
     ...
   ]},
  ...
]}
]
```

Notice that the NativeGraph module functions are gone. There's no longer any conflict.

We can use this technique in the graph_context/1 macro we'll import by default, along with the other GraphCommons.Utils functions:

```
apps/graph_commons/lib/graph_commons/utils.ex
defmacro graph_context(graph_module) do
  quote do
    # unimport any existing graph modules
    import DGraph, only: []
    import NativeGraph, only: []
    import PropertyGraph, only: []
    import RDFGraph, only: []
    import TinkerGraph, only: []
    # import graph module argument
    import unquote(graph_module)
  end
end
```

This macro will effectively do an unimport of all the graph modules and then will import the graph module supplied.

Now if we try this, we see that we have an effective means of switching between graph contexts. At any time, there will only be one graph context accessible without namespacing. Of course, all the graph contexts are available if full namespacing is used.

We can define the function graph_context/0 within the body of the _using_/1 macro in the GraphCommons.Graph module so that it'll be injected into each of the graph modules that call use/1:

```
apps/graph_commons/lib/graph_commons/graph.ex
def graph_context(), do: unquote(graph_module)
```

Since these are imported with the graph module, we can find out which is the default graph context at any time:

```
iex> graph_context PropertyGraph
PropertyGraph

iex> graph_info
%GraphCommons.Service.GraphInfo{
  file: "",
  labels: ["Author", "Book", "Publisher"],
  num_edges: 17,
  num_nodes: 17,
  type: :property
}
```

```
iex> graph_context RDFGraph
RDFGraph

iex> graph_info
%GraphCommons.Service.GraphInfo{
  file: "",
  labels: ["Book", "Organization", "Person"],
  num_edges: 27,
  num_nodes: 8,
  type: :rdf
}
```

This use of a graph context with the query helpers we introduced earlier makes interacting with our graph services a much simpler task. We can now focus on querying the various graph models and switch between graph contexts seamlessly.

Wrapping Up

In this chapter, we covered quite a bit of ground. We reviewed the property graph model, which is perhaps the dominant graph model for representing information within a graph framework.

We set up a new PropertyGraph project for exploring property graphs and used the bolt_sips driver package to communicate with a Neo4j instance.

We met Cypher—the query language for Neo4j property graphs—and the APOC library of procedures for extending Cypher with richer algorithms.

We spent some time looking at the response patterns from bolt_sips and the structures used for returning nodes, relationships, and paths.

We also looked at implementing a graph service for property graphs so that we can use a common API for graph management and for sending queries to the graph service. Lastly, we talked about service contexts that allow us to switch between different graph services seamlessly.

With this in place, we're finally ready to query property graphs.

## CHAPTER 6

Querying Neo4j with Cypher

We're finally ready to query a real graph database—Neo4j. We're going to use Cypher for this.

Let's review the things we've done so far. We've got our graph database (Neo4j) running and a connection to the database (Bolt) set up. We've also created our property graph service API (PropertyGraph) and have added in a query helper cypher!/1 for sending Cypher queries.

Now we want to get down to the business of querying the graph database.

We're going to focus on a couple of simple applications by getting acquainted with Neo4j property graphs using Elixir. We'll start off with some basics for creating and querying nodes, relationships, and paths, and we'll provide a rudimentary test query library.

We'll then create a simple graph—the book graph—and see how this is implemented in Cypher. And then we'll create a larger graph—the ARPANET graph—to look at an example of a real network.

Parameter passing in queries is an important capability so we'll cover that. We'll extend our query API to support parameters and also show some examples of this in action.

We'll round this out with some general remarks on property graphs and schemas and anticipate the RDF schemas that we'll meet in the following chapters.

Getting Started with Cypher

We can't possibly do any real justice to a language as rich as Cypher here. For more information, you should consult the Cypher Query Language[1] developer resource, The Neo4j Cypher Manual,[2] and the openCypher Resources page.[3]

Let's review some basics of Cypher patterns, which are used in CREATE clauses for construction and in MATCH clauses for querying. These patterns are used to specify nodes, relationships, and paths. This should be enough to get us started.

Some Basic Cypher Syntax

As earlier noted, Cypher uses an ASCII art style for writing down its queries. This helps because with Cypher's labels and properties we are essentially dealing with structured values for nodes and relationships.

Nodes

The pattern for creating and matching a node in Cypher is:

```
( variable? :label* {properties}? )
```

Here we use the standard regex quantifiers, ? and *, which show that all parts are optional. The only required syntax is the pair of parentheses, (), which marks a node. The node may be referenced with a variable name, and can optionally be labeled with one or more labels. Additionally, properties may be attached using a property map construct properties, marked with braces, {}, and enclosing a comma-separated list of key/value pairs:

```
{key: value, ...}
```

Here's an example of a node with two labels:

```
iex> "CREATE (a:Foo:Bar)" |> cypher!
%{"labels-added" => 2, "nodes-created" => 1}

iex> "MATCH (a:Foo) RETURN labels(a)" |> cypher!
[%{"labels(a)" => ["Foo", "Bar"]}]

iex> "MERGE (a:Baz) RETURN labels(a)" |> cypher!
[%{"labels(a)" => ["Baz"]}]
```

Note that a variable name is needed for MATCH. (Also note that the MERGE clause here is like a combination of CREATE and MATCH.)

---

1. https://neo4j.com/developer/cypher-query-language/
2. https://neo4j.com/docs/cypher-manual/current/
3. https://www.opencypher.org/resources

Here's an example of an unlabeled node with a property map:

```
iex> "CREATE (a {blue: [1, 2, 3]})" |> cypher!
%{"nodes-created" => 1, "properties-set" => 1}

iex> [%{"n.blue" => blue}] =
...> "MATCH (n) WHERE exists(n.blue) RETURN n.blue" |> cypher! ; blue
[1, 2, 3]
```

Relationships

The pattern for creating and matching a relationship in Cypher is:

```
() - [ variable? :type {properties}? ] - ()
```

Note that the relationship includes the two nodes it links. For CREATE queries, a directed arrow (either -[...]-> or <-[...]-) is required. For MATCH queries, where the direction isn't important, an undirected link (-[...]-) is used.

Here's an example of a relationship with a property map:

```
iex> "CREATE (a)-[r:REL_TYPE {baz: 123}]->(b)" |> cypher!
%{"nodes-created" => 2, "properties-set" => 1, "relationships-created" => 1}
iex> "MATCH ()-[r:REL_TYPE]-() RETURN r" |> cypher!
[
  %{
    "r" => %Bolt.Sips.Types.Relationship{
      end: 22512,
      id: 1518,
      properties: %{"baz" => 123},
      start: 22540,
      type: "REL_TYPE"
    }
  }
]
```

So, variable is used for cross-referencing within a single query part, type is the type for the relationship, and properties is a property map as before.

Paths

The pattern for creating and matching a path in Cypher is:

```
() - [] -> () - [] -> () ...
```

Here's an example of a path with four nodes:

```
iex> """
...> CREATE (a {name: 'a'})-[:X]->()<-[:Y]-()-[:Z]->(b {name: 'b'})
...> """ |> cypher!
%{"nodes-created" => 4, "properties-set" => 2, "relationships-created" => 3}
```

The path syntax is the same as that for a relationship, but it's extended to include all the nodes in the path. As with relationships, the path links use a directed arrow (either -[...]-> or <-[...]-) between node pairs for CREATE queries.

For MATCH queries, where the direction isn't important, an undirected link (-[...]-) is used. It's also possible to specify a path length using the [*n] syntax:

```
iex> "MATCH p = ({name: 'a'})-[*3]-({name: 'b'}) RETURN p" |> cypher!
[
  %{
    "p" => %Bolt.Sips.Types.Path{
      nodes: [ ... ],
      relationships: [ ... ],
      sequence: [1, 1, -2, 2, 3, 3]
    }
  }
]
```

And with that in hand, let's try out some test queries.

First Queries with Cypher

Let's cd back to our ExGraphsBook root and open up IEx:

```
$ iex -S mix
Erlang/OTP 24 [erts-12.3.1] ...
```

We can then use the graph_context/1 macro to switch our context to use the PropertyGraph module:

```
iex> graph_context PropertyGraph
PropertyGraph
```

And we can inspect the graph service with a graph_info/0 call:

```
iex> graph_info
%GraphCommons.Service.GraphInfo{
  file: "",
  labels: ["Movie", "Person"],
  num_edges: 253,
  num_nodes: 171,
  type: :property
}
```

What you see in the graph_info summary will depend on how you've set up your Neo4j instance. If you've installed the demo movies graph that comes with Neo4j, you may see something similar to the summary shown here. But this doesn't matter as long as there is something to query on.

For a simple initial exploration, we've defined some basic graph queries (nodes.cypher, nodes_and_relationships.cypher, paths.cypher, and relationships.cypher) and their variant forms to get a single entity (node1.cypher, node1_and_relationships.cypher, path1.cypher, and relationship1.cypher) in a lib folder under queries in the code listings. But you can also create them here.

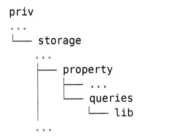

```
priv
...
└── storage
    ...
    ├── property
    │   ├── ...
    │   └── queries
    │       └── lib
    ...
```

Let's create that directory now:

```
$ mkdir -p priv/storage/property/queries/lib
```

You can either copy those queries over from the code listings or create them yourself from the following examples.

You can then list out those queries by filename:

```
iex> list_queries_dir("lib") |> Enum.each(
...> fn f -> IO.puts "* " <> f; read_query("lib/" <> f).data |> IO.puts end
...> )
* node1.cypher
MATCH (n) RETURN n LIMIT 1

* node1_and_relationships.cypher
MATCH (n) MATCH (n)-[r]-() RETURN DISTINCT n, r

* node_id1.cypher
MATCH (n) RETURN n LIMIT 1

* node_ids.cypher
MATCH (n) RETURN DISTINCT id(n)

* nodes.cypher
MATCH (n) RETURN DISTINCT n

* nodes_and_relationships.cypher
MATCH (n) MATCH ()-[r]-() RETURN DISTINCT n, r

* path1.cypher
MATCH p = ()--() RETURN p LIMIT 1

* paths.cypher
MATCH p = ()--() RETURN DISTINCT p

* relationship1.cypher
MATCH ()-[r]-() RETURN r LIMIT 1
```

```
* relationship_ids.cypher
MATCH ()-[r]-() RETURN DISTINCT id(r)

* relationships.cypher
MATCH ()-[r]-() RETURN DISTINCT r

:ok
```

Here's how you might send a query directly from a query file, in this case for a single node:

```
iex> read_query("lib/node1.cypher").data |> cypher!
[
  %{
    "n" => %Bolt.Sips.Types.Node{
      id: 2634,
      labels: ["Person"],
      properties: %{"born" => 1971, "name" => "Regina King"}
    }
  }
]
```

But let's look now at creating our own graph. We'll start with our reference graph—the book graph.

Modeling the Book Graph

We're going to implement our book graph using the property graph model. First, let's remind ourselves what this book graph looks like—take a look at this figure on page 9, which shows our reference book graph.

This book graph can be mapped into the property graph model as shown in the following figure. As you can see, it maps almost exactly.

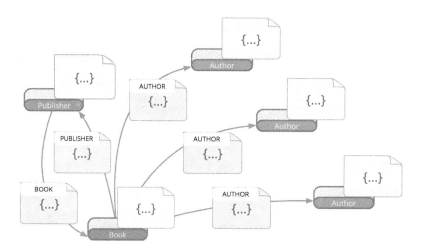

Yes, that's right. It looks like the property graph model has full support for all the features we require.

We can express this book graph in Cypher as:

```
// book 1
CREATE
(bk1:Book {
    id:  "adopting_elixir",
    date: "2018-03-14",
    format: "Paper",
    isbn: "978-1-68050-252-7",
    title: "Adopting Elixir",
    url: "https://pragprog.com/titles/tvmelixir/adopting-elixir/"
}),
(bk1_au1:Author {
    id: "ben_marx",
    name: "Ben Marx",
    url: "https://twitter.com/bgmarx"
}),
(bk1_au2:Author {
    id: "jose_valim",
    name: "José Valim",
    url: "https://twitter.com/josevalim"
}),
(bk1_au3:Author {
    id: "bruce_tate",
    name: "Bruce Tate",
    url: "https://twitter.com/redrapids"
}),
(bk1_pub:Publisher {
    id: "pragmatic",
    name: "The Pragmatic Bookshelf",
    url: "https://pragprog.com/"
})
CREATE
(bk1)-[:AUTHOR { role: "first author" }]->(bk1_au1),
(bk1)-[:AUTHOR { role: "second author" }]->(bk1_au2),
(bk1)-[:AUTHOR { role: "third author" }]->(bk1_au3),
(bk1)-[:PUBLISHER]->(bk1_pub),
(bk1_pub)-[:BOOK]->(bk1)

;
```

Here bk1, bk1_au1, bk1_au2, bk1_au3, and bk1_pub are internal variables being used for cross-referencing in the Cypher query.

Now let's create a new database and import the book graph we just created:

```
iex> graph_delete
%Bolt.Sips.Response{
  ...
  stats: %{"nodes-deleted" => 17, "relationships-deleted" => 17},
  type: "w"
}
iex> graph_create read_graph("book.cypher")
%Bolt.Sips.Response{
  ...
  stats: %{
    "labels-added" => 5,
    "nodes-created" => 5,
    "properties-set" => 21,
    "relationships-created" => 5
  },
  type: "w"
}
```

We can get a summary with the graph_info/0 function:

```
iex> graph_info
%GraphCommons.Service.GraphInfo{
  file: "",
  labels: ["Author", "Book", "Publisher"],
  num_edges: 5,
  num_nodes: 5,
  type: :property
}
```

This confirms that five labeled nodes and five relationships have been created together with 20 properties.

Querying for Nodes

We can now test this graph by querying over all the nodes. Let's get system IDs and labels:

```
iex> "MATCH (n) RETURN id(n), labels(n)" |> cypher!
[
  %{"id(n)" => 0, "labels(n)" => ["Book"]},
  %{"id(n)" => 1, "labels(n)" => ["Author"]},
  %{"id(n)" => 2, "labels(n)" => ["Author"]},
  %{"id(n)" => 3, "labels(n)" => ["Author"]},
  %{"id(n)" => 4, "labels(n)" => ["Publisher"]}
]
```

So let's get system IDs and properties for those nodes with an Author label:

```
iex> "MATCH (n:Author) RETURN id(n), properties(n)" |> cypher!
[
  %{
    "id(n)" => 1,
    "properties(n)" => %{
      "id" => "ben_marx",
      "name" => "Ben Marx",
      "url" => "https://twitter.com/bgmarx"
    }
  },
  %{
    "id(n)" => 2,
    "properties(n)" => %{
      "id" => "jose_valim",
      "name" => "José Valim",
      "url" => "https://twitter.com/josevalim"
    }
  },
  %{
    "id(n)" => 3,
    "properties(n)" => %{
      "id" => "bruce_tate",
      "name" => "Bruce Tate",
      "url" => "https://twitter.com/redrapids"
    }
  }
]
```

It's worth pointing out here that there might be some confusion between the system ID returned by the id(n) function and the id property on a node. One way around this would be to use aliases as:

```
iex> """
...> MATCH (n:Author) RETURN id(n) AS sys_id, properties(n) AS properties
...> """ |> cypher!
[
  %{
    "properties" => %{
      "id" => "ben_marx",
      "name" => "Ben Marx",
      "url" => "https://twitter.com/bgmarx"
    },
    "sys_id" => 1
  },
  ...
```

But let's carry on as we are for now.

Querying for Relationships

Likewise, we can query over all the relationships:

```
iex> "MATCH ()-[r]->() RETURN id(r), type(r)" |> cypher!
[
  %{"id(r)" => 3, "type(r)" => "PUBLISHER"},
  %{"id(r)" => 2, "type(r)" => "AUTHOR"},
  %{"id(r)" => 1, "type(r)" => "AUTHOR"},
  %{"id(r)" => 0, "type(r)" => "AUTHOR"},
  %{"id(r)" => 4, "type(r)" => "BOOK"}
]
```

And we can also query for the properties of a given relationship:

```
iex> "MATCH ()-[r:AUTHOR]->() RETURN id(r), properties(r)" |> cypher!
[
  %{"id(r)" => 0, "properties(r)" => %{"role" => "first author"}},
  %{"id(r)" => 1, "properties(r)" => %{"role" => "second author"}},
  %{"id(r)" => 2, "properties(r)" => %{"role" => "third author"}}
]
```

Querying for Paths

Now let's try querying over paths. Here we look for the path between a node with a :Book label and a node with an :Author label with a :url property of "https://twitter.com/redrapids":

```
iex> nodes = """
...> MATCH p = (n)-[*]->(m)
...> WHERE n.id = "pragmatic" AND m.id = "ben_marx"
...> RETURN nodes(p)
...> """ |> cypher!
[
  %{
    "nodes(p)" => [
      %Bolt.Sips.Types.Node{
        id: 4,
        labels: ["Publisher"],
        properties: %{
          "id" => "pragmatic",
          "name" => "The Pragmatic Bookshelf",
          "url" => "https://pragprog.com/"
        }
      },
      %Bolt.Sips.Types.Node{
        id: 0,
        labels: ["Book"],
        properties: %{
          "date" => "2018-03-14",
          "format" => "Paper",
```

```
              "id" => "adopting_elixir",
              "isbn" => "978-1-68050-252-7",
              "title" => "Adopting Elixir",
              "url" => "https://pragprog.com/titles/tvmelixir/adopting-elixir/"
          }
        },
        %Bolt.Sips.Types.Node{
          id: 1,
          labels: ["Author"],
          properties: %{
            "id" => "ben_marx",
            "name" => "Ben Marx",
            "url" => "https://twitter.com/bgmarx"
          }
        }
      ]
  }
]
iex> nodes |> Enum.map(&(&1["nodes(p)"] |>
...> Enum.reduce([], fn n, acc -> [n.properties["id"] | acc]  end)))
[["ben_marx", "adopting_elixir", "pragmatic"]]
```

Alternatively, we can do this in Cypher using list comprehension:

```
iex> """
...> MATCH p = (n)-[*]->(m)
...> WHERE n.id = "pragmatic" AND m.id = "ben_marx"
...> RETURN [n IN nodes(p) | n.id] AS node
...> """ |> cypher!
[%{"node" => ["pragmatic", "adopting_elixir", "ben_marx"]}]
```

If we want to find the longest path in our graph, we could try listing all unique path lengths:

```
iex> "MATCH p = ()-[*]->() RETURN DISTINCT length(p)" |> cypher!
[%{"length(p)" => 1}, %{"length(p)" => 2}, %{"length(p)" => 3}]
```

Or we could get the longest path length directly as:

```
iex> """
...> MATCH p = ()-[*]->() RETURN DISTINCT length(p)
...> ORDER BY length(p) DESC LIMIT 1
...> """ |> cypher!
[%{"length(p)" => 3}]
```

Of course, we should note that computing all paths in the graph is feasible only for smaller graphs and can quickly become extremely expensive for graphs of any real size.

So, let's see an example of one of those paths of length 1:

```
iex> """
...> MATCH p = ()-[*]->() WHERE length(p) = 1
...> RETURN p LIMIT 1
...> """ |> cypher!
[
  %{
    "p" => %Bolt.Sips.Types.Path{
      nodes: [
        %Bolt.Sips.Types.Node{
          id: 0,
          labels: ["Book"],
          properties: %{
            "date" => "2018-03-14",
            "format" => "Paper",
            "id" => "adopting_elixir",
            "isbn" => "978-1-68050-252-7",
            "title" => "Adopting Elixir",
            "url" => "https://pragprog.com/titles/tvmelixir/adopting-elixir/"
          }
        },
        %Bolt.Sips.Types.Node{
          id: 1,
          labels: ["Author"],
          properties: %{
            "id" => "ben_marx",
            "name" => "Ben Marx",
            "url" => "https://twitter.com/bgmarx"
          }
        }
      ],
      relationships: [
        %Bolt.Sips.Types.UnboundRelationship{
          end: nil,
          id: 0,
          properties: %{"role" => "first author"},
          start: nil,
          type: "AUTHOR"
        }
      ],
      sequence: [1, 1]
    }
  }
]
```

As noted, the book graph is a simple graph, so for more expressive queries, we'll need to upgrade to a more interesting graph such as the ARPANET graph. Let's look at that now.

Recalling the ARPANET

Before there was the Internet, there was the ARPANET. The ARPANET was founded by the Advanced Research Projects Agency (ARPA) of the United States Department of Defense as a prototype of a packet-switched network for connecting computer resources. It would be developed into a coherent computer network and later subsumed into the larger global internetwork—the Internet.

The first connection between a pair of ARPANET hosts was made in October 1969, following the Moon landing in July that same year (with the Woodstock music festival sandwiched somewhere in between). A four-host network appeared in December 1969 and the network was progressively scaled up through the '70s and '80s and finally decommissioned in 1990. This was where the Internet protocol suite and the TCP/IP set of protocols were first born and trialed.

The growth of the fledgling network was described in a series of ARPANET logical maps, which make for compelling reading. These show the nascent network as graphs of (network) nodes and (computer) hosts with lines connecting them, which get progressively more complex. A published example of network topology for December 1972 is given in RFC-432 (Network logical map).[4]

The following figure shows the state of the network in December 1970, with 13 nodes (in blue), 21 hosts (in white), and 40 edges between them. (There are also two user hosts that are connected via the server hosts but aren't shown.)

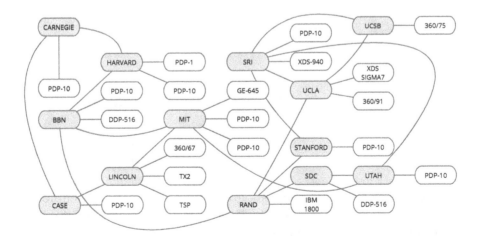

---

4.   https://www.rfc-editor.org/rfc/rfc432.pdf

Let's see how we can model this more simply. To make things easier, let's roll back a couple of years to the four-node network from December of that standout year—1969. In the following figure, we have one host computer at each of the four sites (UCLA, UCSB, SRI, and Utah). Each site has a dedicated minicomputer—the Interface Message Processor (IMP), which functions as a node on the network backbone. The host computers are satellites and are attached directly to the IMPs.

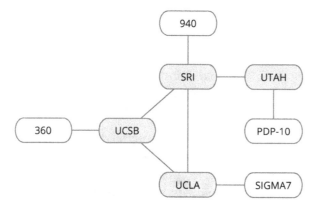

Moving on from name labels to type labels (Node and Host) with ID strings (sri, ucla, and so on) we can represent the graph as shown in the next figure.

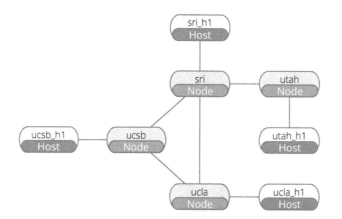

We can model this similar to the book graph from earlier in the chapter. We have two types of (graph) nodes, which we can distinguish with the labels Node and Host. We can then add id and name properties to these nodes, and for the Node nodes we can add a type property as variants of the IMP begin to appear.

The graph is undirected although a direction is needed in Cypher CREATE statements. Also needed but not shown in the diagrams is a type for the relationship. There are two main kinds of links: links between IMP and IMP and links between Host and IMP. There are no obvious unique names for these, so let's go with N_LINK for Node (to Node) links and H_LINK for Host (to Node) links, respectively.

So we can now describe the December 1969 network with this chunk of Cypher:

```
//
// SEGMENT 1 - Outer Circuit (Clockwise from UCLA to SRI)

// Site: UCLA

CREATE (ucla:Node { id: "ucla", type: "IMP", name: "UCLA" })
CREATE (ucla_h1:Host { id: "ucla_h1", name: "SIGMA7" })
CREATE (ucla_h1)-[:H_LINK]->(ucla)

// Site: UCSB

CREATE (ucsb:Node { id: "ucsb", type: "IMP", name: "UCSB" })
CREATE (ucsb_h1:Host { id: "ucsb_h1", name: "360" })
CREATE (ucsb_h1)-[:H_LINK]->(ucsb)

// Site: SRI

CREATE (sri:Node { id: "sri", type: "IMP", name: "SRI" })
CREATE (sri_h1:Host { id: "sri_h1", name: "940" })
CREATE (sri_h1)-[:H_LINK]->(sri)


//
// SEGMENT 2 - Outer Path (Right from SRI to UTAH)

// Site: UTAH

CREATE (utah:Node { id: "utah", type: "IMP", name: "UTAH" })
CREATE (utah_h1:Host { id: "utah_h1", name: "PDP-10" })
CREATE (utah_h1)-[:H_LINK]->(utah)

// NETWORK (3+1=4)

//
// SEGMENT 1 - Outer Circuit (Clockwise from UCLA to SRI)
CREATE (ucla)-[:N_LINK]->(ucsb)
CREATE (ucsb)-[:N_LINK]->(sri)
CREATE (sri)-[:N_LINK]->(ucla)
//
// SEGMENT 2 - Outer Path (Right from SRI to UTAH)
CREATE (sri)-[:N_LINK]->(utah)
```

We can take this out for a spin now. But let's use the slightly more developed network for December 1970, which is formed in the same manner.

We'll first need to read this graph into our graph service:

```
iex> graph_create read_graph("arpa/arpa70.cypher")
%Bolt.Sips.Response{
  ...
  stats: %{
    "labels-added" => 36,
    "nodes-created" => 36,
    "properties-set" => 85,
    "relationships-created" => 40
  },
  ...
}
```

Let's say we want to get the shortest path between two host computers: a PDP-1 at Harvard and an XDS SIGMA7 at UCLA. Here's one way to do that:

```
iex> """
...> MATCH (n), (m), p = shortestPath((n)-[*]-(m))
...> WHERE n.id = "harvard_h1" AND m.id = "ucla_h2"
...> RETURN [n IN nodes(p) | n.name] AS node
...> """ |> cypher!
[%{"node" => ["PDP-1", "HARVARD", "BBN", "RAND", "UCLA", "XDS SIGMA7"]}]
```

We can see this path in the figure marked out with the red line.

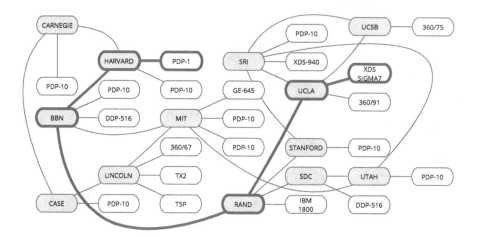

And, of course, we can replace this graph with other graphs of interest by clearing the database and querying with a Cypher query string for creating graphs.

Passing Parameters to Queries

Cypher supports querying with parameters.[5] This simplifies query reuse and makes caching of execution plans easier, in turn leading to faster query execution times.

The Bolt.Sips module allows us to pass our parameters as a map in a third argument to the query/3 function. (The first argument is the database connection, and the second is the query string.)

But the query functions we've created so far take the query string and implicitly supply the database connection. We'll need to do something about that.

Supporting Parameters

We've already updated the GraphCommons.Service behaviour with a couple of optional callbacks:

```
@optional_callbacks query_graph: 2
@optional_callbacks query_graph!: 2

@callback query_graph(GraphCommons.Query.t(), map()) :: any()
@callback query_graph!(GraphCommons.Query.t(), map()) :: any()
```

This allows us to extend the basic PropertyGraph.Service implementation.

We need to add a cypher!/2 query helper in GraphCommons.Utils to pair off with the cypher!/1 query helper:

apps/graph_commons/lib/graph_commons/utils.ex
```
def cypher!(query_string, query_params),
  do: to_query_graph!(PropertyGraph, query_string, query_params)
```

Querying with Parameters

Let's query first for a system ID using the id() function on our nodes:

```
iex> "MATCH (n) WHERE id(n) = $id RETURN n" >| cypher!(%{id: 22484})
[
  %{
    "n" => %Bolt.Sips.Types.Node{
      id: 22484,
      labels: ["Node"],
      properties: %{"id" => "rand", "name" => "RAND", "type" => "IMP"}
    }
  }
]
```

---

5. https://neo4j.com/docs/cypher-manual/current/syntax/parameters/

Here we've added a query parameter using the param map. Note that the actual :id value is a system property and is not guaranteed to be reliable—it'll vary from system to system. We are using it here as a simple illustration.

Here's the corresponding query for a user ID using the :id property of the nodes:

```
iex> "MATCH (n) WHERE n.id = $id RETURN n" |> cypher!(%{id: "rand"})
[
  %{
    "n" => %Bolt.Sips.Types.Node{
      id: 22484,
      labels: ["Node"],
      properties: %{"id" => "rand", "name" => "RAND", "type" => "IMP"}
    }
  }
]
```

Another parametrized query might be a string search. There are many different host computers attached to the network. Let's say we want to search hosts by name—we can use Cypher's STARTS WITH operator. For now, let's insert a variable $char into the query string and then we can run a query with the key :char passed in the parameter map:

```
iex> q = """
...> MATCH (n:Host) WHERE n.name STARTS WITH $char
...> RETURN n.id, n.name
...> """
```

The ARPANET era was also the heyday of minicomputers—especially the PDP from DEC. (And the PDP minicomputer will always resonate strongly with me as the first computer I used. That machine was a PDP-11, although the machines listed here are of an earlier vintage.) So, how many of the hosts were PDPs on our December 1970 map, and where were they?

```
iex> pdp = q |> cypher!(%{char: "PDP"})
[
  %{"n.id" => "bbn_h2", "n.name" => "PDP-10"},
  %{"n.id" => "stanford_h1", "n.name" => "PDP-10"},
  %{"n.id" => "sri_h1", "n.name" => "PDP-10"},
  %{"n.id" => "case_h1", "n.name" => "PDP-10"},
  %{"n.id" => "carnegie_h1", "n.name" => "PDP-10"},
  %{"n.id" => "harvard_h1", "n.name" => "PDP-1"},
  %{"n.id" => "harvard_h2", "n.name" => "PDP-10"},
  %{"n.id" => "utah_h1", "n.name" => "PDP-10"},
  %{"n.id" => "mit_h1", "n.name" => "PDP-10"},
  %{"n.id" => "mit_h2", "n.name" => "PDP-10"}
]
iex> length pdp
```

So, this has been a brief introduction to Cypher as a query language. But what can Cypher do in terms of modeling the data structures used in the graph? Let's turn to that now.

Schemas and Types in Cypher

Obviously, we've barely touched upon the full power of Cypher for building and querying graph stores and its special capabilities to query over paths within the graph. But what about the data models that can be supported in property graphs? Well, Cypher provides some strong data management facilities—schemas and data typing.

Schemas

One aspect that we haven't discussed yet is schemas. Cypher includes support for managing both indexes and constraints over labels, which together constitute a property graph schema.

Indexes

Indexes (both simple and composite) are used for expediting query lookup. For nodes with a given label, an index can be created on a single property (simple) or a number of properties (composite).

Let's say we want an index on the name property for nodes with an Author label, as we have in the book graph:

```
iex> "CREATE INDEX ON :Author(name)" |> cypher!
%{"indexes-added" => 1}
```

Now we'll get a performance boost when we query on that property:

```
iex> "MATCH (n:Author) WHERE n.name = 'Bruce Tate' RETURN n.id" |> cypher!
[%{"n.id" => "bruce_tate"}]
```

We can list out the indexes that are present in the database using a built-in procedure:

```
iex> "CALL db.indexes" |> cypher!
[
  %{
  "description" => "INDEX ON :Author(name)",
  ...
  "type" => "node_unique_property"
},
...
]
```

And we can explicitly remove indexes with the DROP command.

Note that indexes are implicitly created when we set up constraints.

Constraints

Constraints can be used to ensure node property uniqueness, node and relationship property existence, and node keys. The node keys ensure that all nodes with a particular label have a set of defined properties with a unique combined value. Property existence and node key constraints are only available in the Enterprise Edition of Neo4j. We'll look at an example here of a property uniqueness constraint.

Recall the H_2O graph which has two hydrogen atoms with label H and property label H:

```
iex> IO.puts read_graph("h2o.cypher").data
CREATE
(:H {label: 'H'})<-[:BOND]-(:O {label: 'O'})-[:BOND]->(:H {label: 'H'})
:ok
```

If we create that graph and *then* set a constraint that the property labels should be unique, we should get an error. Let's try that:

```
iex> graph_create read_graph("h2o.cypher")
%Bolt.Sips.Response{
  ...
  stats: %{
    "labels-added" => 3,
    "nodes-created" => 3,
    "properties-set" => 3,
    "relationships-created" => 2
  },
  type: "w"
}
```

```
iex> "CREATE CONSTRAINT ON (a:H) ASSERT a.label IS UNIQUE" |> cypher!
** (RuntimeError) ! %Bolt.Sips.Error{code:
"Neo.DatabaseError.Schema.ConstraintCreationFailed", message: "Unable to
create CONSTRAINT ON ( h:H ) ASSERT h.label IS UNIQUE:\nBoth Node(22532) and
Node(22534) have the label `H` and property `label` = 'H'"}
    (property_graph) lib/property_graph/service.ex:98:
PropertyGraph.Service.query_graph!/2
```

And indeed, that is just what we see.

Now if we do this in the normal (expected) order—that is, create the constraint and then the graph—we should fail when we try to create the graph with two property labels H:

```
iex> "CREATE CONSTRAINT ON (a:H) ASSERT a.label IS UNIQUE" |> cypher!
[]

iex> graph_create read_graph("h2o.cypher")

** (Bolt.Sips.Exception) Node(22629) already exists with label `H` and property
`label` = 'H'
    (elixir) lib/process.ex:767: Process.info/2
    (bolt_sips) lib/bolt_sips/query.ex:116: Bolt.Sips.Query.query_commit/3
    (bolt_sips) lib/bolt_sips/query.ex:58: Bolt.Sips.Query.query!/3
    (stdlib) erl_eval.erl:680: :erl_eval.do_apply/6
    (iex) lib/iex/evaluator.ex:257: IEx.Evaluator.handle_eval/5
    (iex) lib/iex/evaluator.ex:237: IEx.Evaluator.do_eval/3
```

And again, this is what we see.

As with indexes, we can list out any constraints in the database.

```
iex> "CALL db.constraints" |> cypher!
[
  %{"description" => "CONSTRAINT ON ( h:H ) ASSERT h.label IS UNIQUE"},
  ...
]
```

We can also remove constraints with the DROP command.

The schema constraint mechanism here is more about data integrity and doesn't support inferencing—the generation of new data—which is something the RDF graphs, which we'll explore in the next chapter, allow for.

Types

The type system used by Cypher is documented on the Values and types page of the Neo4j Cypher Manual.[6]

Property types include:

- numeric—integer, float
- string
- boolean
- spatial—point
- temporal—date, time, datetime, duration, and so on

We'll see later that RDF graphs have a more rigorous datatyping based on XML Schema datatypes for recognized datatypes but are also extensible to allow adding in custom datatypes.

---

6. https://neo4j.com/docs/cypher-manual/current/syntax/values/

Looking for More Cypher Graphs?

If you're looking for more examples of Cypher graphs, note that Neo4j supports a teaching tool format called GraphGists. These are simple text-based documents based on the AsciiDoc[7] format that support GraphGist directives through special comments.

The intention is to build up a library of user-supplied graph models, which can be displayed through the GraphGist application and in a browser for instructional purposes. Check the GraphGists page[8] for examples and also the GitHub project.[9]

Wrapping Up

We've seen in this chapter how we can query property graphs using the Cypher query language. We started off by giving a quick recap of Cypher patterns for building and querying nodes, relationships, and paths. We also showed off a simple test query library.

Next, we looked at our reference book graph and saw how we could implement that in Cypher as a property graph. It turns out that Cypher is expressive enough to capture all the features we want to model. We looked at some basic queries on this simple graph.

To make things a little more interesting, we then turned to the ARPANET graphs and saw how we could render the early ARPANET logical network maps as property graphs. And we got to try out some path queries on those historical networks.

To extend our querying capability, we added support for query parameters and showed some example queries using parameters.

Lastly, we took the opportunity to review some aspects of the Neo4j graph database, such as data types and schema support through indexes and constraints.

At this point, it almost looks like property graphs have everything we could need. But as we'll see in the next chapter, RDF graphs promise much in the way of large-scale data integration—and we're talking here about web-scale data integration. They will also introduce us to a whole new world of reasoning and inference. Semantic graphs are about to get a lot more real.

---

7. http://asciidoc.org/
8. https://neo4j.com/graphgists/
9. https://github.com/neo4j-examples/graphgists

## CHAPTER 7

Graphing Globally with RDF

While property graphs focus on solving a range of immediate tactical problems, the RDF graph model focuses on the longer-term strategic goals of large-scale data integration, especially public data integration. This has been one of the driving forces behind the semantic web vision.

The Resource Description Framework (RDF) is a data model standardized by the W3C for describing resources on the web. But note that it's the descriptions that are on the web, not necessarily the resources that are being described. This means that we can use RDF to describe anything, whether it's online or not. Put simply, we might say anything that can be named. In fact, we can also describe unnamed things too. So, "anything" can be described. And these descriptions are built up using the common web-naming convention—the URI.

Of course, we can also use property graphs to describe things, but here's the real kicker. Without any common naming convention, it's difficult to exchange any meanings except by some prior arrangement, which means an application has to keep track of what goes with what, and what means what. With a common naming system, however, we can freely share our descriptions of things with others—with no ambiguity. And we can share our meanings too, which is a crazy big win.

So how does all this work?

The RDF data model describes resources in terms of statements which can be interpreted as a basic graph structure—a directed labeled graph. The labels used in RDF graphs are URIs. This is that little bit of magic that allows one RDF graph to be added to another RDF graph. This leads to an incredibly simple way of doing data integration. Just add your RDF datasets together—the names, or labels, that are used will take care of joining the data elements together.

By the way, the title of this chapter implies the use of URIs as global names, which allows for building global data structures. In practice, this also allows for building out a global graph, which is kind of awesome. More awesome though is the fact that this global graph already exists in the form of the linked open data (LOD) cloud[1] and is essentially a growing graph of graphs of open data.

Web Names—A Crib Sheet

URL—Uniform Resource Locator
A web document address

URI—Uniform Resource Identifier
A web identifier for a resource, which may also be located

IRI—Internationalized Resource Identifier
An international form for a URI

RDF is a data model and not a data format, which means that we can write out an RDF graph in many different ways. There are a number of standard serializations by the W3C, and these allow for a high degree of interoperability in reading and writing RDF data. We thus have a standard means of sharing RDF graphs and can input and output them with ease.

But there is more to RDF than this. We can also define and express standard schema languages in RDF, and then layer this schema RDF on top of an existing RDF dataset. This allows us to query over a richer graph of data—one that has now been augmented with the actual data model that the data conforms to. And as the schema languages encode a given logic, we can then make inferences over the data and add these new inferred statements back into our graph.

What's Different About RDF?

RDF is about sharing data—essentially sharing descriptions of things. And those descriptions are expressed as graphs.

Two of the most notable features of the RDF graph model seen from a graph perspective are global identity and inference. The first greatly simplifies data integration and the second helps in building out knowledge graphs.

Let's talk about each of these.

---

1. https://lod-cloud.net/

Integrating Data at Scale

RDF uses web names, or URIs, for identifying the nodes and edges in its data model. What does that mean? It means everything.

The URI has been a key development in the ongoing integration of the global telecoms network. It builds on the DNS system for naming computers as nodes on the (inter)network. By extending it with a network protocol scheme and a local address on the host system we can identify (and retrieve) documents using the web. The same URI pattern that we use for documents can also be used to identify data points within an RDF graph. The thinking here is that descriptions of things (that is, documents) can be sent in place of the actual things themselves, which may not be so easy to transmit without Star Trek transporters to beam them down. So, in principle, information about any resource (be it physical or abstract) can be returned. We can build out a global information network.

There's another benefit to using URIs—namespacing. With namespacing based on DNS names, we get naming authorities, branding, and trust, and with the DNS name as the namespace root, we get guarantees of uniqueness. It follows that we effectively have a commons for developing a shared semantics with types and properties all globally namespaced. There is now no confusion as to where names come from.

OK, so far, we've talked about sharing data and the semantics for that data, but we haven't talked about data integration. Let's look at the way data integration happens. If user A makes statements about a subject S, and user B also makes statements about a subject S, then those sets of statements can be simply added together because the subject S is the same in both cases. And we know the subject S is the same because we are using a global name. What we effectively have with RDF are self-joining datasets based on the use of URIs, or global names.

Extracting Knowledge from Graphs

Graphs are an excellent choice for representing knowledge bases as they allow easy and arbitrary connections to be set up between the data items. This naturally leads to the notion of knowledge graphs.

But knowledge graphs are more than fixed data stores. They generally follow an open-world model that allows new data to be added as required, and the shape of the data isn't constrained as is the case in a relational database.

In a sense, they are programmable knowledge stores. New data can be added from the outside, new data can be generated from the inside, and new interpretations over the data can be made. They are more akin to knowledge machines.

RDF builds on common standards for naming, which allows for different datasets to be readily mixed together. Formal reasoning systems from the knowledge representation communities have been layered on top of the basic RDF model. RDF datasets can then be modeled according to RDF schemas (or "ontologies" as they are sometimes called) which are also expressed in RDF. These RDF schemas are built on a formal semantics and a system of logic. This means we can reason over the data, deduce logical inferences, and extract new facts, or statements, which can be added to the dataset. We can thus "grow" the dataset.

At this point, we should probably take a quick look at the RDF data model before we get some real experience with generating RDF from Elixir.

RDF Model

An RDF description is built up of a set of RDF statements where each RDF statement is comprised of a subject, a predicate (or property), and an object—or, as it is called, an RDF triple. Each RDF triple encodes an RDF statement. These RDF statements (or triples) are modeled in graph terms as a node, an edge, and a node as shown in this figure:

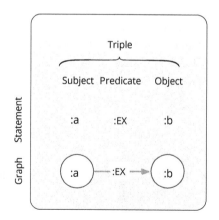

So, subjects link to objects via predicates (or properties). In our simple graph, subject :a links to object :b via the predicate (or property) :EX.

The terms here are all shown in the default namespace (indicated by the empty prefix before the : separator), but usually, each term will be taken from its own namespace. Suppose we have an RDF statement such as the following:

```
ns1:a ns2:EX ns3:b .
```

Here the namespace prefixes ns1:, ns2:, and ns3: are all paired off with URI namespaces. Writing that RDF statement out in its full form would give us this:

```
<http://ns1.com/a> <http://ns2.com/EX> <http://ns3.com/b> .
```

Here the <, > brackets mark out a URI.

This is the RDF triple. And an RDF dataset is a set of RDF triples. In fact, this RDF triple expresses a graph edge between two graph nodes.

Now this RDF triple shows the linkages between things. To add descriptions to these things, we add strings like this:

```
ns1:a ns2:EX_NAME "Example name" .
```

Or, in long form like this:

```
<http://ns1.com/a> <http://ns2.com/EX_NAME> "Example name" .
```

These descriptions are encoded as RDF triples, but with the object now as a string. This is how we add subject attributes in RDF.

Well, right about now, you might want to start coding. Let's crack on with that.

Creating the RDFGraph Project

To get some experience working with RDF graphs from Elixir, we'll set up an RDFGraph project under our umbrella application.

We're also going to need an RDF graph database for local experiments. We'll use the free version of Ontotext GraphDB.[2]

RDFGraph Project/Database Setup
See Appendix 1, Project Setups, on page 245, for details on retrieving a working project with code and data.
And see Appendix 2, Database Setups, on page 247, for help on setting up a local copy of GraphDB.

---

2. https://www.ontotext.com/products/graphdb/

We typically connect to RDF graph databases over the web using SPARQL endpoints, which is what we'll do here. SPARQL is the query language for RDF graphs, and we'll have more to say about this later.

We could use some help to make building and querying RDF from Elixir easier. When I first looked around for any hint of an RDF library in Elixir, I was excited to find the rdf[3] package from Marcel Otto,[4] which has exceptional support for working with RDF. He's also published the sparql[5] and sparql_client[6] packages for querying RDF, as well as the json_ld[7] package for serializing RDF. Check out the RDF on Elixir[8] page for more info.

Without further ado, let's create a new project RDFGraph. Go to the ExGraphsBook home project (see ExGraphsBook Umbrella, on page 16), cd down into the apps directory, and open up the new RDFGraph project:

```
$ mix new rdf_graph --module RDFGraph
```

Note that this time we use the --module option to override the default naming of the module.

We now have an apps directory that looks like this:

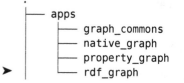

Let's cd into the rdf_graph directory:

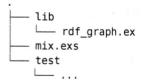

We'll declare a dependency on the sparql_client package (from the SPARQL.Client project) in the mix.exs file. (This will bring in the rdf and sparql package modules

---

3. https://hex.pm/packages/rdf
4. http://marcelotto.net/
5. https://hex.pm/packages/sparql
6. https://hex.pm/packages/sparql_client
7. https://hex.pm/packages/json_ld
8. https://rdf-elixir.dev/

from the RDF.ex and SPARQL.ex projects too.) We'll also use the hackney HTTP client in Erlang as recommended:

```
apps/rdf_graph/mix.exs
defp deps do
  [
    # graph_commons
    {:graph_commons, in_umbrella: true},
    # rdf graphs
    {:sparql_client, "~> 0.4"},
    {:hackney, "~> 1.17"}
  ]
end
```

As usual, use Mix to add in the dependency:

```
$ mix deps.get; mix deps.compile
```

We also need to add in the HTTP client:

```
config :tesla, :adapter, Tesla.Adapter.Hackney
```

Add these lines to the umbrella config.exs file in the main project directory or to an environment-specific import (for example, dev.exs).

Finally, let's wire our graph storage into the RDFGraph module with these use/2 macros:

```
apps/rdf_graph/lib/rdf_graph.ex
use GraphCommons.Graph, graph_type: :rdf, graph_module: __MODULE__
use GraphCommons.Query, query_type: :rdf, query_module: __MODULE__
```

Well, that's our setup. Our plan here is to spend some time first in this chapter looking at building RDF models, which may not be so familiar, and then to get into querying RDF graphs with SPARQL in Chapter 8, Querying RDF with SPARQL, on page 143.

Modeling the Book Graph

Before we start building and querying RDF, we'll want a better understanding of how to work with it. To get a better feel for what the RDF model looks like, let's revisit the book graph we introduced in the first chapter—see this figure on page 9, which shows our reference book graph.

The book graph can be mapped to RDF as shown in the figure on page 122.

One thing that we can immediately see is that RDF is more "graphy" than the property graph we saw earlier in Modeling the Book Graph, on page 98, because labels and attributes are modeled as independent nodes. (The attributes here

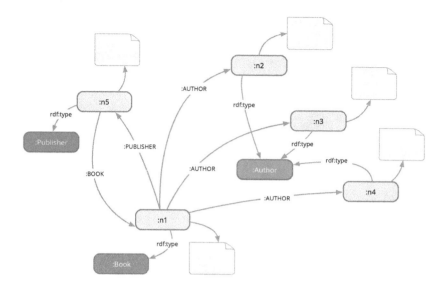

are shown for convenience as a single document icon, but in reality, each attribute is represented with its own node and a link from the original node.) This means an RDF graph is typically much larger than a corresponding property graph because the RDF graph has a more primitive data structure than a property graph. Specifically, in an RDF graph, there are no internal structures.

There are four things to note:

nodes (:n1, :n2, :n3, :n4, :n5) and edges (:AUTHOR, :BOOK, :PUBLISHER)
> are identified with web names, or URIs, shown here in the short-form prefix notation with a : character joining a namespace to a name (an empty namespace is assigned the default namespace)

node labels (:Author, :Book, :Publisher)
> are also identified with web names, or URIs, and are unbundled from the nodes and represented as new nodes in the graph with rdf:type links from the original node to these new label nodes—or types, as RDF calls them

node properties (yellow note)
> are unbundled from the nodes and represented as new nodes in the graph with links from the original node to these new property nodes

edge properties
> are not supported in the RDF model, although RDF*[9]—an extension to RDF—does support edge properties

---

9.   http://blog.liu.se/olafhartig/2019/01/10/position-statement-rdf-star-and-sparql-star/

We've also touched on node properties here. These are shown with a yellow note icon as a single thing to simplify the diagram, but they actually represent a basket of properties, and each property separately will be linked to from the node. In our case, all the property values are simple datatypes. If any of the property values were resources in their own right, they would become a new node in the graph with a URI.

This clearly shows that RDF has a primitive data model, with nodes and edges having URIs for labels but no intrinsic structure. Node labels (or types) and properties are separately managed in an extrinsic manner as part of the graph. The advantage of this from a semantic point of view is that these are global things and are not local to the node. This results from the open-data model of RDF and allows for statements to be added at will to the descriptions.

Enough with the theory. Let's see this in practice.

So, remember we said at the beginning of this chapter that RDF is a data model. Well, we can serialize an instance of this model in many ways, a number of which have been standardized by the W3C.

We're going to use Turtle[10] format, or Terse RDF Triple Language—a user-friendly plain text format for RDF.

We can express our book graph in Turtle as:

```
@prefix : <https://example/> .

<https://pragprog.com/>
    :id "pragmatic" ;
    :name "The Pragmatic Bookshelf" ;
    :url "https://pragprog.com/" ;
    :BOOK <https://pragprog.com/titles/tvmelixir/adopting-elixir/> ;
    a :Publisher .

<https://twitter.com/bgmarx>
    :id "ben_marx" ;
    :name "Ben Marx" ;
    :url "https://twitter.com/bgmarx" ;
    a :Author .

...

<https://pragprog.com/titles/tvmelixir/adopting-elixir/>
    :id "adopting_elixir" ;
    :date "2018-03-14";
    :format "Paper" ;
    :isbn "978-1-68050-252-7" ;
    :title "Adopting Elixir" ;
```

---

10. https://www.w3.org/TR/turtle/

```
:url "https://pragprog.com/titles/tvmelixir/adopting-elixir/" ;
:AUTHOR <https://twitter.com/bgmarx>, <https://twitter.com/josevalim>,
    <https://twitter.com/redrapids> ;
:PUBLISHER <https://pragprog.com/> ;
a :Book .
```

Some things are worth mentioning here. The most important one is that RDF uses URIs for IDs—both for nodes and edges. To make handling URIs simpler, Turtle has a namespace mechanism using prefix declarations, where a base URI can be associated with a namespace prefix. Our default namespace (here <https://example/>) is mapped to an empty namespace prefix. If we were to use an explicit namespace prefix (for example, "ex," although we could use any other prefix name, such as "foo"), we'd need to include a prefix declaration like this:

```
@prefix ex: <https://example/> .

<https://pragprog.com/>
    ex:id "pragmatic" ;
    ex:name "The Pragmatic Bookshelf" ;
    ex:url "https://pragprog.com/" ;
    ex:BOOK <https://pragprog.com/titles/tvmelixir/adopting-elixir/> ;
    a ex:Publisher .

...
```

URIs are delimited with <>, and strings with "". Also, the special form "a" in Turtle is short for rdf:type—a property that relates a class type.

The basic folded pattern shows a subject followed by a set of property/object pairs. If we were to write this out in a long-hand form with each statement written separately as subject/property/object (and with namespace prefixes substituted), we would then arrive at classic RDF triples:

```
<https://pragprog.com/> <https://example/id> "pragmatic" .
<https://pragprog.com/> <https://example/name> "The Pragmatic Bookshelf" .
<https://pragprog.com/> <https://example/url> "https://pragprog.com/" .
<https://pragprog.com/> <http://www.w3.org/1999/02/22-rdf-syntax-ns#type>
    <https://example/Publisher> .
```

This is an example of N-Triples[11] format—a canonical line-based format for RDF. Each triple is an independent statement, which makes it easier to work with but harder to read.

Note that we've also used a standard Turtle abbreviation on repeated properties—in this case, the :AUTHOR property is repeated, and it can be shown just once with a comma-separated list of values.

---

11. https://www.w3.org/TR/n-triples/

Our next step will be to create an RDF graph directly with Elixir. We'll start by generating an RDF vocabulary for our terms and then go on to build up a semantic RDF graph in Elixir.

Building an RDF Graph

We'll switch gears here and see how we can build up an RDF graph using RDF.ex rather than writing out the RDF explicitly as in the examples we just saw.

One of the challenges to working with RDF is managing URI strings. We'll need to deal with node names ourselves (for instance data) as these will generally use application-specific naming. But for edges and node labels, we don't want to be dealing with URI strings every time we add a property or a class name.

We can use one particular aspect of RDF.ex—its support for RDF vocabularies. This will abstract away the URI strings.

Let's see how we might do this.

Adding a SCHEMA Vocabulary for Schema.org Terms

We could generate a set of example terms as used in the previous example. But this would be rather limited. Somebody receiving such a graph using these example terms would have no idea about their meaning. And RDF is fundamentally about sharing graph data—and meanings. So, it's better to use a set of well-known terms that have a standard meaning.

An excellent candidate vocabulary that we could use is Schema.org,[12] which is a community activity founded by Google, Microsoft, Yahoo, and Yandex. Schema.org maintains a fairly large set of schemas. The schemas are a set of "types," each associated with a set of properties. Currently, the vocabulary has almost 800 types and 1500 properties.

We can usefully start by inspecting the Book[13] schema and seeing which terms we could use for our book graph.

Let's see how we might map our book terms into Schema.org terms, as shown in the table on page 126.

---

12. https://schema.org/
13. https://schema.org/Book

	Book Term	**Schema.org Term**
Types	Author	Person
	Book	Book
	Publisher	Organization
Properties	AUTHOR	author
	BOOK	–
	PUBLISHER	publisher
	date	datePublished
	format ("Paper")	bookFormat ("Paperback")
	id	identifier
	url	–
	isbn	isbn
	name	name
	title	name

Let's create a module RDFGraph.Vocab in the lib/rdf_graph/vocab.ex file and add a use RDF.Vocabulary.Namespace declaration:

```
defmodule RDFGraph.Vocab do
  use RDF.Vocabulary.Namespace

  # ...

end
```

Now we can add a defvocab definition block for SCHEMA:

apps/rdf_graph/lib/rdf_graph/vocab.ex
```
defvocab(SCHEMA,
  base_iri: "https://schema.org/",
  terms: ~w[
    Book Organization Person
    author book bookFormat datePublished
    identifier isbn name publisher
  ]
)
```

Note that in the defvocab definition block we have two keywords: base_iri, which is a string specifying the base IRI for the vocabulary, and terms, which takes a word list of the vocabulary terms.

Let's try this out in IEx:

```
iex> alias RDFGraph.Vocab.SCHEMA
RDFGraph.Vocab.SCHEMA
```

```
iex> SCHEMA.name
~I<https://schema.org/name>

iex> SCHEMA.datePublished
~I<https://schema.org/datePublished>
```

So, there we have it, a simple means of generating RDF IRIs in the SCHEMA namespace. Note that RDF.ex maintains IRIs as Elixir structs, which we can inspect by using the i/1 helper in IEx:

```
iex> i SCHEMA.name
Term
  ~I<https://schema.org/name>
Data type
  RDF.IRI
Description
  This is a struct. Structs are maps with a __struct__ key.
Reference modules
  RDF.IRI, Map
Implemented protocols
  ...
```

The ~I sigil is used to provide a simple string representation for the IRI struct. We can access the IRI string by using the value field of the struct:

```
iex> SCHEMA.name.value
"https://schema.org/name"
```

It looks good so far for properties.

Classes behave a little differently. They don't resolve directly to IRIs as properties do but can be made to resolve using the RDF.iri/1 function. They are, however, allowed by RDF.ex in any place that an IRI is expected:

```
iex> SCHEMA.Book
RDFGraph.Vocab.SCHEMA.Book

iex> RDF.iri(SCHEMA.Book)
~I<https://schema.org/Book>

iex> i SCHEMA.Book
Term
  RDFGraph.Vocab.SCHEMA.Book
Data type
  Atom
Raw representation
  :"Elixir.RDFGraph.Vocab.SCHEMA.Book"
Reference modules
  Atom
Implemented protocols
  ...
```

Using the SCHEMA Vocabulary to Build an RDF Graph

Let's put this to use now and build an RDF graph in Elixir. And of course, we'll use the book graph as our example.

Here we use two RDF.ex features: sigils for RDF terms and variant property function calls, which implement a description builder style. To glue it all together, we'll use the Elixir pipe operator |>.

Let's add this book/0 function to our RDFGraph.Vocab module:

apps/rdf_graph/lib/rdf_graph/vocab.ex

```elixir
def book() do
  import RDF.Sigils

  [
    ~I<https://pragprog.com/titles/tvmelixir/adopting-elixir/>
    |> RDF.type(SCHEMA.Book)
    |> SCHEMA.author(
      ~I<https://twitter.com/bgmarx>,
      ~I<https://twitter.com/josevalim>,
      ~I<https://twitter.com/redrapids>
    )
    |> SCHEMA.datePublished("2018-03-14")
    |> SCHEMA.bookFormat(~L"Paperback")
    |> SCHEMA.identifier(~L"adopting_elixir")
    |> SCHEMA.isbn(~L"978-1-68050-252-7")
    |> SCHEMA.publisher(~I<https://pragprog.com/>)
    |> SCHEMA.name(~L"Adopting Elixir"),

    ~I<https://pragprog.com/>
    |> RDF.type(SCHEMA.Organization)
    |> SCHEMA.identifier(~L"pragmatic")
    |> SCHEMA.name(~L"The Pragmatic Bookshelf"),

    ~I<https://twitter.com/bgmarx>
    |> RDF.type(SCHEMA.Person)
    |> SCHEMA.identifier(~L"ben_marx")
    |> SCHEMA.name(~L"Ben Marx"),

    ~I<https://twitter.com/josevalim>
    |> RDF.type(SCHEMA.Person)
    |> SCHEMA.identifier(~L"jose_valim")
    |> SCHEMA.name(~L"José Valim"),

    ~I<https://twitter.com/redrapids>
    |> RDF.type(SCHEMA.Person)
    |> SCHEMA.identifier(~L"bruce_tate")
    |> SCHEMA.name(~L"Bruce Tate")
  ]
end
```

So, briefly, we can construct new RDF terms using the sigils defined in the RDF.Sigils module (which we import):

- ~I for IRIs (for example, ~I<https://pragprog.com/>)
- ~L for literals (for example, ~L"Paperback")

This book/0 function provides RDF descriptions for the five things in our book graph—one book, one publisher, and three authors.

Serializing the RDF Graph

There are various options for reading and writing the RDF descriptions in our book graph as a string or as a file. See the documentation for RDF.Serialization.[14] But the simplest solution for serializing in Turtle format is using the RDF.Turtle[15] module functions.

Let's first create our book graph:

```
iex> book = RDFGraph.Vocab.book
[#RDF.Description<
  <https://pragprog.com/titles/tvmelixir/adopting-elixir/>
      a <https://schema.org/Book> ;
      <https://schema.org/author> <https://twitter.com/bgmarx>,
          <https://twitter.com/josevalim>, <https://twitter.com/redrapids> ;
      <https://schema.org/bookFormat> "Paperback" ;
      <https://schema.org/datePublished> "2018-03-14" ;
      <https://schema.org/identifier> "adopting_elixir" ;
      <https://schema.org/isbn> "978-1-68050-252-7" ;
      <https://schema.org/name> "Adopting Elixir" ;
      <https://schema.org/publisher> <https://pragprog.com/> .
>,
 #RDF.Description<
  <https://pragprog.com/>
      a <https://schema.org/Organization> ;
      <https://schema.org/identifier> "pragmatic" ;
      <https://schema.org/name> "The Pragmatic Bookshelf" .
>,
 #RDF.Description<
  <https://twitter.com/bgmarx>
      a <https://schema.org/Person> ;
      <https://schema.org/identifier> "ben_marx" ;
      <https://schema.org/name> "Ben Marx" .
>,
 #RDF.Description<
  <https://twitter.com/josevalim>
      a <https://schema.org/Person> ;
```

---

14. https://hexdocs.pm/rdf/RDF.Serialization.html
15. https://hexdocs.pm/rdf/RDF.Turtle.html

```
    <https://schema.org/identifier> "jose_valim" ;
    <https://schema.org/name> "José Valim" .
>,
 #RDF.Description<
  <https://twitter.com/redrapids>
      a <https://schema.org/Person> ;
      <https://schema.org/identifier> "bruce_tate" ;
      <https://schema.org/name> "Bruce Tate" .
>]
```

Remember that Turtle has a namespacing mechanism where we can associate a namespace prefix with a namespace URI. Well, we would like to abbreviate all our Schema.org URIs having a "https://schema.org/" base URI with the "schema:" namespace prefix. We can do this by building a prefix map:

```
iex> import RDF.Sigils
RDF.Sigils

iex> prefixes = RDF.PrefixMap.new(schema: ~I<https://schema.org/>)
%RDF.PrefixMap{schema: ~I<https://schema.org/>}
```

And we can add this prefix map to the book graph:

```
iex> graph = RDF.Graph.add_prefixes(RDF.Graph.new(book), prefixes)
#RDF.Graph<name: nil
  @prefix schema: <https://schema.org/> .

  <https://pragprog.com/>
      a schema:Organization ;
      schema:identifier "pragmatic" ;
      schema:name "The Pragmatic Bookshelf" .

  ...
>
```

We can now write out the book graph as a Turtle string:

```
iex> graph |> RDF.Turtle.write_string! |> IO.puts
@prefix schema: <https://schema.org/> .

<https://pragprog.com/>
    a schema:Organization ;
    schema:identifier "pragmatic" ;
    schema:name "The Pragmatic Bookshelf" .

<https://pragprog.com/titles/tvmelixir/adopting-elixir/>
    a schema:Book ;
    schema:author <https://twitter.com/bgmarx>,
        <https://twitter.com/josevalim>, <https://twitter.com/redrapids> ;
    schema:bookFormat "Paperback" ;
    schema:datePublished "2018-03-14" ;
```

```
    schema:identifier "adopting_elixir" ;
    schema:isbn "978-1-68050-252-7" ;
    schema:name "Adopting Elixir" ;
    schema:publisher <https://pragprog.com/> .
<https://twitter.com/bgmarx>
    a schema:Person ;
    schema:identifier "ben_marx" ;
    schema:name "Ben Marx" .

...

:ok
```

There we go—a valid RDF Turtle string with a "schema:" namespace.

While we're here, let's save that down into our graph store. We're going to query against that later.

```
iex> graph |> RDF.Turtle.write_string! |> write_graph("book.ttl")
```

So, that might be perfectly good for sharing with RDF applications, but if we want to share our graph with other applications by using a more familiar serialization, we would probably choose something like JSON. We're in luck. There is a JSON specification that is specifically tailored for expressing linked data—JSON-LD.[16] We also have the JSON-LD Elixir package.

So if we want to write our graph out as a JSON-LD string, we can do that as simply as this:

```
iex> graph |> JSON.LD.write_string!(pretty: true) |> IO.puts
[
  {
    "@id": "https://pragprog.com/",
    "@type": [
      "https://schema.org/Organization"
    ],
    "https://schema.org/identifier": [
      {
        "@value": "pragmatic"
      }
    ],
    "https://schema.org/name": [
      {
        "@value": "The Pragmatic Bookshelf"
      }
    ]
  },
```

---

16. https://json-ld.org/

```
  {
    "@id": "https://pragprog.com/titles/tvmelixir/adopting-elixir/",
    "@type": [
      "https://schema.org/Book"
    ],
    "https://schema.org/author": [
      {
        "@id": "https://twitter.com/bgmarx"
      },
      {
        "@id": "https://twitter.com/josevalim"
      },
      {
        "@id": "https://twitter.com/redrapids"
      }
    ],
    "https://schema.org/bookFormat": [
      {
        "@value": "Paperback"
      }
    ],
    "https://schema.org/datePublished": [
      {
        "@value": "2018-03-14"
      }
    ],
    "https://schema.org/identifier": [
      {
        "@value": "adopting_elixir"
      }
    ],
    "https://schema.org/isbn": [
      {
        "@value": "978-1-68050-252-7"
      }
    ],
    "https://schema.org/name": [
      {
        "@value": "Adopting Elixir"
      }
    ],
    "https://schema.org/publisher": [
      {
        "@id": "https://pragprog.com/"
      }
    ]
  },
  ...
]
:ok
```

Whoa! What's going on here? This is both good and bad. We've got a valid JSON-LD document here, but there's a lot of substructure that we don't want to see.

It turns out that JSON-LD has a neat way to handle this—the "context." This is essentially an instruction set to map simple terms used in a generic JSON format to IRIs used in a specific application format. In JSON-LD we can define our context as an Elixir map:

```
ctxt = %{
  "author" => %{"@id" => "https://schema.org/author", "@type" => "@id"},
  "bookFormat" => "https://schema.org/bookFormat",
  "datePublished" => "https://schema.org/datePublished",
  "identifier" => "https://schema.org/identifier",
  "isbn" => "https://schema.org/isbn",
  "name" => "https://schema.org/name",
  "publisher" => %{"@id" => "https://schema.org/publisher", "@type" => "@id"}
}
```

We won't spend any time here discussing the mapping, except to note that the "@id" term on the "@type" key specifies that type is taken from the referenced object.

Now let's write out that JSON document again but this time passing in our ctxt using the :context keyword:

```
iex> graph |> JSON.LD.write_string!(context: ctxt, pretty: true) |> IO.puts
{
  "@context": {
    "author": {
      "@id": "https://schema.org/author",
      "@type": "@id"
    },
    "bookFormat": "https://schema.org/bookFormat",
    "datePublished": "https://schema.org/datePublished",
    "identifier": "https://schema.org/identifier",
    "isbn": "https://schema.org/isbn",
    "name": "https://schema.org/name",
    "publisher": {
      "@id": "https://schema.org/publisher",
      "@type": "@id"
    }
  },
  "@graph": [
    {
      "@id": "https://pragprog.com/",
      "@type": "https://schema.org/Organization",
      "identifier": "pragmatic",
      "name": "The Pragmatic Bookshelf"
    },
```

```
  {
    "@id": "https://pragprog.com/titles/tvmelixir/adopting-elixir/",
    "@type": "https://schema.org/Book",
    "author": [
      "https://twitter.com/bgmarx",
      "https://twitter.com/josevalim",
      "https://twitter.com/redrapids"
    ],
    "bookFormat": "Paperback",
    "datePublished": "2018-03-14",
    "identifier": "adopting_elixir",
    "isbn": "978-1-68050-252-7",
    "name": "Adopting Elixir",
    "publisher": "https://pragprog.com/"
  },
  ...
  ]
}
:ok
```

Much better. This time it looks more like a regular JSON document with simple keys.

You can experiment further with JSON-LD using the handy JSON-LD Playground.[17]

Now it's time to look at connecting to an actual RDF graph database.

Setting Up a Graph Service

As we did with property graphs, we're going to set up an RDF graph service to abstract over any RDF graph database that we want to query. The graph service will provide us with a common API for graph management and for sending queries to the graph database.

While we'll use a local RDF graph database for testing, many public RDF graph databases are also available for querying. We'd like to try some of these out too. We can query these RDF graph databases through their public SPARQL endpoints. (We'll be covering the RDF query language SPARQL in Chapter 8, Querying RDF with SPARQL, on page 143.)

The SPARQL standard also defines a graph store HTTP protocol for graph admin. Our local RDF graph database supports this. We could use this API directly, but for uniformity, we'd rather bring this under our common graph services API so that we can operate at a higher level of abstraction. This will make for less context switching when swapping between graph services.

---

17. https://json-ld.org/playground/

Let's set up a graph service for our RDFGraph project now. We'll add our new module RDFGraph.Service:

```
defmodule RDFGraph.Service do

  # ...

end
```

The first thing we need to keep track of is which RDF service we are currently querying.

Tracking the Current Graph Store

There are many RDF graph stores we'd like to query, so we could do with a simple means of changing between them. We'll need to keep track of their query endpoints as well as any graph store API endpoints. And we'll need to track the graph store we are currently working with.

We can use the application environment to store this info. Let's define an admin property for the graph store API endpoint and a query property for the query endpoint. We'll record this property pair for each store we are interested in. We can use a graph_store map for this and save each graph store with its own key and the endpoints as a value map:

```
config/config.exs
config :rdf_graph,
  cur_graph_store: :local,
  graph_store: %{
    local: %{
      admin: "http://localhost:7200/repositories/ex-graphs-book/rdf-graphs/"
             <> "service?default",
      query: "http://localhost:7200/repositories/ex-graphs-book",
      update: "http://localhost:7200/repositories/ex-graphs-book/statements"
    },
    dbpedia: %{
      admin: nil,
      query: "https://dbpedia.org/sparql",
      update: nil
    },
    wikidata: %{
      admin: nil,
      query: "https://query.wikidata.org/bigdata/namespace/wdq/sparql",
      update: nil
    }
  }
```

Here we've defined a local graph store.

We've set up a local GraphDB instance—see Appendix 2, Database Setups, on page 247, for help on setting up a local copy of GraphDB and creating a repository. Note that we've created the repository ex-graphs-book for working on this book. The config shows the query and update endpoints for this repository, as well as an admin endpoint. We've also defined a couple of well-known RDF graph stores: DBpedia[18] and Wikidata.[19] Note that we only have query endpoints for these so we set the admin property as nil.

We've added a cur_graph_store field to track the current graph store. We need a couple of functions to read this—rdf_store/0 for reading and rdf_store/1 for writing:

```
apps/rdf_graph/lib/rdf_graph/service.ex
def rdf_store do
  Application.get_env(:rdf_graph, :rdf_store)
end
def rdf_store(store) do
  Application.put_env(:rdf_graph, :rdf_store, store )
end
```

We also need a helper function list_rdf_stores/0 to list out the graph stores:

```
apps/rdf_graph/lib/rdf_graph/service.ex
def list_rdf_stores do
  Map.keys Application.get_env(:rdf_graph, :graph_store)
end
```

Lastly, we need a couple of functions—rdf_store_admin/0 and rdf_store_query/0—to return the current admin and query endpoints, respectively:

```
apps/rdf_graph/lib/rdf_graph/service.ex
def rdf_store_admin do
  store = rdf_store()
  Application.get_env(:rdf_graph, :graph_store)[store][:admin]
end
def rdf_store_query do
  store = rdf_store()
  Application.get_env(:rdf_graph, :graph_store)[store][:query]
end
def rdf_store_update do
  store = rdf_store()
  Application.get_env(:rdf_graph, :graph_store)[store][:update]
end
```

We can make these more accessible via delegates in our top-level RDFGraph module:

---

18. https://wiki.dbpedia.org/
19. https://www.wikidata.org/

```
apps/rdf_graph/lib/rdf_graph.ex
defdelegate rdf_store(), to: RDFGraph.Service, as: :rdf_store
defdelegate rdf_store(arg), to: RDFGraph.Service, as: :rdf_store
defdelegate list_rdf_stores(), to: RDFGraph.Service, as: :list_rdf_stores
defdelegate rdf_store_admin(), to: RDFGraph.Service, as: :rdf_store_admin
defdelegate rdf_store_query(), to: RDFGraph.Service, as: :rdf_store_query
defdelegate rdf_store_update(), to: RDFGraph.Service, as: :rdf_store_update
```

We can now select the rdf_store for querying:

```
iex> RDFGraph.rdf_store :local
:ok
```

Then we switch to the graph service which imports the RDFGraph module:

```
iex>  import GraphCommons.Utils
GraphCommons.Utils

iex> graph_context RDFGraph
RDFGraph
```

Or better still, add that to the IEx startup file .iex.exs.

But, of course, we'll need some functionality to operate the API.

Graph API

We can define our graph services API as follows:

```
apps/rdf_graph/lib/rdf_graph/service.ex
def graph_create(%GraphCommons.Graph{} = graph) do
  if rdf_store_admin() do
    graph_delete()
    graph_update(graph)
  else
    {:error, rdf_store()}
  end
end

def graph_delete() do
  if rdf_store_admin() do
    {:ok, env} = Tesla.delete(rdf_store_admin())
    GraphCommons.Graph.new(env.body, "", :rdf)
    env
  else
    {:error, rdf_store()}
  end
end

def graph_read() do
  if rdf_store_admin() do
    {:ok, env} = Tesla.get(rdf_store_admin())
    GraphCommons.Graph.new(env.body, "", :rdf)
```

```elixir
    else
      {:error, rdf_store()}
    end
end

def graph_update(%GraphCommons.Graph{} = graph) do
  if rdf_store_admin() do
    {:ok, env} = Tesla.post(rdf_store_admin(),
                    graph.data, headers: [{"content-type", "text/turtle"}])
    GraphCommons.Graph.new(env.body, "", :rdf)
  else
    {:error, rdf_store()}
  end
end
```

This defines the API for CRUD operations, although we can expand the API further with an optional reporting function graph_info/0.

Graph Info

To get some metrics over the graph service, we'll first define some module attributes with SPARQL query strings:

apps/rdf_graph/lib/rdf_graph/service.ex
```elixir
@sparql_count_nodes """
SELECT (count(DISTINCT ?vertex) AS ?total)
WHERE
{
  { ?vertex ?p [] }
  UNION
  {
    [] ?p ?vertex
    FILTER(!IsLiteral(?vertex))
  }
}
"""

@sparql_count_edges """
SELECT (count(?vertex) AS ?total)
WHERE
{
  ?vertex ?edge []
}
"""

@sparql_list_types """
SELECT distinct ?type
WHERE
{
  ?vertex a ?type
}
"""
```

Here the SPARQL query bodies are stubbed out to save space, but look into the project if you're interested.

The graph_info/0 function makes use of the Query API we'll define next.

apps/rdf_graph/lib/rdf_graph/service.ex
```elixir
def graph_info() do
  import RDFGraph, only: [new_query: 1]
  if rdf_store_admin() do

    {:ok, %SPARQL.Query.Result{results: [%{"total" => total}]}} =
      @sparql_count_nodes
      |> new_query
      |> query_graph

    nodes = RDF.Literal.value(total)

    {:ok, %SPARQL.Query.Result{results: [%{"total" => total}]}} =
      @sparql_count_edges
      |> new_query
      |> query_graph

    edges = RDF.Literal.value(total)

    {:ok, %SPARQL.Query.Result{results: types}} =
      @sparql_list_types
      |> new_query
      |> query_graph

    labels =
      types
      |> Enum.map(fn t ->
        %{"type" => type} = t
        URI.parse(type.value).path |> Path.basename
      end)
      |> Enum.sort

    %GraphCommons.Service.GraphInfo{
      type: :rdf,
      file: "",
      num_nodes: nodes,
      num_edges: edges,
      labels: labels
    }
  else
    {:ok, rdf_store()}
  end
end
```

Query API

Now it's time to look at the query API.

This is something additional to the graph API which is only used for graph management. Here we'd like to query *within* the current graph. To make this separation between the two APIs clearer, we'll use the differently named query_graph/1 function instead of the graph_*/1 and graph_*/0 naming:

```
apps/rdf_graph/lib/rdf_graph/service.ex
def query_graph(%GraphCommons.Query{} = query, params \\ []) do
  :rdf = query.type
  SPARQL.Client.query(query.data, rdf_store_query(), params)
end

def query_graph!(%GraphCommons.Query{} = query, params \\ []) do
  :rdf = query.type

  update = Keyword.has_key?(params, :update) && Keyword.get(params, :update)

  unless update do
    SPARQL.Client.query(query.data, rdf_store_query(), params)
      |> case do
        {:ok, response} -> response
        {:error, message} -> raise "! #{message}"
      end
  else
    SPARQL.Client.update(query.data, rdf_store_update(), raw_mode: true)
      |> case do
        :ok -> :ok
        {:error, message} -> raise "! #{message}"
      end
  end
end
```

API Demo

As a demo, let's add our default graph to the RDF graph service. We'll start by importing our RDFGraph functions via the graph_context/1 macro:

```
iex> graph_context RDFGraph
RDFGraph
```

We'll use the read_graph/1 function to read the default graph from the graph store:

```
iex> default_graph = read_graph("default.ttl")
#GraphCommons.Graph<type: rdf, file: "...", data: "@prefix ex: <htt...">
```

We can then simply pipe this into the graph_create/1 function to create our default graph in the graph service:

```
iex> graph_create default_graph
#GraphCommons.Graph<type: rdf, file: "", data: "">
```

We can use the graph_info/0 function to confirm the service graph:

```
iex> graph_info
%GraphCommons.Service.GraphInfo{
  file: "",
  labels: [],
  num_edges: 1,
  num_nodes: 2,
  type: :rdf
}
```

And we can query this as before:

```
iex> "SELECT * WHERE {?s ?p ?o}" |> new_query |> query_graph!
%SPARQL.Query.Result{
  results: [
    %{
      "o" => ~I<http://example/b>,
      "p" => ~I<http://example/EX>,
      "s" => ~I<http://example/a>
    }
  ],
  variables: ["s", "p", "o"]
}
```

Let's see now how to do that query more simply without all the boilerplate so we can focus more clearly on the query itself.

Query Helper

As we've seen earlier (see Query Helper, on page 88), we can define a query helper to make querying simpler:

```
apps/graph_commons/lib/graph_commons/utils.ex
def sparql!(query_string), do: to_query_graph!(RDFGraph, query_string)
```

To simplify access to this helper function, let's import the GraphCommons.Utils module in our IEx startup file .iex.exs:

```
  import GraphCommons
► import GraphCommons.Utils ; alias GraphCommons.Utils
```

Let's try this now:

```
iex> "SELECT * WHERE {?s ?p ?o}" |> sparql!
%SPARQL.Query.Result{
  results: [
    ...
  ],
  variables: ["s", "p", "o"]
}
```

We'll use this query form when we start querying with SPARQL in the next chapter. And we'll also use SPARQL to query against a local RDF graph database as well as public RDF graph databases using our RDF graph service.

Wrapping Up

In this chapter, we briefly reviewed the RDF data model, which underlies the semantic web and its linked data offspring—W3C standardized approaches to connecting and querying data from across the web. We saw that RDF's common naming system and primitive data model simplify public data sharing, which more readily leads to global semantics and data integration at web scale. These factors together with the support for formal reasoning provide a useful basis for building knowledge graphs.

We then set up a new RDFGraph project for exploring RDF graphs.

Next, we used RDF.ex to define an RDF vocabulary for the Schema.org book schema. Using this vocabulary, we saw how to build a set of RDF descriptions for the book graph and how to serialize this both as an RDF Turtle string and as a JSON-LD document.

Finally, we implemented a graph service for RDF graphs so that we can use our common API for graph management and for sending queries to the graph service. And since there are many public query endpoints for RDF graphs, we also saw how we can simply configure our graph service to point to any of those.

We're now ready for SPARQL—the query language for RDF.

## CHAPTER 8

Querying RDF with SPARQL

In the previous chapter, we talked about the rdf package from the RDF.ex project for RDF processing in Elixir. But there is also a sparql_client package for querying RDF graph stores with SPARQL. So let's have a look at that. In fact, there are two SPARQL packages: sparql[1] (from the SPARQL.ex project) for querying in-memory RDF models and sparql_client[2] (from the SPARQL.Client project) for dispatching queries to RDF graph databases, or RDF triplestores as they're usually referred to. We're going to focus here on querying graph services using the sparql_client package, although we'll also discuss querying in-memory models with the sparql package.

Getting Started with SPARQL

Let's start with some background. The query language for RDF is known as SPARQL, and there is an accompanying graph admin language, SPARQL Update. (The name SPARQL, by the way, is a recursive acronym—"SPARQL Protocol and RDF Query Language.") We'll focus on the query language here for reasons of space.

SPARQL

SPARQL looks nominally a bit like SQL, which was an intentional move to help foster a wider acceptance. A SPARQL query provides a number of graph patterns for matching against. In essence, a SPARQL query simply scans a set of RDF triples and provides filtered values as solutions.

There are four query forms—two major and two minor—as shown in the table on page 144. The major query forms return either a table of values (SELECT) or

---

1. https://hex.pm/packages/sparql
2. https://hex.pm/packages/sparql_client

a graph of triples (CONSTRUCT). The minor query forms support testing (ASK) and inspection (DESCRIBE).

Query Form	Query Purpose	Return Type
SELECT	extract values	table
CONSTRUCT	create graph	graph
ASK	test graph	boolean
DESCRIBE	inspect nodes	(server dependent)

The majority of queries tend to use the SELECT form to return a value set in table form, although a more canny use of SPARQL will prefer the CONSTRUCT form to generate a new graph from the existing graph.

SPARQL Update

SPARQL Update allows for graph admin operations and can be seen as a kind of write complement to SPARQL, which is a read-only language. It allows for specifying and executing updates to RDF graphs in a graph store and supports two categories of update operations: graph update (INSERT DATA, DELETE DATA, DELETE/INSERT, and so on) and graph management (CREATE, DROP, COPY, MOVE, and so on). But here we'll focus on the SPARQL query language.

And that concludes our brief introduction to SPARQL. Now let's see it in action.

Querying the Local RDF Service

We're going to need some RDF data. To keep it simple, we'll take the RDF description we generated in the previous chapter for a book resource—the book graph:

```
iex> graph_context RDFGraph
RDFGraph

iex> graph_create read_graph("book.ttl")
#GraphCommons.Graph<type: rdf, file: "", data: "">

iex> graph_info
%GraphCommons.Service.GraphInfo{
  file: "",
  labels: ["Book", "Organization", "Person"],
  num_edges: 27,
  num_nodes: 8,
  type: :rdf
}
```

Here we selected the RDFGraph graph service and then created a new graph using the book.ttl stored graph.

Now let's have a look at the SELECT and CONSTRUCT query forms.

SELECT

Let's use a simple SELECT query that returns all the RDF terms under the variables ?s, ?p, and ?o:

```
iex> IO.puts (select_q = read_query("lib/select.rq").data)
SELECT ?s ?p ?o
WHERE {
  ?s ?p ?o
}

:ok
```

We've saved that query string as the variable select_q.

Now send this SPARQL query select_q to your local graph service. The result is a SPARQL.Query.Result struct:

```
iex> result = select_q |> sparql!
%SPARQL.Query.Result{
  results: [
    %{
      "o" => ~I<https://schema.org/Organization>,
      "p" => ~I<http://www.w3.org/1999/02/22-rdf-syntax-ns#type>,
      "s" => ~I<https://pragprog.com/>
    },
    ...
  ],
  variables: ["s", "p", "o"]
}
```

You can process this query result using, for example, the get/2 function from the SPARQL.Query.Result module:

```
iex> result |> SPARQL.Query.Result.get(:o)
[~I<https://schema.org/Organization>, ~I<https://schema.org/Book>,
 ~I<https://schema.org/Person>, ~I<https://schema.org/Person>,
 ~I<https://schema.org/Person>,
 %RDF.Literal{literal: %RDF.XSD.String{value: "pragmatic", lexical:
 "pragmatic"}, valid: true},
 %RDF.Literal{literal: %RDF.XSD.String{value: "adopting_elixir", lexical:
 "adopting_elixir"}, valid: true},
 ...]
```

CONSTRUCT

Let's now use a simple CONSTRUCT query that creates a new graph from the variables ?s, ?p, and ?o:

```
iex> IO.puts (construct_q = read_query("lib/construct.rq").data)
CONSTRUCT { ?s ?p ?o }
WHERE {
  ?s ?p ?o
}
:ok
```

We've saved that query string as the variable construct_q.

Sending the SPARQL query construct_q to your local graph service returns an RDF.Graph struct:

```
iex> result = construct_q |> sparql!
#RDF.Graph<name: nil
  @prefix rdf: <http://www.w3.org/1999/02/22-rdf-syntax-ns#> .
  @prefix rdfs: <http://www.w3.org/2000/01/rdf-schema#> .
  @prefix schema: <https://schema.org/> .
  @prefix xsd: <http://www.w3.org/2001/XMLSchema#> .

  <https://pragprog.com/>
      a schema:Organization ;
      schema:identifier "pragmatic" ;
      schema:name "The Pragmatic Bookshelf" .

  <https://pragprog.com/titles/tvmelixir/adopting-elixir/>
      a schema:Book ;
      ...
      }
```

You can access this RDF.Graph data structure by using some of the RDF.ex data accessors—see RDF Data Structures[3] for more info:

```
iex> result |> RDF.Graph.get(~I<https://pragprog.com/>) |>
...> RDF.Description.get(~I<https://schema.org/name>)
[%RDF.Literal{literal: %RDF.XSD.String{value: "The Pragmatic Bookshelf",
lexical: "The Pragmatic Bookshelf"}, valid: true}]
```

We can simplify this further by using the SCHEMA vocabulary we defined earlier (see Adding a SCHEMA Vocabulary for Schema.org Terms, on page 125):

```
iex> alias RDFGraph.Vocab.SCHEMA
RDFGraph.Vocab.SCHEMA

iex> result |> RDF.Graph.get(~I<https://pragprog.com/>) |>
...> RDF.Description.get(SCHEMA.name)
[%RDF.Literal{literal: %RDF.XSD.String{value: "The Pragmatic Bookshelf",
lexical: "The Pragmatic Bookshelf"}, valid: true}]
```

---

3.   https://rdf-elixir.dev/rdf-ex/data-structures.html

Well, those are the two major query forms. Now let's take a look at the two minor query forms. And by the way, we'll also see examples of all these query forms in action later in the chapter.

ASK

Here's a simple ASK query that tests a graph with the graph pattern it supplies:

```
iex> IO.puts (ask_q = read_query("lib/ask.rq").data)
ASK
WHERE {
  ?s ?p ?o
}

:ok
```

We've saved that query string as the variable ask_q.

In this case, we are simply asking if any triple exists within the graph.

Sending the SPARQL query ask_q to your local graph service returns a single boolean result wrapped in a SPARQL.Query.Result struct:

```
iex> result = ask_q |> sparql!
%SPARQL.Query.Result{results: true, variables: nil}

iex> result.results
true
```

You could almost think of the ASK result as being a degenerate table with a single cell. In this case, however, there are no variable bindings—just a single boolean value.

Lastly, we have DESCRIBE.

DESCRIBE

Here's a qualified DESCRIBE query that inspects a resource matched via a graph pattern:

```
iex> IO.puts (describe_q = read_query("lib/describe.rq").data)
DESCRIBE ?s
WHERE {
  ?s ?p "Bruce Tate"
}

:ok

iex> IO.puts (RDF.Turtle.write_string! (describe_q |> sparql!))
@prefix rdf: <http://www.w3.org/1999/02/22-rdf-syntax-ns#> .
@prefix rdfs: <http://www.w3.org/2000/01/rdf-schema#> .
@prefix schema: <https://schema.org/> .
@prefix xsd: <http://www.w3.org/2001/XMLSchema#> .
```

```
<https://pragprog.com/titles/tvmelixir/adopting-elixir/>
    schema:author <https://twitter.com/redrapids> .

<https://twitter.com/redrapids>
    a schema:Person ;
    schema:identifier "bruce_tate" ;
    schema:name "Bruce Tate" .

:ok
```

We've saved that query string as the variable describe_q.

Often, however, DESCRIBE will be used with a direct value, for example:

```
iex> "DESCRIBE <https://twitter.com/redrapids>" |> sparql!
#RDF.Graph<name: nil
  @prefix rdf: <http://www.w3.org/1999/02/22-rdf-syntax-ns#> .
  @prefix rdfs: <http://www.w3.org/2000/01/rdf-schema#> .
  @prefix schema: <https://schema.org/> .
  @prefix xsd: <http://www.w3.org/2001/XMLSchema#> .

  <https://pragprog.com/titles/tvmelixir/adopting-elixir/>
      schema:author <https://twitter.com/redrapids> .

  <https://twitter.com/redrapids>
      a schema:Person ;
      schema:identifier "bruce_tate" ;
      schema:name "Bruce Tate" .
>
```

Now that we've seen these query forms, let's see them again in action.

Querying In-Memory RDF Graphs

By the way, we're using the sparql_client package here to query graph services through their published SPARQL endpoints. In this chapter, we're querying a local service as well as a couple of remote services. Because we're accessing the local service via its web interface, the only real difference from a remote service is that we have admin control over the data and write access to the graph database.

But what if you don't have access to a local graph database or don't wish to install one? Well in that case you can use the sparql package to query in-memory RDF graphs. There are some limitations in terms of coverage of SPARQL features supported, [4] but some of these limitations may be worked around either by using emulated query forms or by coding over result sets.

---

4.   https://rdf-elixir.dev/sparql-ex/limitations.html

Case #1: Tokyo Metro

Rail networks make for great examples of applied graphs. In the early years of RDF development, I felt compelled to model the London Underground (or Tube) map as an RDF graph. (I'm surely not the only person who ever tried that.) Here we are going to use an example of the Tokyo Metro that has been modeled as an RDF graph and published as public domain open data—see RDF datasets from DataDock.[5] There are three separate RDF datasets for the lines, stations, and stops listed as tokyo_metro-*.nt.gz. You can simply download, unzip, and concatenate those files into a single source file tokyo_metro.nt. These are in RDF N-Triples format, a subset of the RDF Turtle format.

So now, we've got a local copy of the graph, and we can save that to the graph store. We'll also want to build some queries and save them to the graph store as well. (You can get the queries from either the code listings or the examples as we get to them.) Let's put both the graph and queries under their own metro directory.

Next, let's load our graph into the graph service:

```
iex> graph_context RDFGraph
RDFGraph

iex> graph_create read_graph("metro/tokyo_metro.nt")
#GraphCommons.Graph<type: rdf, file: "", data: "">

iex> graph_info
%GraphCommons.Service.GraphInfo{
  file: "",
  labels: [],
  num_edges: 1065,
  num_nodes: 520,
  type: :rdf
}
```

We can also list out the queries we're going to use:

```
iex> list_queries_dir("metro")
["list-line-names-english.rq", "list-line-names.rq", "list-properties.rq",
 "list-station-names-on-line.rq", "list-types.rq"]
```

Querying the Graph

One of the first things we can do with a new graph is inspect the types of its nodes:

```
iex> IO.puts (types_q = read_query("metro/list-types.rq").data)
SELECT DISTINCT ?type
```

---

5.   http://datadock.io/kal/data/

```
WHERE {
  ?s a ?type .
}
ORDER BY ?type

:ok
```

Here we use the special keyword 'a' which is shorthand for rdf:type. We also sort the result set with ORDER BY and deduplicate with DISTINCT.

Now try this query:

```
iex> result = types_q |> sparql!
%SPARQL.Query.Result{results: [], variables: ["type"]}
```

And we get nothing. It turns out that this RDF dataset contains instances only and includes no type information. We'll see soon how we can add type information to the graph.

Our next strategy will be to list out all the predicates:

```
iex> IO.puts (properties_q = read_query("metro/list-properties.rq").data)
SELECT DISTINCT ?p
WHERE {
  ?s ?p ?o .
}
ORDER BY ?p

:ok
```

Let's try this query:

```
iex> result = properties_q |> sparql!
%SPARQL.Query.Result{
  results: [
    %{"p" => ~I<http://.../dataset/tokyo_metro_stations.csv#on_line>},
    %{"p" => ~I<http://.../dataset/tokyo_metro_stops.csv#at_station>},
    %{"p" => ~I<http://.../dataset/tokyo_metro_stops.csv#on_line>},
    %{"p" => ~I<http://.../dataset/tokyo_metro_stops.csv#seealso>},
    %{"p" => ~I<http://.../definition/line_colour>},
    %{"p" => ~I<http://.../definition/line_name>},
    %{"p" => ~I<http://.../definition/line_name_english>},
    %{"p" => ~I<http://.../definition/line_name_french>},
    %{"p" => ~I<http://.../definition/station_name>},
    %{"p" => ~I<http://.../definition/station_name_english>}
  ],
  variables: ["p"]
}
```

This time, we have a list of properties. Note that we're showing the predicate URLs here truncated in the middle for display purposes only.

What if we try to get a list of line names using the line_name property?

```
iex> IO.puts (lines_q = read_query("metro/list-line-names.rq").data)
PREFIX schema: <http://.../definition/>

SELECT ?line_name
WHERE {
  ?s schema:line_name ?line_name .
}

:ok
```

We use prefix notation to make the query more readable. Again, here we're truncating the namespace URL in the middle.

Let's try this query:

```
iex> result = lines_q |> sparql!
%SPARQL.Query.Result{
  results: [
    %{"line_name" => ~L"千代田線"},
    %{"line_name" => ~L"副都心線"},
    %{"line_name" => ~L"銀座線"},
    %{"line_name" => ~L"日比谷線"},
    %{"line_name" => ~L"丸ノ内線"},
    %{"line_name" => ~L"丸ノ内線分岐線"},
    %{"line_name" => ~L"南北線"},
    %{"line_name" => ~L"東西線"},
    %{"line_name" => ~L"有楽町線"},
    %{"line_name" => ~L"半蔵門線"}
  ],
  variables: ["line_name"]
}
```

Well, this is fine. But maybe we could add in some English names as well:

```
iex> IO.puts (line-english_q =
...> read_query("metro/list-line-names-english.rq").data)
PREFIX schema: <http://.../definition/>

SELECT ?line_name ?line_name_english
WHERE {
  ?s schema:line_name ?line_name .
  ?s schema:line_name_english ?line_name_english .
}

:ok
```

Let's try this query:

```
iex> result = line-english_q |> sparql!
%SPARQL.Query.Result{
  results: [
    %{"line_name_english" => ~L"Chiyoda Line", "line_name" => ~L"千代田線"},
```

```
    %{"line_name_english" => ~L"Fukutoshin Line", "line_name" => ~L"副都心線"},
    %{"line_name_english" => ~L"Ginza Line", "line_name" => ~L"銀座線"},
    %{"line_name_english" => ~L"Hibiya Line", "line_name" => ~L"日比谷線"},
    %{"line_name_english" => ~L"Marunouchi Line", "line_name" => ~L"丸ノ内線"},
    %{
      "line_name_english" => ~L"Marunouchi Line Branch Line",
      "line_name" => ~L"丸ノ内線分岐線"
    },
    %{"line_name_english" => ~L"Namboku Line", "line_name" => ~L"南北線"},
    %{"line_name_english" => ~L"Tōzai Line", "line_name" => ~L"東西線"},
    %{"line_name_english" => ~L"Yūrakuchō Line", "line_name" => ~L"有楽町線"},
    %{"line_name_english" => ~L"Hanzōmon Line", "line_name" => ~L"半蔵門線"}
  ],
  variables: ["line_name", "line_name_english"]
}
```

So, those are the line names in Japanese and English for this RDF dataset.

Maybe we could now try listing the stations on a given line, the Ginza line, for example. Here's a query that will do that:

```
iex> IO.puts (stations_q =
...> read_query("metro/list-station-names-on-line.rq").data)
PREFIX schema: <http://.../definition/>
PREFIX stations: <http://.../dataset/tokyo_metro_stations.csv#>

SELECT ?station_name ?station_name_english
WHERE {
  BIND ("Ginza Line" AS ?line_name_english)
  ?line schema:line_name_english ?line_name_english .
  ?s stations:on_line ?line .
  ?s schema:station_name ?station_name .
  ?s schema:station_name_english ?station_name_english .
}
```

There are a couple of things to note. We're using BIND to assign a value to the variable ?line_name_english. And we're using the property on_line in the stations: namespace, which relates stations to lines.

This query gives us the expected result:

```
iex> result = stations_q |> sparql!
%SPARQL.Query.Result{
  results: [
    %{
      "station_name" => ~L"三越前駅",
      "station_name_english" => ~L"Mitsukoshimae"
    },
    ...
  ],
  variables: ["station_name", "station_name_english"]
}
```

If we want to grab only the station_name values, we can use the get/2 function in the SPARQL.Query.Result module:

```
iex> names = result |> SPARQL.Query.Result.get(:station_name)
[~L"三越前駅", ~L"上野広小路駅", ~L"上野駅", ~L"京橋駅",
 ~L"外苑前駅", ~L"新橋駅", ~L"日本橋駅", ~L"末広町駅",
 ~L"浅草駅", ~L"渋谷駅", ~L"溜池山王駅", ~L"田原町駅",
 ~L"神田駅", ~L"稲荷町駅", ~L"虎ノ門駅", ~L"表参道駅",
 ~L"赤坂見附駅", ~L"赤坂見附駅", ~L"銀座駅",
 ~L"青山一丁目駅", ~L"青山一丁目駅"]
```

We can do likewise for the station_name_english values:

```
iex> names_english = result |> SPARQL.Query.Result.get(:station_name_english)
[~L"Mitsukoshimae", ~L"Ueno-Hirokōji", ~L"Ueno", ~L"Kyōbashi", ~L"Gaiemmae",
 ~L"Shimbashi", ~L"Nihombashi", ~L"Suehirochō", ~L"Asakusa", ~L"Shibuya",
 ~L"Tameike-Sannō", ~L"Tawaramachi", ~L"Kanda", ~L"Inarichō", ~L"Toranomon",
 ~L"Omotesandō", ~L"Akasaka-Mitsuke", ~L"Akasaka-mitsuke", ~L"Ginza",
 ~L"Aoyama-Itchōme", ~L"Aoyama-itchōme"]
```

And we can always zip these two lists together as:

```
iex> Enum.zip(names, names_english)
[
  {~L"三越前駅", ~L"Mitsukoshimae"},
  {~L"上野広小路駅", ~L"Ueno-Hirokōji"},
  {~L"上野駅", ~L"Ueno"},
  {~L"京橋駅", ~L"Kyōbashi"},
  {~L"外苑前駅", ~L"Gaiemmae"},
  {~L"新橋駅", ~L"Shimbashi"},
  {~L"日本橋駅", ~L"Nihombashi"},
  {~L"末広町駅", ~L"Suehirochō"},
  {~L"浅草駅", ~L"Asakusa"},
  {~L"渋谷駅", ~L"Shibuya"},
  {~L"溜池山王駅", ~L"Tameike-Sannō"},
  {~L"田原町駅", ~L"Tawaramachi"},
  {~L"神田駅", ~L"Kanda"},
  {~L"稲荷町駅", ~L"Inarichō"},
  {~L"虎ノ門駅", ~L"Toranomon"},
  {~L"表参道駅", ~L"Omotesandō"},
  {~L"赤坂見附駅", ~L"Akasaka-Mitsuke"},
  {~L"赤坂見附駅", ~L"Akasaka-mitsuke"},
  {~L"銀座駅", ~L"Ginza"},
  {~L"青山一丁目駅", ~L"Aoyama-Itchōme"},
  {~L"青山一丁目駅", ~L"Aoyama-itchōme"}
]
```

Enriching the Graph

Do you remember that we said this RDF dataset had no types? Well, we can fix that.

This query uses the SPARQL form CONSTRUCT to return a graph. We'll say that any subject that has a schema:line_name property is a line type.

For this demo, we'll add a type Line from an example namespace ex: to any matched subjects:

```
iex> IO.puts (line_types_q = read_query("metro/add-line-types.rq").data)
PREFIX ex: <http://example/>
PREFIX schema: <http://datadock.io/kal/data/id/definition/>

CONSTRUCT {
  ?s a ex:Line
}
WHERE {
  ?s schema:line_name ?line_name .
}

:ok
```

The query returns an RDF.Graph struct:

```
iex> result = line_types_q |> sparql!
#RDF.Graph{name: nil
    ~I<http://datadock.io/kal/data/id/resource/line/tokyo-metro-C>
        ~I<http://www.w3.org/1999/02/22-rdf-syntax-ns#type>
            ~I<http://example/Line>
    ...
    ~I<http://datadock.io/kal/data/id/resource/line/tokyo-metro-Z>
        ~I<http://www.w3.org/1999/02/22-rdf-syntax-ns#type>
            ~I<http://example/Line>}
```

We can generate an RDF Turtle string from this struct and add that to the graph service by piping through the new_graph/1 function:

```
iex> (RDF.Turtle.write_string! result) |> new_graph |> graph_update
#GraphCommons.Graph<type: rdf, file: "", data: "">
```

We've now added an ex:Line type in our dataset using the local graph service.

We can verify that by querying:

```
iex> result = read_query("metro/list-types.rq").data |> sparql!
%SPARQL.Query.Result{
  results: [%{"type" => ~I<http://example/Line>}],
  variables: ["type"]
}
```

Let's look now at a couple of remote graph services where we will only have read access.

Querying a Remote RDF Service

Let's try querying a remote RDF graph store. We're going to use DBpedia[6] and the DBpedia SPARQL endpoint[7] for our remote querying. So, we use the rdf_store/1 function we defined in the RDFGraph module with the atom :dbpedia as our key:

```
iex> rdf_store :dbpedia
:ok
```

Now if we check with the graph_info/0 function, we don't get a %GraphCommons.Service.GraphInfo{} struct returned as we would with a local graph store, but instead we get a tuple returning the store token:

```
iex> graph_info
{:ok, :dbpedia}
```

Note that later in A Graph-to-Graph Example, on page 207, we'll also be querying against Wikidata[8] and using the Wikidata SPARQL endpoint.[9]

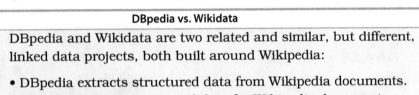

DBpedia vs. Wikidata

DBpedia and Wikidata are two related and similar, but different, linked data projects, both built around Wikipedia:

• DBpedia extracts structured data from Wikipedia documents.
• Wikidata creates structured data for Wikipedia documents.

Before we get into querying, you might want to experiment with the SPARQL query form at the DBpedia SPARQL endpoint. There is also a DBpedia ontology[10] which models the instances, types, and relationships found in the DBpedia dataset.

Let's put together a simple "Hello World" query. Fortunately, most resources in DBpedia are named under a "http://dbpedia.org/resource/" namespace. So, we can expect a "Hello World" page to be named "http://dbpedia.org/resource/Hello_World".

```
iex> hello_q = """
PREFIX dbr: <http://dbpedia.org/resource/>

CONSTRUCT { ?s ?p ?o }
WHERE {
```

---

6. https://wiki.dbpedia.org/
7. https://dbpedia.org/sparql/
8. https://www.wikidata.org/
9. https://query.wikidata.org/bigdata/namespace/wdq/sparql
10. https://www.dbpedia.org/resources/ontology/

```
  BIND (dbr:Hello_World AS ?s)
  ?s ?p ?o
}
FILTER (isLiteral(?o) && langMatches(lang(?o), "en"))
"""
```

This will query the dbr:Hello_World resource at the DBpedia SPARQL endpoint and will construct a new graph with any statements that have English-language values.

So, let's try it:

```
iex> result = hello_q |> sparql!
#RDF.Graph{name: nil
    ~I<http://dbpedia.org/resource/Hello_World>
        ~I<http://www.w3.org/2000/01/rdf-schema#label>
            ~L"Hello World"en}
```

Of course, we'll be able to read that better if we convert it to a Turtle string:

```
iex> IO.puts (RDF.Turtle.write_string! result)
@prefix dbr: <http://dbpedia.org/resource/> .
@prefix rdfs: <http://www.w3.org/2000/01/rdf-schema#> .

dbr:Hello_World
    rdfs:label "Hello World"@en .

:ok
```

Great. We just queried DBpedia and parsed the result set for English language strings. We got one: "Hello World."

Now we're ready for something else. We're going to take a (short) random walk through DBpedia. We're going to do this in two different ways—first by querying DBpedia as we've already done and second by browsing DBpedia. Let's start with querying.

Case #2: Graph Walk (Querying)

The first thing we'll do is create a new module. Create a new folder examples/ under our rdf_graph/lib/rdf_graph/ folder and under that create a walk_query.ex file.

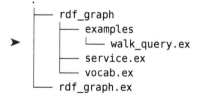

```
.
├── rdf_graph
│   ├── examples
│   │   └── walk_query.ex
│   ├── service.ex
│   └── vocab.ex
└── rdf_graph.ex
```

Then create a new module:

```
defmodule RDFGraph.Examples.WalkQuery do

  # ...

end
```

Now add in a walk_query/2 function as follows:

apps/rdf_graph/lib/rdf_graph/examples/walk_query.ex

```
Line 1  def walk_query(link \\ "http://dbpedia.org/resource/Bob_Dylan", count \\ 0)
     -  def walk_query(_, count) when count >= 7, do: :ok
     -
     -  def walk_query(link, count) do
     5    IO.puts link
     -    query =
     -    ~S"""
     -      PREFIX dbo: <http://dbpedia.org/ontology/>
     -      SELECT DISTINCT ?new_link
    10      WHERE
     -      {
     -        BIND (<LINK> AS ?link)
     -        ?link dbo:wikiPageWikiLink ?new_link
     -      }
    15    """
     -    query = String.replace(query, "LINK", link)
     -    store = RDFGraph.Service.rdf_store_query()
     -    list = with {:ok, result} = SPARQL.Client.query(query, store),
     -         do: SPARQL.Query.Result.get(result, :new_link)
    20    if Enum.empty?(list) do
     -      :ok
     -    else
     -      link = Enum.random(list) |> RDF.IRI.to_string
     -      walk_query(link, count + 1)
    25    end
     -  end
```

It's important to note a few things. We've defined our walk_query/2 function at line 1 with two optional parameters: a link for our graph start node (and defaulting to "http://dbpedia.org/resource/Bob_Dylan") and a count to control our path length (and defaulting to 0). We're going to recursively call this function until we reach our maximum path length as set by the guard at line 2, or until nothing more is returned.

The SPARQL query is defined at line 6, and we replace the LINK placeholder text with the link value at line 16. We match on the dbo:wikiPageWikiLink[11] property, which links a wiki page (bound to ?link) with another wiki page (the as yet unbound ?new_link).

---

11. https://dbpedia.org/ontology/wikiPageWikiLink

The rdf_store name is read at line 17, and we query with SPARQL.Client.query/3 at line 18 with any matched new_link values added to the list.

Lastly, on line 20 we test the list and, if empty, return :ok or else call walk_query/2 again with a random link from the list. (Note that this is a simpler strategy than trying to return a random link directly from the query because of server-side caching. Without the caching we could have returned a single random link from the query.)

OK, it's time to try this out. To make things simpler, let's import that module:

```
iex> import RDFGraph.Examples.WalkQuery
RDFGraph.Examples.WalkQuery
```

So, try first with our default subject:

```
iex> walk_query
http://dbpedia.org/resource/Bob_Dylan
http://dbpedia.org/resource/John_Lennon
http://dbpedia.org/resource/I_Met_the_Walrus
http://dbpedia.org/resource/The_Omni_King_Edward_Hotel
http://dbpedia.org/resource/Yoko_Ono
http://dbpedia.org/resource/Flipside_(Canadian_TV_program)
http://dbpedia.org/resource/Queen's_University_at_Kingston
:ok
```

And try again, but this time we reach a dead end:

```
iex> walk_query
http://dbpedia.org/resource/Bob_Dylan
http://dbpedia.org/resource/Category:American_folk_singers
:ok
```

Now try with a different start point:

```
iex> walk_query "http://dbpedia.org/resource/Black_hole"
http://dbpedia.org/resource/Black_hole
http://dbpedia.org/resource/Einstein_field_equations
http://dbpedia.org/resource/Schwarzschild_metric
http://dbpedia.org/resource/Schwarzschild_coordinates
http://dbpedia.org/resource/Pressure
http://dbpedia.org/resource/Solid
http://dbpedia.org/resource/Periodic_table
:ok
```

Honestly, this is just way too much fun. We could easily keep looking for new examples.

Now, this is all well and good and shows that we can walk the graph. But we are querying against a public SPARQL endpoint so there's nothing too surprising here. We ran a query, and we got some results. More surprising will be to navigate the graph without querying a central database, only by touching each node and getting a new node in the graph. This is linked data (or distributed data) in action, and we'll try that out now.

Browsing Linked Data

By definition, graphs connect data. (IDs, labels, and other attributes will either be implicit or explicit.) But since RDF graphs use URIs for node names, they can typically be dereferenced, that is they may return a document when the link is followed. What's more, the document they return is a graph—a graph of semantically linked data.

One could say that a web page usually returns a graph via its DOM model, but this is just a structure for HTML documents—there is no real semantics beyond the operational parse tree. One could also say that any web page may link to additional web pages through HTML links and these links actually form a graph.

And while this may be true, HTML links are anonymous—there are no names, no meaning. We're missing semantics again.

What we mean by linked data here is that a given node in the graph can be inspected—it'll return a graph fragment describing its local context. And this graph fragment can be queried locally, and further nodes can be dereferenced to obtain another graph fragment. And so on. So, essentially, we retrieve graph fragments and query locally. We can thus walk the graph in a meaningful way. We know what the links mean.

Case #3: Graph Walk (Browsing)

Let's build a small toy—a linked data explorer. We're going to look up Wikipedia links in DBpedia and see if there's a link from one Wikipedia page to another. We can then follow our nose and see if that link is linked to another Wikipedia page, and so on.

Create a new walk_links.ex file under the rdf_graph/lib/rdf_graph/examples/ folder:

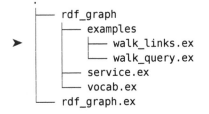

```
.
├── rdf_graph
│   ├── examples
│   │   ├── walk_links.ex
│   │   └── walk_query.ex
│   ├── service.ex
│   └── vocab.ex
└── rdf_graph.ex
```

And create a new module:

```
defmodule RDFGraph.Examples.WalkLinks do
  use Tesla

  # ...

end
```

Note that we add a use Tesla macro as we'll be using the Tesla framework for HTTP requests.

We can then add a couple of middleware plugs to follow redirects and to set our preferred content type as:

apps/rdf_graph/lib/rdf_graph/examples/walk_links.ex
```
plug Tesla.Middleware.FollowRedirects, max_redirects: 3
plug Tesla.Middleware.Headers, [{"accept", "text/turtle"}]
```

Now let's add in a walk_links/2 function as follows:

apps/rdf_graph/lib/rdf_graph/examples/walk_links.ex
```
Line 1  def walk_links(link \\ "http://dbpedia.org/resource/Bob_Dylan", count \\ 0)
     -  def walk_links(_, count) when count >= 7, do: :ok
     -
     -  def walk_links(link, count) do
     5    IO.puts link
     -    {:ok, result} = get(link)
     -    id = String.slice(link, 28..-1)
     -    RDFGraph.write_graph(result.body, "walk/" <> id <> ".ttl")
     -    graph = RDF.Turtle.read_string!(result.body)
    10    query = ~S"""
     -      PREFIX dbo: <http://dbpedia.org/ontology/>
     -      SELECT DISTINCT ?new_link
     -      WHERE
     -      {
    15        BIND (<LINK> AS ?link)
     -        ?link dbo:wikiPageWikiLink ?new_link
     -      }
     -      """
     -    query = String.replace(query, "LINK", link)
    20    list = SPARQL.execute_query(graph, query) |>
     -             SPARQL.Query.Result.get(:new_link)
     -    if Enum.empty?(list) do
     -      :ok
     -    else
    25      link = Enum.random(list) |> RDF.IRI.to_string
     -      walk_links(link, count + 1)
     -    end
     -  end
     -  end
```

This is similar to the walk_query/2 function we discussed earlier in Case #2: Graph Walk (Querying), on page 156). There are two main differences though. After line 5, where we write out the node link, there is a short section between lines 6 and 9 where we first use Tesla.get/1 to retrieve the document at link. Then we get the local ID by stripping out the "http://dbpedia.org/resource/" namespace, which we can then use as a filename for saving the document into our RDF storage. Then finally, at line 9 we read the RDF Turtle in the document into a graph variable.

The second difference is at line 20 where we use SPARQL.execute_query/2 to apply our query against the graph, but this time, the query is local and is run against the in-memory graph, rather than querying DBpedia itself.

OK, it's time to try this out. To make things simpler, let's import the module:

```
iex> import RDFGraph.Examples.WalkLinks
RDFGraph.Examples.WalkLinks
```

Let's try first with our default resource:

```
iex> walk_links
http://dbpedia.org/resource/Bob_Dylan
http://dbpedia.org/resource/Cinéma_vérité
http://dbpedia.org/resource/Dziga_Vertov
http://dbpedia.org/resource/Ukrainian_language
http://dbpedia.org/resource/Vistula_Land
http://dbpedia.org/resource/Scorched_earth
http://dbpedia.org/resource/1999_East_Timorese_crisis
:ok
```

And try again. This time we hit a dead end:

```
iex> walk_links
http://dbpedia.org/resource/Bob_Dylan
http://dbpedia.org/resource/William_Shakespeare
http://dbpedia.org/resource/Category:17th-century_English_male_actors
:ok
```

Now try with a new start node:

```
iex> walk_links "http://dbpedia.org/resource/Renoir"
http://dbpedia.org/resource/Renoir
http://dbpedia.org/resource/Pierre-Auguste_Renoir
http://dbpedia.org/resource/Diego_Velázquez
http://dbpedia.org/resource/Hans-Adam_II,_Prince_of_Liechtenstein
http://dbpedia.org/resource/Prince_Alfred_of_Liechtenstein
http://dbpedia.org/resource/Franz_Joseph_II,_Prince_of_Liechtenstein
http://dbpedia.org/resource/Liechtenstein
:ok
```

Repeat as required.

But note that in the meantime we are also building up a small graph library in our RDF storage:

```
iex> list_graphs_dir("walk")
["A&M_Records.ttl", "Barbara_Carroll.ttl", "Black_Bottom_(dance).ttl",
 "Bob_Dylan.ttl", "Brian_Griffin.ttl", "Broadway_theatre.ttl",
 "Bruce_Springsteen.ttl", "Carroll_Dickerson.ttl",
 ...
 "Music_from_Big_Pink.ttl", "Satchmo.ttl",
 "Sgt._Pepper's_Lonely_Hearts_Club_Band.ttl", "The_Stooges.ttl",
 "Thurgood_Marshall.ttl", "Traditional_pop.ttl",
 "We_Have_All_the_Time_in_the_World.ttl", "Édouard_Vuillard.ttl"]
```

And we can read these graphs back in and query against them.

Wrapping Up

In this chapter, we looked at the SPARQL query language and saw how it can be used to query RDF graphs.

Specifically, we used the sparql_client package to query RDF graph services from Elixir. (We also discussed querying in-memory RDF data structures using the sparql package.)

We queried a local graph service using our book graph RDF model and also a public RDF dataset for the Tokyo Metro. And since we control the local graph service, we can also write to it. We saw an example of enriching the RDF dataset by adding in rdf:type statements which are used for classifying entities.

A number of public SPARQL endpoints on the web are available for querying. We used our sparql! function to query a couple of them. First, we demonstrated a simple "Hello World" query on DBpedia. We then tried our hand at a random walk over DBpedia, first querying DBpedia directly and then using DBpedia's built-in support for linked data to browse the graph.

The special thing about RDF graphs is that they are uniquely designed for publishing and sharing. The use of global identifiers means that any RDF datasets from whatever source can be merged together with no supervision at all. When you think about it, that's heady stuff.

But we still want to cover another couple of graph query languages that we can access from Elixir: Gremlin and GraphQL.

## CHAPTER 9

Traversing Graphs with Gremlin

Cypher and SPARQL are the two main declarative query languages for graphs, but for directly traversing graphs, perhaps the best-known language used by graph databases is Gremlin.[1] And as an imperative language, Gremlin may even provide a performance boost in some cases, as its execution is more finely controlled.

Gremlin is the graph traversal language of the Apache TinkerPop project.[2] This traversal language is supported on many different graph implementations and is something of a de facto standard in the graph query landscape. So we'll definitely want to get acquainted with it.

We need to clarify a couple of terms: TinkerPop and TinkerGraph. TinkerPop is the underlying graph framework that is distributed by the Apache project, while TinkerGraph is an in-memory reference implementation that is deployed with TinkerPop. We'll be using TinkerGraph with our graph service.

We're going to create our own TinkerGraph project so that we can play with Gremlin queries. And we'll implement a graph service for the project using our common graph services API.

But first, let's have a quick look at Gremlin itself.

Using Gremlin

Gremlin is a graph traversal language for property graphs that is being developed by the Apache TinkerPop project and is supported by various graph system vendors for both OLTP graph databases and OLAP graph processors.

---

1. https://tinkerpop.apache.org/gremlin.html
2. http://tinkerpop.apache.org/

Gremlin traverses the graph by following a sequence of steps, with each step performing a single operation on the data. The basic steps are transforms (which modify data), filters (which exclude data), or compute steps (which provide stats, and so on).

The Apache TinkerPop distribution is written in Java, and as such it supports a Groovy-based query syntax with methods for steps and method chaining for sequencing the steps. Here's an example of a Gremlin query string piped into a Gremlin client:

```
iex> "g.V().hasLabel('Book').out().values('name').dedup()" |> gremlin!
["O'Reilly Media", "Amy E. Hodler", "Mark Needham",
 "The Pragmatic Bookshelf", "Ben Marx", "José Valim", "Bruce Tate",
 "Ben Wilson", "Bruce Williams", "James Edward Gray II"]
```

We can break this down as:

1. g: use the current graph traversal
2. V(): for all nodes (that is, vertices) in the graph
3. hasLabel('Book'): filter nodes with the label Book
4. out(): traverse outgoing edges from Book nodes
5. values('name'): get the name property of the outgoing nodes
6. dedup(): deduplicate the list of names

We'll see some more examples of this shortly.

For more information on querying with Gremlin, check out the excellent online book "Practical Gremlin: An Apache TinkerPop Tutorial"[3] by Kelvin R. Lawrence.

Now let's see this in practice.

Creating the TinkerGraph Project

Fortunately, there already is an Elixir package we can use to test out querying Gremlin—the gremlex[4] package by CarLabs[5] which provides an Elixir client for Apache TinkerPop. For a general introduction to Gremlex, be sure to see the post "Introducing Gremlex" by Kevin Moore.[6]

3.   https://kelvinlawrence.net/book/Gremlin-Graph-Guide.html
4.   https://hex.pm/packages/gremlex
5.   https://www.carlabs.ai/
6.   https://medium.com/carlabs/introducing-gremlex-6f685adf73bd

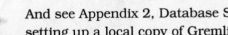

TinkerGraph Project/Database Setup

See Appendix 1, Project Setups, on page 245, for details on retrieving a working project with code and data.

And see Appendix 2, Database Setups, on page 247, for help on setting up a local copy of Gremlin Server.

So, without further ado, let's create a new project, TinkerGraph. Go to the ExGraphsBook home project (see ExGraphsBook Umbrella, on page 16), cd down into the apps directory, and open up the new TinkerGraph project:

```
$ mix new tinker_graph
```

You should have an apps directory that looks like this:

```
.
├── apps
│   ├── graph_commons
│   ├── native_graph
│   ├── property_graph
│   ├── rdf_graph
│   └── tinker_graph
```

Now cd into the tinker_graph directory:

```
.
├── lib
│   └── tinker_graph.ex
├── mix.exs
└── test
    └── ...
```

You need to declare a dependency on gremlex by adding the line {:gremlex, "~> 0.3"} to the mix.exs file:

apps/tinker_graph/mix.exs
```
defp deps do
  [
    # graph_commons
    {:graph_commons, in_umbrella: true},

    # tinker graphs
    {:gremlex, "~> 0.3"},
    {:httpoison, "~> 1.8", override: true}
  ]
end
```

Note that we also added the line {:httpoison, ~> 1.8", override: true} to the mix.exs file as gremlex has a fixed dependency for an earlier version of httpoison.

Now use Mix to add in the dependencies:

```
$ mix deps.get
Resolving Hex dependencies...
```

Then add the connection details to your config:

```
config :gremlex,
  host: "127.0.0.1",
  port: 8182,
  path: "/gremlin",
  pool_size: 10,
  secure: false,
  ping_delay: 90_000
```

Finally, wire the graph storage into the TinkerGraph module with these use/2 macros:

apps/tinker_graph/lib/tinker_graph.ex
```
use GraphCommons.Graph, graph_type: :tinker, graph_module: __MODULE__
use GraphCommons.Query, query_type: :tinker, query_module: __MODULE__
```

And with that, we're all set to do some querying.

Querying with Gremlin

Let's start with some basic Gremlin queries to get an idea of what to expect.

The gremlex package provides two main modules: Gremlex.Graph and Gremlex.Client.

We'll first bring these modules into our default namespace to make for easier handling in IEx:

```
iex> alias Gremlex.{Client,Graph}
[Gremlex.Client, Gremlex.Graph]
```

Now that that's done, here's a sample graph build and query:

```
iex> Graph.g() |> Graph.add_v("Foo") |> Client.query
{:ok, [%Gremlex.Vertex{id: 0, label: "Foo", properties: %{}}]}
```

The Graph module supports some, but not all, Gremlin functions and is still in early development. For the sake of brevity, we'll focus here on sending raw Gremlin queries using the Client module and receiving results back as Elixir data structures.

So here's the same graph build using a Gremlin traversal:

```
iex> "g.addV('Foo')" |> Client.query
{:ok, [%Gremlex.Vertex{id: 919, label: "Foo", properties: %{}}]}
```

We'll start by wiping the current graph:

```
iex> "g.V().drop()" |> Client.query
{:ok, []}
```

If we now inspect the Gremlin graph instance, we'll see that it's empty:

```
iex> "graph" |> Client.query
{:ok, [%{"edges" => [], "vertices" => []}]}
```

We can also inspect the graph traversal object:

```
iex> "g.toString()" |> Client.query
{:ok, ["graphtraversalsource[tinkergraph[vertices:0 edges:0], standard]"]}
```

Now let's read a graph from our graph store:

```
iex> IO.puts (default = read_graph("default.groovy").data)
// Default graph

a = graph.addVertex('a')
b = graph.addVertex('b')
a.addEdge('EX', b)

:ok
```

This is our standard default graph with two nodes and one edge:

```
iex> default |> Client.query
{:ok,
 [
   %Gremlex.Edge{
     id: 949,
     in_vertex: %Gremlex.Vertex{id: 948, label: "b", properties: nil},
     label: "EX",
     out_vertex: %Gremlex.Vertex{id: 947, label: "a", properties: nil},
     properties: %{}
   }
 ]}
```

We can inspect the Gremlin graph instance again:

```
iex> "graph" |> Client.query
{:ok,
 [
   %{
     "edges" => [
       %{
         "@type" => "g:Edge",
         "@value" => %{
           "id" => %{"@type" => "g:Int64", "@value" => 934},
           "inV" => %{"@type" => "g:Int64", "@value" => 933},
           "inVLabel" => "b",
           "label" => "EX",
```

```
            "outV" => %{"@type" => "g:Int64", "@value" => 932},
            "outVLabel" => "a"
          }
        }
      ],
      "vertices" => [
        %{
          "@type" => "g:Vertex",
          "@value" => %{
            "id" => %{"@type" => "g:Int64", "@value" => 932},
            "label" => "a"
          }
        },
        %{
          "@type" => "g:Vertex",
          "@value" => %{
            "id" => %{"@type" => "g:Int64", "@value" => 933},
            "label" => "b"
          }
        }
      ]
    }
  ]}
```

Now let's query the graph traversal object for nodes:

```
iex> "g.V()" |> Client.query
{:ok,
 [
   %Gremlex.Vertex{id: 932, label: "a", properties: %{}},
   %Gremlex.Vertex{id: 933, label: "b", properties: %{}}
 ]}
```

Let's do the same for edges:

```
iex> "g.E()" |> Client.query
{:ok,
 [
   %Gremlex.Edge{
     id: 934,
     in_vertex: %Gremlex.Vertex{id: 933, label: "b", properties: nil},
     label: "EX",
     out_vertex: %Gremlex.Vertex{id: 932, label: "a", properties: nil},
     properties: %{}
   }
 ]}
```

Well, we've covered the basics. We'll now want to create some larger graphs and use Gremlin's traversal object for more elaborate querying. But before that, let's set up our own graph service to abstract away the Gremlex API so that we can more easily switch between different graph types.

Setting Up a Graph Service

As we've done with the previous graph types, we'll layer our own graph service API over the Gremlex API so that we can focus on the Gremlin query language itself and not be concerned with the details of any particular package API. The other reason for defining our own API is to achieve a certain brevity as we are particularly focused on querying graphs interactively with IEx.

Graph API

We can set up our TinkerGraph graph service API by simply wrapping the Gremlex.Client.query/2 function. The TinkerGraph graph service functions are now defined as:

apps/tinker_graph/lib/tinker_graph/service.ex
```
def graph_create(graph) do
  graph_delete()
  graph_update(graph)
end

def graph_delete() do
  Gremlex.Client.query("g.V().drop()")
end

def graph_read() do
end

def graph_update(%GraphCommons.Graph{type: :tinker} = graph) do
  Gremlex.Client.query(graph.data)
end
```

This gives us our basic graph service API.

Graph Info

We'll also want a graph_info/0 function:

apps/tinker_graph/lib/tinker_graph/service.ex
```
def graph_info() do
  {:ok, [num_vertices]} = Gremlex.Client.query("g.V().count()")
  {:ok, vertex_labels} = Gremlex.Client.query("g.V().label().dedup()")
  {:ok, [num_edges]} = Gremlex.Client.query("g.E().count()")
  {:ok, edge_labels} = Gremlex.Client.query("g.E().label().dedup()")

  %GraphCommons.Service.GraphInfo{
    type: :tinker,
    num_nodes: num_vertices,
    num_edges: num_edges,
    labels: vertex_labels ++ edge_labels
  }
end
```

This gives us a simple means to introspect graphs.

Query API

Finally, let's create a couple of simple wrappers for our query functions:

apps/tinker_graph/lib/tinker_graph/service.ex
```
def query_graph(%GraphCommons.Query{type: :tinker} = query) do
  Gremlex.Client.query(query.data)
end

def query_graph!(%GraphCommons.Query{type: :tinker} = query) do
  Gremlex.Client.query(query.data)
  |>
  case do
    {:ok, response} -> response
    {:error, message} -> raise "! #{message}"
  end
end
```

OK, we're good to query.

But let's add one last touch. As before, we can define a query helper gremlin!/1 in GraphCommons.Utils as:

apps/graph_commons/lib/graph_commons/utils.ex
```
def gremlin!(query_string), do: to_query_graph!(TinkerGraph, query_string)
```

This function takes a query string and calls the private function to_query_graph!/1 (also in GraphCommons.Utils) to convert the query string into a %GraphCommons.Query struct:

apps/graph_commons/lib/graph_commons/utils.ex
```
defp to_query_graph!(graph_module, query_string)
    when is_module(graph_module) do
  query_string
  |> graph_module.new_query()
  |> graph_module.query_graph!()
end
```

This function uses the is_module/1 guard to ensure that the graph_module argument is one of the valid graph modules:

apps/graph_commons/lib/graph_commons/utils.ex
```
defguard is_module(graph_module)
  when graph_module in [DGraph, NativeGraph, PropertyGraph, RDFGraph,
  TinkerGraph]
```

So now we're all set to do some querying.

API Demo

Let's try our API out. But first, let's switch our graph context and import the TinkerGraph module:

```
iex> graph_context TinkerGraph
TinkerGraph
```

We'll need some data, so let's reload our default graph from the graph store.

```
iex> graph_create read_graph("default.groovy")
{:ok,
 [
   %Gremlex.Edge{
     id: 937,
     in_vertex: %Gremlex.Vertex{id: 936, label: "b", properties: nil},
     label: "EX",
     out_vertex: %Gremlex.Vertex{id: 935, label: "a", properties: nil},
     properties: %{}
   }
 ]}
```

Now we can query this simply as:

```
iex> "g.V()" |> gremlin!
[
  %Gremlex.Vertex{id: 3, label: "a", properties: %{}},
  %Gremlex.Vertex{id: 4, label: "b", properties: %{}}
]
```

This gives us the nodes in the graph.

And to get the edges we can query as:

```
iex> "g.E()" |> gremlin!
[
  %Gremlex.Edge{
    id: 2,
    in_vertex: %Gremlex.Vertex{id: 1, label: "b", properties: nil},
    label: "EX",
    out_vertex: %Gremlex.Vertex{id: 0, label: "a", properties: nil},
    properties: %{}
  }
]
```

Now let's get some counts:

```
iex> "g.V().count()" |> gremlin!
[2]

iex> "g.E().count()" |> gremlin!
[1]
```

That's right—we have two nodes and one edge, exactly as we expected.

We're able to read and write into our graph service and query over that. So let's move on to a slightly larger graph.

Creating the Book Graph

In this section, we're going to use Gremlin to query over the book graph we've been using as our reference graph. We'll also see how that differs from the other query languages we've seen.

As Gremlin models a property graph, we can expect our graph model to be pretty much the same as the one we modeled earlier with Cypher—see Modeling the Book Graph, on page 98, for a reminder of how that looked.

We can simply create our book graph in Gremlin, using the addVertex and addEdge steps on our graph instance and listing out the properties on both nodes and edges:

```
// Book 1
adopting_elixir = graph.addVertex(label, 'Book',
  'id', 'adopting_elixir',
  'date', '2018-03-14',
  'format', 'Paper',
  'isbn', '978-1-68050-252-7',
  'title', 'Adopting Elixir',
  'url', 'https://pragprog.com/titles/tvmelixir/adopting-elixir/',
)
ben_marx = graph.addVertex(label, 'Author',
  'id', 'ben_marx',
  'name', 'Ben Marx',
  'url', 'https://twitter.com/bgmarx',
)
jose_valim = graph.addVertex(label, 'Author',
  'id', 'jose_valim',
  'name', 'José Valim',
  'url', 'https://twitter.com/josevalim',
)
bruce_tate = graph.addVertex(label, 'Author',
  'id', 'bruce_tate',
  'name', 'Bruce Tate',
  'url', 'https://twitter.com/redrapids',
)
pragmatic = graph.addVertex(label, 'Publisher',
  'id', 'pragmatic',
  'name', 'The Pragmatic Bookshelf',
  'url', 'https://pragprog.com/',
)

// add  edges
adopting_elixir.addEdge('AUTHOR', ben_marx,
  'role', 'first author',
)
adopting_elixir.addEdge('AUTHOR', jose_valim,
  'role', 'second author',
)
```

```
adopting_elixir.addEdge('AUTHOR', bruce_tate,
  'role', 'third author',
)
adopting_elixir.addEdge('PUBLISHER', pragmatic,
)
pragmatic.addEdge('BOOK', adopting_elixir,
)
// Book 2
...
```

Let's save this down into the graph store in the file books.groovy. We can now load this into our graph service as:

```
iex> graph_create read_graph("books.groovy")
{:ok,
 [
   %Gremlex.Edge{
     ...
   }
 ]}
```

And we can check the status of our graph service as:

```
iex> graph_info
%GraphCommons.Service.GraphInfo{
  file: nil,
  labels: ["Book", "Author", "Publisher", "AUTHOR", "PUBLISHER", "BOOK"],
  num_edges: 17,
  num_nodes: 14,
  type: :tinker
}
```

Now let's query the book graph using the graph traversal object. Let's check on one of the authors using the name property:

```
iex> "g.V().has('name', 'Ben Marx').values('name')" |> gremlin!
["Ben Marx"]
```

Yup, he's there.

We can list out properties for this author as:

```
iex> "g.V().has('name', 'Ben Marx').properties()" |> gremlin!
[
  %Gremlex.VertexProperty{
    id: 845,
    label: "url",
    value: "https://twitter.com/bgmarx",
    vertex: nil
  },
```

```
%Gremlex.VertexProperty{
  id: 846,
  label: "name",
  value: "Ben Marx",
  vertex: nil
},
%Gremlex.VertexProperty{
  id: 402,
  label: "id",
  value: "ben_marx",
  vertex: nil
}
]
```

And if we want to list all the author names, we can query for the label Author and get the name property:

```
iex> "g.V().hasLabel('Author').values('name')" |> gremlin!
["Amy E. Hodler", "Mark Needham", "Ben Marx", "José Valim", "Bruce Tate",
 "Bruce Williams", "Ben Wilson", "James Edward Gray II"]
```

As a property graph query, let's say we want to get all the third authors of our books by querying for edges with a third_author value for the role property:

```
iex> "g.E().has('role', 'third author')" |> gremlin!
[
  %Gremlex.Edge{
    id: 861,
    in_vertex: %Gremlex.Vertex{id: 851, label: "Author", properties: nil},
    label: "AUTHOR",
    out_vertex: %Gremlex.Vertex{id: 837, label: "Book", properties: nil},
    properties: %{}
  }
]
```

Note that this gives us the edges, but we want to just get the in_vertex:

```
iex> "g.E().has('role', 'third author').inV().values('name')" |> gremlin!
["Bruce Tate"]
```

At this point, you'll probably want to go off and create some more interesting graphs to query against. Gremlin is a rich query language with plenty to learn.

Wrapping Up

In this chapter, we've seen how to use the graph traversal language Gremlin from Elixir.

We've used the gremlex package to query against a TinkerGraph model maintained by a local Gremlin Server. As before, we built a graph service to abstract away the specific interface details so that we could focus more on the graph model and query language.

We've also seen how our reference book graph can be modeled using Gremlin's query syntax, and we tried out some queries to get an overall feel for what this looks like in practice.

Truth be told, we could spend a lot more time experimenting with Gremlin and graph traversals, but I'm sure we're eager at this point to continue with the last of the graph query types we'll be meeting in this book—GraphQL.

## CHAPTER 10

Delivering Data with Dgraph

These days whenever we talk about web APIs, GraphQL[1] invariably springs to mind. Created by Facebook and open-sourced since 2015, GraphQL supports data access through APIs for reading, writing, and subscribing to changes to data.

It sounds like we have a new graph query language to play with. But despite the suggestive name, GraphQL isn't strictly a query language for graphs. The name comes from its ability to query over a mixed-source object graph, although it isn't limited to any particular backend data model. Rather it defines a query interface in which queries are tree-shaped affairs and result sets are returned as document trees. Users get to specify the data items and the shapes that they need. In short, GraphQL acts essentially like a mixing desk for data.

It would be great if there were a GraphQL interface to an actual graph database. Enter Dgraph.

Dgraph[2] is a transaction-distributed graph database. It is written in Go and is open-sourced under the Apache 2.0 license. It shards data horizontally and provides shard rebalancing with an automated synchronous replication. With its flexible schema model, it can break queries down and run them in parallel to achieve low latency and reliably high throughput.

Dgraph has developed its own variant of GraphQL, originally named GraphQL+- and now renamed DQL (Dgraph Query Language), which it has tailored specifically for graph databases.

---

1. https://graphql.org/
2. https://dgraph.io/

> **What Is GraphQL?**
>
> GraphQL provides a graph layer over backend data sources and provides a query language that traverses the data graph to produce a query result tree. In the case of Dgraph, however, there is no abstraction layer, and the query language interrogates a graph database directly.
>
> For more information about using GraphQL with Elixir, see *Craft GraphQL APIs in Elixir with Absinthe [WW18]* by Bruce Williams and Ben Wilson.

With a couple of Elixir packages for interfacing to Dgraph, this looks like an excellent opportunity for us to contrast a GraphQL-like query syntax with SQL-based query syntaxes such as Cypher and SPARQL. (In passing, we note that Dgraph has declared intentions to also provide support for Cypher and Gremlin.)

Dgraph supports an RDF-like data ingest model, but it also supports facets on edges similar to a regular property graph model. So it seems to be implementing some kind of hybrid graph data model. Let's see what's going on.

But first, let's see how DQL differs from GraphQL.

GraphQL and DQL

GraphQL provides a nested object query language that looks nominally like a JSON template, with the resulting format being an actual JSON document. Queries are built up from types and fields, which are declared in a schema using GraphQL's Schema Definition Language (SDL). GraphQL also provides a means to modify data using what it calls mutations, which use the query language format and tap into the schema data definitions. Queries and mutations are also declared in the schema and may be introspected.

This gives the client a lot of flexibility in how it requests data. Clients can query for the query forms and then request just the types and fields that they have an interest in.

DQL extends the GraphQL query and schema styles with some additions and omissions. It adds these features: transactions, upserts, variables (query blocks), math functions, aggregations, group by, facets, geo, datetime, and i18n. The removed features include enums, interfaces, unions, strong types, and introspection.

For more information, see the blog post "Building a Native GraphQL Database: Challenges, Learnings and Future" by Manish Jain,[3] and also the article "New to Dgraph? DQL vs. GraphQL, Endpoints, Headers, and Schema Translation" by Anthony Master.[4]

Let's take a look now at DQL and the Dgraph data model.

Dgraph Model

The Dgraph data model is a little curious. Superficially, it resembles RDF in that nodes connect to both nodes and literal values via edges. But critically, it does away with RDF's key feature—external IDs. This is the very feature that allows for web-scale data integration. As such, it corresponds to an RDF that uses blank nodes.

Dgraph's Take on RDF

 Dgraph uses an RDF-like N-Triples syntax for data mutations. (The documentation talks about N-Quads, although all the examples are in N-Triples format.) Note that this isn't strictly RDF as properties are typically expressed using local names, whereas RDF requires properties to be identified using absolute URI names. Be warned also that this RDF mutation format won't validate with an RDF parser. It does, however, provide a simple means of expressing edges.

Mutation

To update data in Dgraph or add new data, we need to perform a mutation. Dgraph has two mutation formats: RDF and JSON. We'll show the RDF format here because it's more compact.

This is what a simple graph looks like in Dgraph's RDF mutation format:

```
{
  set {
    # triples in here
  }
}
```

And here are the RDF triples:

```
# object predicates
_:n1 <FOO> _:m1 .
_:n1 <FOO> _:m2 .
```

3. https://dgraph.io/blog/post/building-native-graphql-database-dgraph/
4. https://discuss.dgraph.io/t/new-to-dgraph-dql-vs-graphql-endpoints-headers-and-schema-translation/10443

```
# string predicates
_:n1 <foo> "bar" .
_:n1 <foo> "baz" .
```

Here we have one node _:n1 that links to nodes _:m1 and _:m2 via the <FOO> object predicate. It also adds two simple string values via the <foo> string predicate. We're using a simple convention here with object predicates labeled in uppercase and string predicates labeled in lowercase, although this isn't required. In fact, the only real difference between the two is that object predicates are of type uid whereas string values are one of the scalar types such as int or string.

The example shows one main divergence from the property graph model. Like the RDF graph model, properties are added as edges pointing at literal values, rather than being attributes of the node itself.

And in a nod to the property graph model, Dgraph supports properties on edges via facets. This is what facets look like in Dgraph's RDF mutation format:

```
# object predicates
_:n1 <FOO> _:m1 (test="one") .
_:n1 <FOO> _:m2 (test="two") .
# string predicates
_:n1 <foo> "bar" (test="three") .
_:n1 <foo> "baz" (test="four") .
```

Here we've added a facet test to the edges with string values.

Schema

A Dgraph schema lists out the predicates and types separately. Predicates are indicated using the following form, which declares the scalar type:

```
FOO: uid .
foo: string .
```

These may be further enhanced using directives to specify indexing and other features, for example:

```
foo: string @index(term).
```

Object types are defined using a GraphQL-like syntax:

```
type Test {
  FOO
  foo
}
```

Each attribute in an object type will have a predicate definition.

Schema mutations are used to add or modify a schema. If no schema is provided, then Dgraph will generate default predicate definitions. Typically, however, a schema will be added before any data mutation.

Query

Queries in Dgraph use GraphQL's nested object query language. They are always named, and use one of DQL's built-in functions:

```
{
  test_query(func: has(foo)) {
    foo
  }
}
```

The test_query here uses the has() built-in function after a func: key and returns all objects with a foo predicate. With the data listed earlier, this would return the following JSON document:

```
{
  "data": {
    "test_query": [
      {
        "foo": "bar"
      },
      {
        "foo": "baz"
      }
    ]
  },
  ...
}
```

Of course, there's a lot more to DQL but this example here gives the essence of querying in Dgraph. So, let's set up a new project now to try this out.

Creating the DGraph Project

We're going to be using the dlex[5] package by Dmitry Russ[6] which provides a gRPC-based Dgraph client for Elixir. (This was inspired by the earlier ex_dgraph[7] package by Ole Spaarmann.[8])

---

5. https://hex.pm/packages/dlex
6. https://github.com/liveforeverx
7. https://hex.pm/packages/ex_dgraph
8. https://twitter.com/olespaarmann

DGraph Project/Database Setup

See Appendix 1, Project Setups, on page 245, for details on retrieving a working project with code and data.

And see Appendix 2, Database Setups, on page 247, for help on setting up a local copy of Dgraph.

Let's create a project DGraph. Go to the ExGraphsBook home project (see ExGraphsBook Umbrella, on page 16), cd down into the apps directory, and open up the new DGraph project:

```
$ mix new d_graph --sup
```

Note that we are using the --sup flag as we're going to use a supervised process. This will add in a new d_graph app:

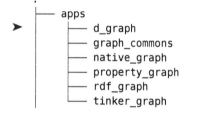

```
.
├── apps
│   ├── d_graph
│   ├── graph_commons
│   ├── native_graph
│   ├── property_graph
│   ├── rdf_graph
│   └── tinker_graph
```

Let's cd into the d_graph directory:

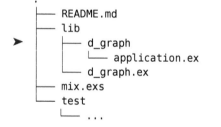

```
.
├── README.md
├── lib
│   ├── d_graph
│   │   └── application.ex
│   └── d_graph.ex
├── mix.exs
└── test
    └── ...
```

Note that the --sup flag has generated an extra directory d_graph under lib with an application.ex file. Now let's add the :dlex dependency into mix.exs:

```
apps/d_graph/mix.exs
defp deps do
  [
    # graph_commons
    {:graph_commons, in_umbrella: true},

    # dgraph graphs
    {:dlex, "~> 0.5"},
    {:protobuf, "~> 0.5.0"}
  ]
end
```

Note that we've also added a dependency restriction on protobuf as the latest version isn't compatible with dlex.

As usual, use Mix to add in the dependencies:

```
$ mix deps.get; mix deps.compile
```

We'll also need to start up our DGraph.Application module:

```
def application do
  [
    extra_applications: [:logger],
➤   mod: { DGraph.Application, [] }
  ]
end
```

The :mod option specifies the application callback module, followed by any arguments to be passed on application start. The application callback module is any module that implements the Application behaviour.

And we update the start/2 function in lib/d_graph/application.ex as:

```
apps/d_graph/lib/d_graph/application.ex
def start(_type, _args) do
  children = [
    {Dlex, Application.get_env(:dlex, Dlex, [])},
  ]

  opts = [strategy: :one_for_one, name: DGraph.Service]
➤ {:ok, pid} = Supervisor.start_link(children, opts)
  [{_, child_pid, _, _}] = Supervisor.which_children(pid)
  Application.put_env(:dlex, PID, child_pid)
  {:ok, pid}
end
```

The application will now be started automatically.

Note that we get the pid of the supervisor process and use that to get the child_pid of the Dlex process which we then save into our application environment.

We can then define a simple get_pid/0 accessor function in a DGraph.Service module:

```
apps/d_graph/lib/d_graph/service.ex
def get_pid() do
  Application.get_env(:dlex, PID)
end
```

Whenever we want a database connection, we can simply call this function:

```
iex> conn = DGraph.Service.get_pid
#PID<0.284.0>
```

Finally, let's wire our graph storage into the DGraph module with these use/2 macros:

apps/d_graph/lib/d_graph.ex
```
use GraphCommons.Graph, graph_type: :dgraph, graph_module: __MODULE__
use GraphCommons.Query, query_type: :dgraph, query_module: __MODULE__
```

At this point, we're all set to store and query our first graph. We'll start by opening up a new IEx session and getting our database connection:

```
iex> conn = DGraph.Service.get_pid
#PID<0.378.0>
```

To ensure we start off with a clean slate, let's drop any previous schemas and data:

```
iex> Dlex.alter!(conn, %{drop_all: true})
""
```

We can now define our default graph with two nodes and one edge between them and use the Dlex.mutate/2 function to ingest it:

```
iex> default = "_:a <EX> _:b ."
"_:a <EX> _:b ."
iex> Dlex.mutate(conn, %{set: default})
{:ok, %{queries: %{}, uids: %{"a" => "0x4fff", "b" => "0x5000"}}}
```

We can go ahead and query as follows:

```
iex> default_q = """
...> {
...>   q(func: has(EX)) {
...>     uid
...>     EX { uid }
...>   }
...> }
...> """
"{\n  q(func: has(EX)) {\n    uid\n    EX { uid }\n  }\n}\n"
iex> Dlex.query(conn, default_q)
{:ok, %{"q" => [%{"EX" => [%{"uid" => "0x5000"}], "uid" => "0x4fff"}]}}
```

You can see that Dgraph has automatically added a predicate EX to the schema:

```
iex> Dlex.query(conn, "schema {}")
{:ok,
 %{
```

```
  "schema" => [
    %{"list" => true, "predicate" => "EX", "type" => "uid"},
    . . .
  ],
  "types" => [
    . . .
  ]
}}
```

Note that there is a handy wrapper Dlex.query_schema/1 function which will return the same result. But the basic Dlex.query/4 function allows us to query our schema by predicate or type with pred and type args, respectively:

```
iex> Dlex.query(conn, "schema(pred: EX) {}")
{:ok,
 %{"schema" => [%{"list" => true, "predicate" => "EX", "type" => "uid"}]
 }}
```

So that's a quick run-through of some of the standard Dlex library functions. Now we're going to hide them away behind our common graph services API.

Setting Up a Graph Service

To use the graph services API, we're going to define some wrapper functions for the Dlex library functions.

Schema API

First, let's add a special function to the DGraph.Service module to upload our Dgraph schema:

apps/d_graph/lib/d_graph/service.ex
```
def schema_update(%GraphCommons.Graph{} = graph) do
  Dlex.alter(DGraph.Service.get_pid(), graph.data)
end
```

We'll use a %GraphCommons.Graph{} struct to hold the schema data, which we'll access with the usual read_graph/1 function. We can then retrieve the schema body and pass that to Dlex.alter/3.

Graph API

The graph service functions are simply defined as:

apps/d_graph/lib/d_graph/service.ex
```
def graph_create(graph) do
  graph_delete()
  graph_update(graph)
end
```

```
def graph_delete() do
  Dlex.alter!(DGraph.Service.get_pid(), %{drop_all: true})
end

def graph_read() do
  #
end

def graph_update(%GraphCommons.Graph{} = graph) do
  Dlex.mutate(DGraph.Service.get_pid(), %{set: graph.data})
end
```

Note that with graph_delete/0 we clear both schemas and data.

Query API

Let's also create a simple wrapper for our query function:

```
def query_graph(%GraphCommons.Query{} = query) do
  :dgraph = query.type

  Dlex.query(DGraph.Service.get_pid(), query.data)
  |> case do
    {:ok, response} -> response
    {:error, error} -> raise "! #{inspect error}"
  end
end
```

And as before, we can define a query helper for this as:

```
def dgraph!(query_string), do: to_query_graph(DGraph, query_string)
```

API Demo

Let's try our API out. But first, let's switch our graph context and import the DGraph module:

```
iex> graph_context DGraph
DGraph
```

We'll need some data, so let's reload our default graph.

```
iex> read_graph("default.dgraph") |> graph_create
{:ok, %{queries: %{}, uids: %{"a" => "0x4eba", "b" => "0x4ebb"}}}
```

Now we can query this using one of two built-in functions: has() or uid(). The has() function will query over a predicate, while the uid() function will query over a node UID. (And if we had defined custom types, we could have used a type() function.)

Let's try both approaches. First, we'll try querying by predicate EX:

```
iex> """
...> {
...>   q(func: has(EX)) {
...>     uid
...>     EX { uid }
...>   }
...> }
...> """ |> dgraph!
  %{"q" => [%{"EX" => [%{"uid" => "0x4ebb"}], "uid" => "0x4eba"}]}
```

Now that we have the UIDs we can query by UID:

```
iex> """
...> {
...>   q(func: uid(0x4eba)) {
...>     uid
...>     EX { uid }
...>   }
...> }
...> """ |> dgraph!
%{"q" => [%{"EX" => [%{"uid" => "0x4ebb"}], "uid" => "0x4eba"}]}
```

Yes, this works just fine. We are ready to query. So now we need some graphs.

Modeling the Book Graph

Once again, let's go back to our book graph—see this figure on page 9 which shows our reference book graph.

The following figure shows how this reference graph can be mapped in Dgraph.

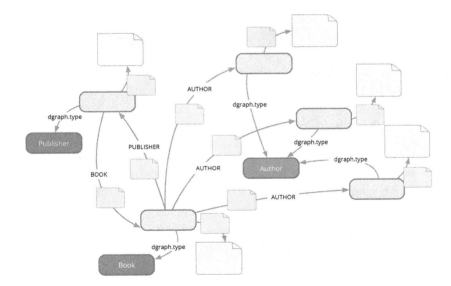

Note that this resembles the RDF graph but with properties added to the edges.

We have some choices in how we load our book graph. We can load the data directly, and Dgraph will auto-generate predicates for us. A more principled way of proceeding would be to define a schema with types and predicates and to load that first.

Again, we have another choice. We can define a GraphQL schema, and Dgraph will auto-generate a DQL schema, or we can define a DQL schema and use that directly. We're going to look at both approaches to creating a DQL schema.

Loading a Schema into Dgraph

Let's have a look at a simple GraphQL schema for our book graph:

```
type Book {
    id: ID!
    date: DateTime
    format: String
    isbn: String
    title: String! @search(by: [term])
    url: String
    AUTHORED_BY: [Author]!
    PUBLISHED_BY: Publisher!
}
type Author {
  id: ID!
  name: String! @search(by: [term])
  url: String
}
type Publisher {
  id: ID!
  name: String! @search(by: [term])
  url: String
}
```

Here we've defined three types (Author, Book, and Publisher) with the fields we require.

We can post this up to the /admin/schema endpoint using Postman or some other tool. This will auto-generate a DQL schema which can be inspected from our service using Dlex:

```
iex> "schema(pred: Author.url) {}" |> dgraph!
%{"schema" => [%{"predicate" => "Author.url", "type" => "string"}]}
```

```
iex> "schema(type: Author) {}" |> dgraph!
%{
  "types" => [
    %{
      "fields" => [%{"name" => "Author.name"}, %{"name" => "Author.url"}],
      "name" => "Author"
    }
  ]
}
```

One thing to note is that Dgraph adds a type namespace to auto-generated DQL predicates, that is title becomes Author.title. We can override this action by using a @dgraph directive as follows:

```
title: String! @search(by: [term]) @dgraph(pred: "title")
```

We can add this to each of the predicates if we want to use simple predicate names.

The advantage of using a GraphQL schema is that we'll be then able to query Dgraph using its GraphQL endpoint (/graphql) with standard tools such as GraphiQL or Insomnia.

But let's put that aside and focus on querying with DQL and let's ingest a DQL schema. This is similar to the GraphQL schema but the predicates and types are separately specified:

```
iex> IO.puts (books_schema = read_graph("schemas/books.schema")).data
date: dateTime .
format: string @index(term) .
isbn: string @index(exact) .
name: string @index(term) .
title: string @index(term) .
url: string @index(exact) .

AUTHORED_BY: [uid] .
PUBLISHED_BY: [uid] .

type Book {
  date
  format
  isbn
  title
  url
  AUTHORED_BY
  PUBLISHED_BY
}
type Author {
  name
  url
}
```

```
type Publisher {
  name
  url
}
:ok

iex> books_schema |> schema_update
{:ok, ""}
```

And we can query the predicates and types again as shown earlier.

Loading Data into Dgraph

We'll now want to load some data. We're going to use our standard book graph which is expressed in Dgraph's RDF mutation format:

```
iex> IO.puts (books_graph = read_graph "books.dgraph").data
# Book 1
_:adopting-elixir <date> "2018-03-14" .
_:adopting-elixir <format> "Paper" .
_:adopting-elixir <isbn> "978-1-68050-252-7" .
_:adopting-elixir <title> "Adopting Elixir" .
_:adopting-elixir <url> "https://pragprog.com/titles/tvmelixir/adopting-elixir/" .
_:adopting-elixir <dgraph.type> "Book" .

_:bgmarx <name> "Ben Marx" .
_:bgmarx <url> "https://twitter.com/bgmarx" .
_:bgmarx <dgraph.type> "Author" .

_:josevalim <name> "José Valim" .
_:josevalim <url> "https://twitter.com/josevalim" .
_:josevalim <dgraph.type> "Author" .

_:redrapids <name> "Bruce Tate" .
_:redrapids <url> "https://twitter.com/redrapids" .
_:redrapids <dgraph.type> "Author" .

_:pragprog <name> "The Pragmatic Bookshelf" .
_:pragprog <url> "https://pragprog.com/" .
_:pragprog <dgraph.type> "Publisher" .
```
➤
```
_:adopting-elixir <AUTHORED_BY> _:bgmarx (role="first author") .
_:adopting-elixir <AUTHORED_BY> _:josevalim (role="second author") .
_:adopting-elixir <AUTHORED_BY> _:redrapids (role="third author") .
_:adopting-elixir <PUBLISHED_BY> _:pragprog .
...

:ok
```

You'll notice that a fourth term is present in the mutation format for facets as highlighted.

Let's load this into our graph service:

```
iex> graph_update books_graph
{:ok,
 %{
   queries: %{},
   uids: %{
     "JEG2" => "0x4fa7",
     "adopting-elixir" => "0x4fa0",
     "amyhodler" => "0x4fab",
     "benwilson512" => "0x4faa",
     "bgmarx" => "0x4fa9",
     "craft-graphql" => "0x4fa3",
     "designing-elixir" => "0x4fa5",
     "graph-algorithms" => "0x4fa8",
     "josevalim" => "0x4fa1",
     ...
   }
 }}
```

Querying Dgraph

We're ready to do some querying. Let's read back a query that we saved earlier:

```
iex> IO.puts (query = read_query("books.dql")).data
{
  books(func: type(Book)) {
    uid
    date
    format
    isbn
    title
    url
    AUTHORED_BY { uid expand(_all_)} @facets(role)
    PUBLISHED_BY { uid expand(_all_)}
  }
}

:ok

iex> result = query.data |> dgraph!
%{
  "books" => [
    %{
      "AUTHORED_BY" => [
        %{
          "AUTHORED_BY|role" => "second author",
          "name" => "José Valim",
          "url" => "https://twitter.com/josevalim",
          "uid" => "0x4fa1"
        },
        %{
          "AUTHORED_BY|role" => "third author",
          "name" => "Bruce Tate",
```

```
        "url" => "https://twitter.com/redrapids",
        "uid" => "0x4fa6"
      },
      %{
        "AUTHORED_BY|role" => "first author",
        "name" => "Ben Marx",
        "url" => "https://twitter.com/bgmarx",
        "uid" => "0x4fa9"
      }
    ],
    "PUBLISHED_BY" => [
      %{
        "name" => "The Pragmatic Bookshelf",
        "url" => "https://pragprog.com/",
        "uid" => "0x4fa2"
      }
    ],
    "date" => "2018-03-14T00:00:00Z",
    "format" => "Paper",
    "isbn" => "978-1-68050-252-7",
    "title" => "Adopting Elixir",
    "url" => "https://pragprog.com/titles/tvmelixir/adopting-elixir/",
    "uid" => "0x4fa0"
  },
  ...
  ]
}
```

Note that the edge properties (facets) are included in this response by namespacing the facet name with the predicate name, that is AUTHORED_BY|role.

Facets

Now let's look at querying over facets. Let's say we want to find all books with second authors. Well, we can filter on a predicate using a @facets directive:

```
iex> IO.puts (q = read_query("books_facets.dql")).data
{
  q(func: has(title)) {
    uid
    title
    AUTHORED_BY @facets(eq(role, "second author")) {
      uid
      name
    }
  }
}
:ok
```

```
iex> q.data |> dgraph!
%{
  "q" => [
    %{
      "AUTHORED_BY" => [%{"name" => ["José Valim"], "uid" => "0x4f0e"}],
      "title" => "Adopting Elixir",
      "uid" => "0x4f07"
    },
    %{
      "AUTHORED_BY" => [%{"name" => ["Bruce Tate"], "uid" => "0x4f08"}],
      "title" => "Designing Elixir Systems with OTP",
      "uid" => "0x4f10"
    },
    ...
  ]
}
```

It works. We can query by facets. It's time now for another graph.

Reaching Back to the ARPANET

We're going to revisit another graph we've seen before, the ARPANET, and look at some additional DQL features: inverses, paths, and recursion. So, let's set up a Dgraph schema for this.

We start by clearing out the graph service of schemas and data:

```
iex> graph_delete
""
```

We can now read our Dgraph schema from the graph store:

```
iex> IO.puts (arpa70_schema = read_graph "schemas/arpa70.schema").data
name: string @index(term) .
type: string @index(term) .

H_LINK: [uid] @reverse .
N_LINK: [uid] .

type Host {
  name
  type
  <~H_LINK>
}

type Node {
  name
  type
  N_LINK
}
:ok
```

No surprise here, apart from the @reverse directive set on the H_LINK predicate. Also, note the ~ syntax used to indicate an inverse predicate in the type Host. We can add this schema using our schema_update/1 function:

```
iex> schema_update arpa70_schema
{:ok, ""}
```

Now we're ready to ingest our ARPANET graph. We'll read that back from the graph store:

```
iex> IO.puts (arpa70 = read_graph "arpa70.dgraph").data
...
## SEGMENT 1 - Outer Circuit (Clockwise from UCLA to RAND)
# Site: UCLA

_:ucla <dgraph.type> "Node" .
_:ucla <type> "IMP" .
_:ucla <name> "UCLA" .
_:ucla_h1 <dgraph.type> "Host" .
_:ucla_h1 <name> "360/91" .
_:ucla_h2 <dgraph.type> "Host" .
_:ucla_h2 <name> "XDS SIGMA7" .
_:ucla_h1 <H_LINK> _:ucla .
_:ucla_h2 <H_LINK> _:ucla .
...

## SEGMENT 1 - Outer Circuit (Clockwise from UCLA to RAND)
_:ucla <N_LINK> _:sri .
_:sri <N_LINK> _:utah .
_:utah <N_LINK> _:mit .
_:mit <N_LINK> _:lincoln .
_:lincoln <N_LINK> _:case .
_:case <N_LINK> _:carnegie .
_:carnegie <N_LINK> _:harvard .
_:harvard <N_LINK> _:bbn .
_:bbn <N_LINK> _:rand .
...

:ok
```

And we can ingest the graph:

```
iex> graph_update arpa70
{:ok,
 %{
   queries: %{},
   uids: %{
   "sri" => "0x5088",
   "ucsb_h1" => "0x5089",
   "harvard_h1" => "0x5096",
   "lincoln_h1" => "0x5098",
   "ucsb" => "0x508c",
```

```
    "case" => "0x50a3",
    "ucla_h2" => "0x50aa",
    "rand" => "0x50a0",
    "sdc_h1" => "0x5087",
    ...
    }
  }}
```

So we can now query for all ARPANET nodes and the hosts attached to them by using a query like this:

```
iex> IO.puts (query = read_query("arpa70.dql")).data
{
  arpa70(func: type(Node)) {
    uid
    name
    type
    <~H_LINK> { uid expand(_all_)}
    N_LINK { uid expand(_all_)}
  }
}

:ok
```

Sending that query we get a result set as follows:

```
iex> query.data |> dgraph!
%{
  "arpa70" => [
    %{
      "N_LINK" => [%{"name" => "SRI", "type" => "IMP", "uid" => "0x4ff4"}],
      "name" => "STANFORD",
      "type" => "IMP",
      "uid" => "0x4fd7",
      "~H_LINK" => [%{"name" => "PDP-10", "uid" => "0x4fd8"}]
    },
    %{
      "N_LINK" => [
        %{"name" => "RAND", "type" => "IMP", "uid" => "0x4fe1"},
        %{"name" => "MIT", "type" => "IMP", "uid" => "0x4fe3"}
      ],
      "name" => "BBN",
      "type" => "IMP",
      "uid" => "0x4fdc",
      "~H_LINK" => [
        %{"name" => "DDP-516", "uid" => "0x4fd6"},
        %{"name" => "PDP-10", "uid" => "0x4fe0"}
      ]
    },
    ...
  ]
}
```

The next thing to try with DQL is path queries.

Paths

With DQL we can also do shortest path queries as:

```
iex> IO.puts (path_query = read_query "arpa70-path.dql").data
{
  A as var(func: eq(name, "HARVARD"))
  B as var(func: eq(name, "UCLA"))

  path as shortest(from: uid(A), to: uid(B), numpaths: 1) {
    N_LINK
  }
  path(func: uid(path)) {
    name
  }
}
:ok
```

Note that we're using the query variables A, B, and path.

```
iex> path_query.data |> dgraph!
%{
  "_path_" => [
    %{
      "N_LINK" => %{
        "N_LINK" => %{"N_LINK" => %{"uid" => "0x4fe7"}, "uid" => "0x4fe1"},
        "uid" => "0x4fdc"
      },
      "_weight_" => 3.0,
      "uid" => "0x4ff9"
    }
  ],
  "path" => [
    %{"name" => "HARVARD"},
    %{"name" => "BBN"},
    %{"name" => "RAND"},
    %{"name" => "UCLA"}
  ]
}
```

So that's how we do path queries.

Recursion

Sometimes we'll want to follow a predicate until we reach a boundary in the graph (no further edges) or until some depth has been met. We can do this with the @recurse directive:

```
iex> q = """
...> {
...>   q(func: has(type), first: 1) @recurse(depth: 5, loop: true)
...>   {
...>     uid
...>     expand(_all_)
...>   }
...> }
...> """
"{\n  q(func: has(type), first: 1) @recurse(depth: 5, loop: true)
  {\nuid\n    expand(_all_)\n  }\n}\n"

iex> q |> dgraph!
%{
  "q" => [
    %{
      "N_LINK" => [
        %{
          "N_LINK" => [
            %{
              "N_LINK" => [
                %{
                  "N_LINK" => [
                    %{"name" => "CASE", "type" => "IMP", "uid" => "0x5078"}
                  ],
                  "name" => "LINCOLN",
                  "type" => "IMP",
                  "uid" => "0x5080"
                }
              ],
              "name" => "MIT",
              "type" => "IMP",
              "uid" => "0x5075"
            }
          ],
          "name" => "UTAH",
          "type" => "IMP",
          "uid" => "0x506f"
        }
      ],
      "name" => "SRI",
      "type" => "IMP",
      "uid" => "0x5066"
    }
  ]
}
```

Note that some care is required to keep the result set manageable and ensure this doesn't get out of hand.

Well, this seems like a useful place to stop. We've seen some features that Dgraph has to offer above and beyond GraphQL, although there is still much more to be explored.

Wrapping Up

Let's recap what we've done in this chapter. We worked with Dgraph—a distributed graph database that supports GraphQL as a native database query language. This is impressive as not only do we have GraphQL as a standard API but we also have those same structures down at the database level. It's GraphQL all the way down.

We also tried out DQL—the Dgraph version of GraphQL. We ran those mutations and queries using Elixir functions guided by the schemas we created.

There's still some way to go for Dgraph to integrate DQL and GraphQL together. But this is a rather interesting development in graph databases that warrants a lot more attention.

That effectively concludes our survey of the different graph models and how to access them from Elixir. Next, we'll move on to Part III to apply what we've learned so far and to build out a couple of extended applications that deal with graph-to-graph and graph-to-compute scenarios.

Part III

Graph to Graph

How do we repurpose graphs from one model type to another? We'll look at how to transform graphs and how to move graphs from one graph database to another.

We'll also review how Elixir supports concurrency by managing supervision networks. We'll see how to set up dynamic graphs using Elixir processes as active graph nodes.

We'll show these two use cases with a couple of worked examples which should give us a good feel for how we can work with graphs using Elixir.

## CHAPTER 11

Transforming Graph Models

In Part II, we looked at different graph models, but we skimmed over how they could be serialized and saved to our graph store. Each of these models can be expressed in their own various ways.

In this chapter, we'll first talk about some ways to serialize graphs and also list the pros and cons of using common formats such as CSV for exchanging graph data.

We'll then go on to work through a more robust solution with the Neo4j plugin neosemantics (n10s), which supports importing and exporting RDF graphs into and out of a property graph store and querying RDF graph models using the Cypher query language.

Lastly, we'll touch briefly on the topic of federated querying, which is querying against multiple graph databases.

Serializing Graphs

Let's start with the main reason for wanting to serialize graphs, which is to be able to share graphs across space (different graph databases), across time (different graph instances), and across models (different graph data structures).

There are many different means available for expressing graphs. They extend from visualizations and layouts to algorithms, query and data definition languages, and dedicated graph languages and formats. Some of these are proprietary formats or de facto standards. Others have been through the standards mill.

We won't be so much concerned here with visualizations as with capturing annotations attached to the graph. The layout of graphs is a whole subject in itself, although in Storing Graphs in the Graph Store, on page 41, we saw one format supported by libgraph, the DOT format. The DOT language not only expresses graph topologies and annotations but also provides a language for graph layouts. Currently, the libgraph library only supports export graphs in DOT format, so this isn't available for use as an interchange format.

If we consider graph topology, the most common algorithms for graph representations are the adjacency list, adjacency matrix, and incidence matrix. These provide techniques for capturing the node and edge sets. What they don't especially address are the labels and attributes which are often overlaid onto a basic graph structure—the information. We get wiring but no meaning. These forms can be extended to capture annotations, but we are hampered by a lack of reference implementations. This is bespoke territory. Each application will generally need its own definition.

One example of this algorithmic approach is the edgelist, a variant of the adjacency list, which is the other format supported in libgraph. This provides some limited potential, but only for export. Only a serializer is provided but no deserializer.

Moving beyond algorithms and on to data structures, a common graph exchange format is CSV. We can use a format like CSV to encode the nodes, edges, and attributes of a graph. The upside of this is that CSV is a common format for data interchange. The downside is that the details of how those graph elements are arranged in the CSV form are application-dependent. The contract is with the importing database and not with the serialization format.

A good example of this is the CSV import and export capability in Neo4j. Note that this is defined for Neo4j only. We'd need to construct a CSV instance according to the prevailing Neo4j specifications. This would be one way to import into and export from a Neo4j database, but it's somewhat brittle.

Further along, we have attempts at specific languages for expressing graphs. These may be text-based, such as JSON, or markup-based, such as XML. There are no official standards here, although some attempts are better known than others, for example, GraphML,[1] which is based on XML. Support for these languages for describing graphs depends on the libraries and databases that are being used.

Other means for expressing graphs use the graph query language. For example, Neo4j supports importing and exporting of property graphs as Cypher scripts, while Gremlin can also read in Groovy scripts. We could also generate RDF graphs using SPARQL CONSTRUCT queries and SPARQL Update INSERT queries.

---

1. http://graphml.graphdrawing.org/

But this isn't the way that RDF graphs are generally shared. RDF has a rich set of serialization formats that have been standardized by the W3C and are well supported by various RDF libraries. And we've already seen these with the rdf package for Elixir.

So these RDF formats are suited to the interchange of RDF graphs. But the RDF model doesn't support all graph types. Especially missing are edge properties. More recently, however, the RDF* extension to RDF is being developed and would provide support for these cases.

Well, this has been the briefest of summaries of graph serializations; the best approach for you depends on your use case. One direction we could explore would be to define a CSV serializer extension for libgraph (and a corresponding deserializer would also be useful), but this would entail following some particular specification, such as that used by Neo4j, so maybe that's best left as a reader exercise.

Instead, we're going to go down another road. We're going to make RDF serializations as standard formats for graph interchange. We already know that these formats can be used with RDF graph databases and are well supported in Elixir with the rdf package. And Neo4j now also supports importing and exporting of graphs using RDF formats. So, let's first see how that works, and then we'll try a larger example of exchanging graphs between property graph and RDF graph databases.

Importing RDF with n10s—A Neo4j Plugin

We looked earlier at property graphs in Chapter 5, Navigating Graphs with Neo4j, on page 71, and RDF graphs in Chapter 7, Graphing Globally with RDF, on page 115. These may seem to be separate worlds we would need to bridge, but there is a way.

You'll recall from earlier that RDF provides a number of standard serializations. This should make graph interchange simpler. Neosemantics (n10s) is a Neo4j plugin for importing and exporting RDF graphs into Neo4j—a property graph store—and claims to do that losslessly. That sounds perfect. Let's explore it.

There is a super helpful Neosemantics (n10s) User Guide[2] to help you get started. Installation is simple. You copy the neosemantics jar file into the plugins/ folder of your local Neo4j instance, update the Neo4j config file, and restart the server. For details, see the Installation[3] guidelines.

---

2. https://neo4j.com/labs/neosemantics/4.0/
3. https://neo4j.com/labs/neosemantics/4.0/install/

At this point, you may want to look back at the section on APOC, on page 78, where we installed the APOC library. You may also want to review your security settings.

Let's cd back to our ExGraphsBook root now and open up IEx:

```
$ iex -S mix
Erlang/OTP 24 [erts-12.3.1] ...
```

So, we'll first switch our graph service to PropertyGraph:

```
iex> graph_context PropertyGraph
PropertyGraph
```

Let's now check on the n10s procedures to see if they are loaded:

```
iex> """
...> CALL dbms.procedures()
...> YIELD name WITH * WHERE name CONTAINS 'n10s'
...> RETURN *
...> """ |> cypher!
[
  ...
  %{"name" => "n10s.graphconfig.drop"},
  %{"name" => "n10s.graphconfig.init"},
  %{"name" => "n10s.graphconfig.set"},
  %{"name" => "n10s.graphconfig.show"},
  ...
  %{"name" => "n10s.rdf.export.cypher"},
  %{"name" => "n10s.rdf.export.spo"},
  %{"name" => "n10s.rdf.import.fetch"},
  %{"name" => "n10s.rdf.import.inline"},
  ...
]
```

Well, indeed they are. There are more procedures than shown but these are the ones we'll be using initially.

The first order of business is to prepare Neo4j for importing an RDF graph. For this, we need a graph config object. This is simply managed by calling the n10s.graphconfig.init procedure:

```
iex> "CALL n10s.graphconfig.init()" |> cypher!
[
  %{"param" => "handleVocabUris", "value" => "SHORTEN"},
  %{"param" => "handleMultival", "value" => "OVERWRITE"},
  %{"param" => "handleRDFTypes", "value" => "LABELS"},
  ...
]
```

Note that there are multiple parameters, each of which can be set with the n10s.graphconfig.set procedure. There are also procedures for deleting the graph config (n10s.graphconfig.drop) and for displaying it (n10s.graphconfig.show).

Let's check the state of our graph service:

```
iex> graph_info
%GraphCommons.Service.GraphInfo{
  file: "",
  labels: ["_GraphConfig"],
  num_edges: 0,
  num_nodes: 1,
  type: :property
}
```

We have one node for the graph config (_GraphConfig).

Now we can try importing some RDF. For this, there is the n10s.rdf.import.fetch procedure, and we'll also need an RDF document at an HTTP endpoint. Here I just copied over the book.ttl graph we created in Serializing the RDF Graph, on page 129, onto my local webserver:

```
iex> """
...> CALL n10s.rdf.import.fetch("http://localhost/~tony/book.ttl",
...> "Turtle")
...> """ |> cypher!
[
  %{
    "callParams" => %{},
    "extraInfo" => "",
    "namespaces" => %{"ns0" => "https://schema.org/"},
    "terminationStatus" => "OK",
    "triplesLoaded" => 22,
    "triplesParsed" => 22
  }
]
```

Well, it looks like we've successfully loaded something. Let's try our graph_info/0 function to see what we have:

```
iex> graph_info
%GraphCommons.Service.GraphInfo{
  file: "",
  labels: ["Resource", "_GraphConfig", "_NsPrefDef", "ns0__Book",
   "ns0__Organization", "ns0__Person"],
  num_edges: 4,
  num_nodes: 7,
  type: :property
}
```

So, there are seven nodes. Let's see what they are:

```
iex> "MATCH (n) RETURN n" |> cypher!
[
  %{
    "n" => %Bolt.Sips.Types.Node{
      id: 0,
      labels: ["_GraphConfig"],
      properties: %{
        "_applyNeo4jNaming" => false,
        "_classLabel" => "Class",
        "_dataTypePropertyLabel" => "Property",
        ...
      }
    }
  },
  %{
    "n" => %Bolt.Sips.Types.Node{
      id: 1,
      labels: ["_NsPrefDef"],
      properties: %{"ns0" => "https://schema.org/"}
    }
  },
  %{
    "n" => %Bolt.Sips.Types.Node{
      id: 2,
      labels: ["Resource", "ns0__Person"],
      properties: %{
        "ns0__identifier" => "jose_valim",
        "ns0__name" => "José Valim",
        "uri" => "https://twitter.com/josevalim"
      }
    }
  },
  ...
]
```

This shows us that there's one node for the graph config (_GraphConfig) and one node for the namespace table (_NsPrefDef), and then there are five more nodes for our graph data with three-person nodes (ns0_Person), an organization node (ns0_Organization), and a book node (ns1_Book).

We can verify that with a query like this:

```
iex> "MATCH (n) RETURN labels(n)" |> cypher!
[
  %{"labels(n)" => ["_GraphConfig"]},
  %{"labels(n)" => ["_NsPrefDef"]},
  %{"labels(n)" => ["Resource", "ns0__Person"]},
  %{"labels(n)" => ["Resource", "ns0__Person"]},
```

```
  %{"labels(n)" => ["Resource", "ns0__Organization"]},
  %{"labels(n)" => ["Resource", "ns0__Book"]},
  %{"labels(n)" => ["Resource", "ns0__Person"]}
]
```

Or we can also query for a specific property—ns0_name:

```
iex> "MATCH (n) RETURN n.ns0__name" |> cypher!
[
  %{"n.ns0__name" => nil},
  %{"n.ns0__name" => nil},
  %{"n.ns0__name" => "José Valim"},
  %{"n.ns0__name" => "Ben Marx"},
  %{"n.ns0__name" => "The Pragmatic Bookshelf"},
  %{"n.ns0__name" => "Adopting Elixir"},
  %{"n.ns0__name" => "Bruce Tate"}
]
```

Yes, that looks a lot like our RDF graph, but now queried as a property graph with Cypher. Note that we didn't find a ns0_name property for the _GraphConfig and _NsPrefDef nodes.

We could have omitted those control nodes by restricting our query to resource nodes, or nodes with Resource labels:

```
iex> "MATCH (n:Resource) RETURN n.ns0__name" |> cypher!
[
  %{"n.ns0__name" => "José Valim"},
  ...
]
```

Let's move on to something a little more elaborate.

A Graph-to-Graph Example

As a better example of a graph-to-graph exercise, let's try our hand at an extended journey.

We've already seen that there are public endpoints for RDF data. Let's scoop up some of that RDF data, mix it together, and then add that into a local property graph database. For good measure, we'll operate on that property graph in some way and then what? Well, let's get that graph out of our local property graph database, add it back into a local RDF graph database, and operate on it some more as an RDF graph.

The figure on page 208 shows our user and the endpoints we'll be querying. The remote endpoints A and B are shown with a cloud frame, whereas local endpoints C and D are shown without.

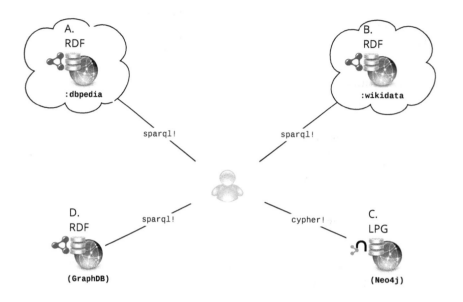

Of course, as we are querying over HTTP there is no essential difference between remote and local endpoints. The remote endpoints are SPARQL endpoints serving RDF data, and we have no special knowledge of the backend systems. On the other hand, our local endpoints are serviced by a pair of local graph databases, one an RDF graph store (GraphDB) and the other a (labeled) property graph, or LPG, store (Neo4j). We'll query the RDF endpoints with SPARQL (using our sparql!/1 function) and the LPG endpoint with Cypher (using our cypher!/1 function).

Our plan is to combine multiple graphs into a single graph, transform that into a new graph model, extend that graph, and then transform it back into the original graph model and extend that graph again.

Let's break that journey down like this:

- 1st stage

  - step 1—query remote SPARQL endpoints for RDF *(A and B)*
  - step 2—put RDF into the local property graph database *(C)*
  - step 3—modify RDF in the local property graph database *(C)*
- 2nd stage

  - step 4—get RDF out of the local property graph database *(C)*
  - step 5—put RDF into the local RDF graph database *(D)*
  - step 6—modify RDF in the local RDF graph database *(D)*

The letters *A to D* reference the separate endpoints shown in the figure.

The main takeaways we're aiming to demonstrate here are the following:

- data integration
- model transformation

Data integration will be shown by querying multiple remote endpoints for separate graphs and merging those graphs into a single graph.

Model transformation will be shown by roundtripping RDF through a property graph database using the n10s library from Neo4j.

So, let's get started on that journey.

Stage 1: Getting RDF into an LPG Store

This stage of the journey will be to import RDF data into a property graph database. The first step is obviously to acquire some RDF data.

In the top part of the previous figure, you saw the remote endpoints we will query to get some RDF data. The following figure shows just that part again.

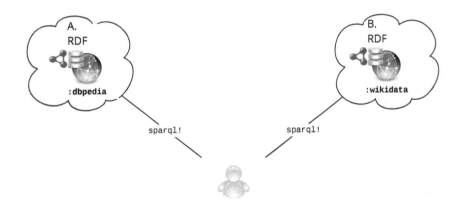

Step 1—Querying Remote SPARQL Endpoints for RDF

We are going to query two public SPARQL endpoints for data: DBpedia and Wikidata. We're going to get a separate RDF graph from each of these two endpoints and then merge those two graphs into a single RDF graph for further processing.

So, let's switch our graph service to RDFGraph:

```
iex> graph_context RDFGraph
RDFGraph
```

We're now ready to query for RDF.

It's probably useful at this point to mention that both databases maintain graphs of things with properties and relationships to other things. These things (and their properties) are identified with URIs and can be queried to return different RDF serializations through HTTP content negotiation. By default, they will redirect to an HTML page view for easy browsing.

We're going to query in this example for the "Bob Dylan" thing. And to short-circuit any long discovery process, we'll simply list the IDs for this concept here:

Service	Concept URL
DBpedia	http://dbpedia.org/resource/Bob_Dylan
Wikidata	http://www.wikidata.org/entity/Q392

If you try entering either of these URLs into a web browser, you'll be redirected to a linked data page URL:

Service	Page URL
DBpedia	http://dbpedia.org/page/Bob_Dylan
Wikidata	https://www.wikidata.org/wiki/Special:EntityData/Q392 => https://wikidata.org/wiki/Q392

You can either use the linked data browser to discover the concept URLs, or query against the SPARQL endpoint and look for a "Bob Dylan" string, but you'll probably need to look instead for the string "Bob Dylan"@en with a language tag.

See Linked Data Access[4] and Wikidata:Data access[5] for DBpedia and Wikidata linked data naming practices, respectively.

To get started, you can use the concept URLs listed above.

Querying DBpedia

First, we're going to query DBpedia. Let's switch the RDF store now to :dbpedia to set our graph service:

```
iex> rdf_store :dbpedia
:ok
```

Let's try querying on that using a DESCRIBE query form as we discussed in Querying the Local RDF Service, on page 144:

4. https://www.dbpedia.org/resources/linked-data/
5. https://www.wikidata.org/wiki/Wikidata:Data_access

```
iex> bob1 = "DESCRIBE <http://dbpedia.org/resource/Bob_Dylan>" |> sparql!
#RDF.Graph<name: nil
  @prefix ns219: <http://dbpedia.org/resource/Amazing_Journey:> .
  ...
  @prefix owl: <http://www.w3.org/2002/07/owl#> .

  ...

  dbr:Thunder_on_the_Mountain
      dbo:artist dbr:Bob_Dylan ;
      dbo:wikiPageWikiLink dbr:Bob_Dylan ;
      dbo:writer dbr:Bob_Dylan ;
      dbp:artist dbr:Bob_Dylan .

  ...

  dbr:Bob_Dylan
      ...
      dbp:birthDate "1941-05-24"^^xsd:date ;
      ...

  ...
>
```

You can see that this DESCRIBE result includes both incoming (dbr:Thunder_on_the_Mountain) and outgoing links (dbr:Bob_Dylan), so there's some useful context here.

Now let's see if we have a link to our Wikidata URL. We can use a DESCRIBE query form again:

```
iex> "DESCRIBE <http://www.wikidata.org/entity/Q392>" |> sparql!
#RDF.Graph<name: nil
  @prefix dbr: <http://dbpedia.org/resource/> .
  @prefix owl: <http://www.w3.org/2002/07/owl#> .
  @prefix wikidata: <http://www.wikidata.org/entity/> .

  dbr:Bob_Dylan
      owl:sameAs wikidata:Q392 .
>
```

Ah, a match! So, we have a link for this entity in DBpedia to an entity in Wikidata. We can see that the entity named as dbr:Bob_Dylan is owl:sameAs (or the "same as") the entity known as wikidata:Q392.

So that's our bob1.

Querying Wikidata

Now let's try the same exercise in Wikidata. But first, we'll reset our rdf_store:

```
iex> rdf_store :wikidata
:ok
```

We do a DESCRIBE again on our Wikidata URL:

```
iex> bob2 = "DESCRIBE <http://www.wikidata.org/entity/Q392>" |> sparql!
#RDF.Graph<name: nil
  @prefix geo: <http://www.opengis.net/ont/geosparql#> .
  ...
  @prefix owl: <http://www.w3.org/2002/07/owl#> .

  ...

  wd:Q109954776
      wdt:P175 wd:Q392 ;
      wdt:P5202 wd:Q392 ;
      wdt:P676 wd:Q392 ;
      wdt:P86 wd:Q392 .

  ...

  wd:Q392

    ...
    wdt:P569 "1941-05-24T00:00:00Z"^^xsd:dateTime ;
    ....

  ...
>
```

And again we have both incoming (wd:Q109954776) and outgoing (wd:Q392) links.

Now, do we also have a link to our DBpedia entity?

```
iex> "DESCRIBE <http://dbpedia.org/resource/Bob_Dylan>" |> sparql!
#RDF.Graph<name: nil
  @prefix geo: <http://www.opengis.net/ont/geosparql#> .
  ...
  @prefix owl: <http://www.w3.org/2002/07/owl#> .
>
```

Nothing there. It looks like we have no link from the Wikidata entity to the DBpedia entity. But at least we have the one assertion that the DBpedia entity is the same as the Wikidata entity.

Wikidata Names

One thing that's worth noting here is that Wikidata uses opaque names (here Q392), which can be challenging to work with. But naming practices aren't something we're investigating here, so let's use what we've got. It's enough that we have a stable ID.

We have a lot of opaque names, for sure, but that's our bob2.

Merging the Graphs

OK. So, we have a couple of Bobs—bob1 and bob2. Let's save them before we do anything else:

```
iex> bob1_graph = (RDF.Turtle.write_string! bob1) |> write_graph("bob1.ttl")
#GraphCommons.Graph<type: rdf, file: "bob1.ttl", data: "@prefix rdf: <ht...">

iex> bob2_graph = (RDF.Turtle.write_string! bob2) |> write_graph("bob2.ttl")
#GraphCommons.Graph<type: rdf, file: "bob2.ttl", data: "@prefix rdf: <ht...">
```

We can also look at the number of edges for each graph:

```
iex> Enum.each [bob1, bob2],
...>    fn g -> IO.puts RDF.Graph.triple_count(g) end
13
3386
10609
:ok
```

Now let's merge those graphs.

Remember this is RDF. We're using global names so we can merge our graphs by simple string concatenation. How cool is that?

```
iex> (bob1_graph.data <> bob2_graph.data) |> write_graph("bob.ttl")
```

So we've stored our merged graph in Turtle format:

```
iex> bob_graph = read_graph("bob.ttl")
#GraphCommons.Graph<type: rdf, file: "bob.ttl", data: "@prefix rdf: <ht...">
```

And we can read this merged graph back into an RDF.Graph as:

```
iex> bob = RDF.Serialization.read_string!(bob_graph.data, [format: :turtle])
#RDF.Graph<name: nil
  ...
>
```

Let's check the number of RDF statements:

```
iex> RDF.Graph.triple_count bob
14008
```

And that's bob.

Of course, we can also just merge the RDF.Graph structs directly as:

```
iex> bob = Enum.reduce([bob1, bob2], fn(g, acc) -> RDF.Graph.add(g, acc) end)
#RDF.Graph<name: nil
  ...
>
```

Same old bob.

Using a Script to Query

If we wanted to replay that set of queries for batch querying, we could just put the commands into a script:

```
apps/graph_commons/priv/scripts/elixir/bob.exs
import GraphCommons.Utils, only: [sparql!: 1]
import RDFGraph, only: [rdf_store: 1, write_graph: 2]

# query :dbpedia
rdf_store :dbpedia
bob1 = "DESCRIBE <http://dbpedia.org/resource/Bob_Dylan>" |> sparql!

# query :wikidata
rdf_store :wikidata
bob2 = "DESCRIBE <http://www.wikidata.org/entity/Q392>" |> sparql!

# write to graph store
bob1_graph = (RDF.Turtle.write_string! bob1) |> write_graph("bob1.ttl")
bob2_graph = (RDF.Turtle.write_string! bob2) |> write_graph("bob2.ttl")

# write graph merge to graph store
(bob1_graph.data <> bob2_graph.data) |> write_graph("bob.ttl")
```

We can then simply run that script as:

```
$ mix run priv/scripts/elixir/bob.exs
```

If all goes well, we'll have some new files added to our RDF graph store.

Step 2—Putting RDF into the Local Property Graph Database

We're going to switch now to our PropertyGraph service. Let's do that and clear out any current state:

```
iex> graph_context PropertyGraph
PropertyGraph

iex> graph_delete
%Bolt.Sips.Response{
  ...
  stats: %{"nodes-deleted" => 10, "relationships-deleted" => 7},
  type: "w"
}

iex> graph_info
%GraphCommons.Service.GraphInfo{
  file: "",
  labels: [],
  num_edges: 0,
  num_nodes: 0,
  type: :property
}
```

Blank slate. Ready to go.

As before, let's set the n10s graph config:

```
iex> "CALL n10s.graphconfig.init()" |> cypher!
[
  %{"param" => "handleVocabUris", "value" => "SHORTEN"},
  %{"param" => "handleMultival", "value" => "OVERWRITE"},
  %{"param" => "handleRDFTypes", "value" => "LABELS"},
  ...
]
```

Now we can try importing some RDF:

```
iex> bob_uri = "file://" <> bob_graph.path
```

```
iex> "CALL n10s.rdf.import.fetch('" <> bob_uri <> "', 'Turtle')" |> cypher!
[
  %{
    "callParams" => %{},
    "extraInfo" => "",
    "namespaces" => %{
      ...
    },
    "terminationStatus" => "OK",
    "triplesLoaded" => 13,
    "triplesParsed" => 13
  }
]
```

Now let's see what we've got:

```
iex> graph_info
%GraphCommons.Service.GraphInfo{
  file: "",
  labels: ["ns7__WikicatPopSingers", "ns7__WikicatJewishAmericanMusicians",
   "ns7__WikicatAmericanHarmonicaPlayers", "ns7__WikicatFolkSingers",
   ...
   "ns7__WikicatAmericanRockGuitarists", "ns7__WikicatActors", ...],
  num_edges: 13199,
  num_nodes: 10777,
  type: :property
}
```

Yes, we've got that RDF graph imported into our property graph database.

Simpler RDF Import into the LPG Store

To import RDF into our property graph database, we don't have to save our RDF graphs and then merge them before importing. We could just as well have done this for each graph in a single step by importing directly from the SPARQL endpoint and using a GET request for the SPARQL query (or from a linked data URI dereference). The fact that the data is already modeled as RDF will allow the merge to succeed directly on import.

Step 3—Modifying RDF in the Local Property Graph Database

Now that we've got the RDF in our property graph database, let's do something with it.

One obvious candidate for augmenting the RDF graph would be one of the APOC procedures we discussed earlier in APOC, on page 78.

Let's do something trivial as a simple proof of concept. Let's add a uuid property to the node with ID http://dbpedia.org/resource/Bob_Dylan.

But hang on! Since we're dealing with RDF data, we really want to give a global name to this property. Let's say we want to add the property http://example/uuid, or in prefix notation ex:uuid.

One way to do this is to add a new prefix to the namespace prefix table. This n10s method returns the current list of namespaces that are registered:

```
iex> "CALL n10s.nsprefixes.list()" |> cypher!
[
  %{"namespace" => "http://purl.org/dc/terms/", "prefix" => "dct"},
  %{"namespace" => "http://www.w3.org/ns/prov#", "prefix" => "ns14"},
  ...
  }
]
```

We can then add our ex namespace prefix as:

```
iex> "CALL n10s.nsprefixes.add(\"ex\", \"http://example/\")" |> cypher!
  %{"namespace" => "http://www.w3.org/2002/07/owl#", "prefix" => "owl"},
  %{"namespace" => "http://www.w3.org/2004/02/skos/core#", "prefix" => "skos"},
  ...
  %{"namespace" => "http://example/", "prefix" => "ex"},
  ...
]
```

And now we can create an ex_uuid property following the standard n10s naming pattern for RDF properties:

```
iex> """
...> MATCH (n {uri: "http://dbpedia.org/resource/Bob_Dylan"})
...> SET n.ex__uuid = apoc.create.uuid()
...> RETURN n
...> """ |> cypher!
[
  %{
    "n" => %Bolt.Sips.Types.Node{
      id: 9221,
      ...
```

➤
```
        "ex__uuid" => "e029be4e-49ee-4830-9cfb-907b15663d8f",
        ...
      }
    }
]
```

This isn't especially exciting but it does at least prove the point. Note that we could have instead used a SPARQL CONSTRUCT query to add an ex:uuid property before we imported the RDF.

Stage 2: Getting RDF out of an LPG Store

Given that we've successfully modified our RDF graph directly, let's move on to the next stage and extract the new graph from the property graph database and import it into an RDF graph database.

Let's look again at the bottom part of the earlier figure. The following figure shows the local endpoints over our RDF and LPG graph databases.

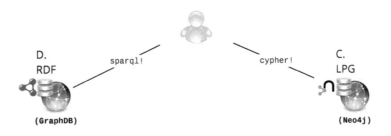

Step 4—Getting RDF out of the Local Property Graph Database

We can export RDF data from Neo4j by using the /rdf endpoint.

We can do this in three main ways. We can select a single node in the graph by its unique identifier, we can select a group of nodes by label and property value, or we can use a Cypher query. We'll show each method for a neo4j database.

Export by Node ID

We can query by a given subject ID like this:

```
:GET http://localhost:7474/rdf/neo4j/describe/{ID}
```

This is a GET request directed at the neo4j database that will pull statements for a given ID. This ID is either the Neo4j system-generated ID for a created node, or the %-encoded URI for an imported node.

Export by Label and Property Value

We can query by a given label and property value:

```
:GET http://localhost:7474/rdf/neo4j/describe/find/{Label}/{poperty}/{value}
```

This is a GET request directed at the neo4j database that will pull statements for a given label and property value.

Export by Cypher Query

We can query by a Cypher query:

```
:POST http://localhost:7474/rdf/neo4j/cypher
```

This is the most general form for extracting RDF from a property value database. In this case, we use a POST request with a JSON map as the payload body with a cypher key and Cypher query as a value. This is also directed at the neo4j database.

Note that we already have tesla in our umbrella app dependency graph (we loaded that with the rdf dependency), so let's go ahead and use the Tesla client directly for this API.

To make things simpler for querying, I've disabled authentication on my local Neo4j instance. This can be done by updating the neo4j.conf file that comes with the server:

```
# To disable authentication, uncomment this line
dbms.security.auth_enabled=false
```

We can now query without using credentials.

In our case, we'd like to get the complete graph back. So, we'll need to use the Cypher query method to return all nodes and edges. We can build a simple JSON map to do this as:

```
iex> data = """
...> { "cypher" : "MATCH (n:Resource)-[r]-(m) RETURN *" }
...> """
"{ \"cypher\" : \"MATCH (n:Resource)-[r]-(m) RETURN *\" }\n"
```

We can post that up as:

```
iex> result = Tesla.post!("http://localhost:7474/rdf/neo4j/cypher", data)
%Tesla.Env{
  client: %Tesla.Client{adapter: nil, fun: nil, post: [], pre: []},
  module: Tesla,
  body: "@prefix owl: <http://www.w3.org/2002/07/owl#> ...",
  headers: [
    {"date", "Mon, 24 May 2021 12:28:00 GMT"},
```

```
    {"access-control-allow-origin", "*"},
    {"content-type", "application/rdf+xml"},
    {"transfer-encoding", "chunked"}
  ],
  method: :post,
  opts: [],
  query: [],
  status: 200,
  url: "http://localhost:7474/rdf/neo4j/cypher"
}
```

We can extract the body with a simple pattern match:

```
iex> %Tesla.Env{body: bob_neo} = result
%Tesla.Env{
  ...
}
```

So, we then have the extracted RDF as:

```
iex> IO.puts bob_neo
@prefix owl: <http://www.w3.org/2002/07/owl#> .
@prefix skos: <http://www.w3.org/2004/02/skos/core#> .
...
<http://dbpedia.org/resource/Changing_of_the_Guards> ns6:artist
    <http://dbpedia.org/resource/Bob_Dylan>;
  ns2:artist <http://dbpedia.org/resource/Bob_Dylan>;
  ns2:writer <http://dbpedia.org/resource/Bob_Dylan>;
  ns6:wikiPageWikiLink <http://dbpedia.org/resource/Bob_Dylan>;
  ns6:writer <http://dbpedia.org/resource/Bob_Dylan> .
...
```

Now that we've got the RDF out, let's save it back to our RDF service.

Step 5—Putting RDF into the Local RDF Graph Database

We'll switch the graph context back to our RDFGraph service:

```
iex> graph_context RDFGraph
RDFGraph
```

Now we can write that RDF back to our graph store:

```
iex> bob_neo |> write_graph("bob_neo.ttl")
#GraphCommons .Graph<type: rdf, file: "neo.ttl", data: "@prefix owl: <ht...">
```

Let's also switch the RDF endpoint to our :local RDF graph service:

```
iex> rdf_store :local
:ok
```

And let's read back the RDF graph we just stored and add that to the :local RDF service:

```
iex> read_graph("bob_neo.ttl") |> graph_create
#GraphCommons .Graph<type: rdf, file: "neo.ttl", data: "@prefix owl: <ht...">
```

We can now query over the RDF graph:

```
iex> """
...> PREFIX ex: <http://example/>
...> SELECT * WHERE { ?s ex:uuid ?uuid }
...> """ |> sparql!
%SPARQL.Query.Result{
  results: [
    %{
      "s" => ~I<http://dbpedia.org/resource/Bob_Dylan>,
      "uuid" => %RDF.Literal{literal: %RDF.XSD.String{value: "65f2ac53-b1e0-
      4351-8a2e-dddc0075dd40", lexical: "65f2ac53-b1e0-4351-8a2e-
      dddc0075dd40"}, valid: true}
    }
  ],
  variables: ["s", "uuid"]
}
```

Look at that. We've got an RDF statement here in our local GraphDB graph database (or triplestore, if you will) as an RDF graph that was created in our Neo4j graph database as a property graph.

This goes to show that we can indeed move semantic graphs around.

Step 6—Modifying RDF in the Local RDF Graph Database

Now let's modify the RDF graph we just ingested. Suppose we want to add an ex:count property to all nodes with multiple edges. Since this is RDF, an edge may connect a node with another object node or with a string value. Let's count the object nodes.

We could do this with the following SPARQL Update query:

```
PREFIX ex: <http://example/>
INSERT {
  ?s ex:count ?count .
}
WHERE {
  {
    SELECT ?s (count(?s) as ?count)
    WHERE { ?s ?p ?o FILTER (isIRI(?o)) }
    GROUP BY ?s
  }
  FILTER (?count > 1)
}
```

Let's add that SPARQL Update query to our query store as add_count.ru:

```
iex> IO.puts (add_count_update = read_query("add_count.ru").data)
PREFIX ex: <http://example/>
INSERT {
  ?s ex:count ?count .
}
WHERE {
  ...
}
:ok
```

We can update the RDF graph service as:

```
iex> add_count_update |> sparql!(update: true)
...
```

Here we're using the update: keyword to signal that this is an update query so that it'll be passed to the update endpoints and not the regular query endpoint.

Let's query to see if that update was applied. And in this case, let's query against those resources with the UUIDs we added to the property graph database:

```
iex> """
...> PREFIX ex: <http://example/>
...> CONSTRUCT { ?s ex:uuid ?uuid ; ex:count ?count }
...> WHERE {
...>   ?s ex:uuid ?uuid
...>   OPTIONAL { ?s ex:count ?count }
...> }
...> """ |> sparql!
#RDF.Graph<name: nil
  @prefix rdf: <http://www.w3.org/1999/02/22-rdf-syntax-ns#> .
  @prefix rdfs: <http://www.w3.org/2000/01/rdf-schema#> .
  @prefix xsd: <http://www.w3.org/2001/XMLSchema#> .

  <http://dbpedia.org/resource/Bob_Dylan>
      <http://example/count> 1226 ;
      <http://example/uuid> "65f2ac53-b1e0-4351-8a2e-dddc0075dd40" .
>
```

Note that we include the keyword OPTIONAL for our ex:count properties as these may not have multiple instances.

So, here we have one property added in the RDF graph database and another property added in the property graph database. While a property graph formalism would treat both of these properties as node attributes, in RDF they are both treated as edges. We could, of course, have added new object nodes which would be treated as edges in both graph models.

Federated Querying

Something we've not touched on before is a neat feature of SPARQL that opens up the game—federated querying. This extension to SPARQL allows for a portion of a query to be directed to any other SPARQL endpoint.

This means that instead of making two separate queries to two separate endpoints in the example we just walked through, we could have done this within a single query.

Let's see how.

Well, we need to wrap a portion of a SPARQL query with the SERVICE keyword, followed by the endpoint URI. So, we could have queried both endpoints with a single query like this:

```
CONSTRUCT {
  ?s ?p ?o
}
WHERE {
    {
        SERVICE <https://dbpedia.org/sparql> {
            BIND (<http://dbpedia.org/resource/Bob_Dylan> AS ?s)
            ?s ?p ?o .
        }
    }
    UNION
    {
        SERVICE <https://query.wikidata.org/bigdata/namespace/wdq/sparql> {
            BIND (<http://www.wikidata.org/entity/Q392> AS ?s)
            ?s ?p ?o .
        }
    }
}
```

Let's try this out. If we've previously saved that query into our graph store, we can read it back as:

```
iex> IO.puts (federated_q = read_query("federated.rq").data)
CONSTRUCT {
  ?s ?p ?o
}
...
:ok
```

Let's switch our RDF service to the :local RDF service:

```
iex> rdf_store :local
:ok
```

Now we can run this federated query as:

```
iex> two_g = federated_q |> sparql!
#RDF.Graph<name: nil
  @prefix rdf: <http://www.w3.org/1999/02/22-rdf-syntax-ns#> .
  @prefix rdfs: <http://www.w3.org/2000/01/rdf-schema#> .
  @prefix xsd: <http://www.w3.org/2001/XMLSchema#> .

  <http://dbpedia.org/resource/Bob_Dylan>
    ...

  <http://www.wikidata.org/entity/Q392>
    ...
```

Yes, we're getting stuff back. We can get a quick count of the RDF statements in the result set as:

```
iex> RDF.Graph.triple_count two_g
2391
```

So, as you can see from this example, SPARQL can do distributed querying. This has been a key feature of the SPARQL toolkit for over the last decade.

Nice. Although we should also note that there may be some limitations on the size of the datasets that can be realistically returned from this type of query.

For balance, note that Neo4j has also recently introduced an extension to support federated querying and data sharding. This feature is known as Fabric,[6] although at the time of this writing this feature is only available in the Neo4j Enterprise Edition.

Wrapping Up

In this chapter, we've taken a brief look at how graphs can be serialized and exchanged.

A great advantage of RDF is its number of standardized serializations, which makes exchanging graphs a simple process. The caveat is that these are targeted at RDF graphs that build on the RDF model, URIs for nodes and edges, and so on.

We then ran through a worked example which demoed how we can query multiple RDF graph stores for a single thing and then simply add that data together—a trivial matter now since all the names are global. We then imported this into the Neo4j property graph store using their n10s library for mapping an RDF graph onto a property graph. Here we used an APOC

---

6. https://neo4j.com/docs/operations-manual/current/fabric/

procedure to do something on the new property graph and exported the result out as an RDF graph that we then stored in our RDF graph store as well as in a local RDF service for further enrichment.

Then, to cap things off, we touched on one of SPARQL's lesser-known features—federated querying.

Now that we've looked at transforming graphs with essentially static graph descriptions, we're going to move on to dealing with dynamic graphs in the next chapter.

## CHAPTER 12

Processing the Graph

In the previous chapter, we looked at converting graph models. Now it's time to come back to Elixir. We're going to return to native graphs. And we're going to use some parts of OTP machinery—agents, generic servers (or genservers), and supervisors.

We're going to have some fun.

Remember back in Basic Workout, on page 37, when we said that libgraph nodes could contain any Elixir term? Well, that also means we could use an Elixir process as a graph node.

Let's try something here. Let's try to create a graph with processes for nodes and then build a supervision tree over that graph. We'll use genservers for those processes and attach them to a supervisor to manage the process lifecycle.

To keep things simple, let's reuse one of our example graphs and map that to a process graph. And we'll save the example graph node term in the process graph node state.

So, if we have the new process graph under a supervision tree, we should be able to terminate any of the processes and have that automatically restored. But there are a couple of issues we need to deal with. The new process will have no memory. When this process is generated, it won't have any state that was carried by the old process. And worse, it will fall outside of the process graph—it won't be connected to any other node.

But we can fix these issues. We simply need a couple more processes (agents in this case) one to cache the state of any failing process and another to save the process graph itself. The figure on page 226 shows the notion.

At the top left, we have a regular graph data structure built using libgraph. We are going to map this to a new libgraph data structure as shown at the bottom where

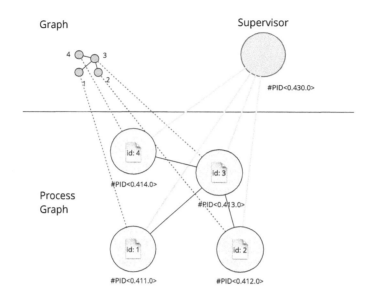

each source node is mapped to a target node instantiated as a process (genserver) with its state capturing the source node term in its id field. So here, for example, in our source graph, we have the source nodes 1, 2, 3, and 4 which are mapped to processes #PID<0.411.0>, #PID<0.412.0>, #PID<0.413.0>, and #PID<0.414.0>. These processes maintain the original source terms in their id field, as shown. The edges connecting the nodes are mapped from source to target so that the target graph has the same graph structure as the source graph.

So far, so good. We have one graph mapped to another graph—the process graph. But we also have a supervisor in its own process #PID<0.430.0>, as shown at the top right. We will create our graph processes under this supervisor. To make this easier, we will use a dynamic supervisor and build these supervision links at process create time. So the supervisor is watching over the nodes in our process graph, but not the edges. We'll get to that later.

And with that, let's get started.

Creating the GraphCompute Project

Follow the usual drill for creating the new project GraphCompute:

```
$ mix new graph_compute --sup
```

This will generate an app with a supervision tree and an application callback. We'll be using the GraphCompute.Application module to set up the supervision tree.

You should now have an apps directory that looks like this:

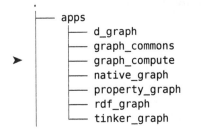

```
.
├── apps
│       ├── d_graph
│       ├── graph_commons
➤       ├── graph_compute
│       ├── native_graph
│       ├── property_graph
│       ├── rdf_graph
│       └── tinker_graph
```

Now cd into the graph_compute directory:

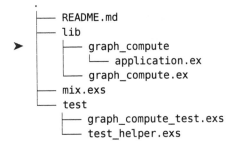

```
.
├── README.md
├── lib
➤   │   ├── graph_compute
│       │       └── application.ex
│       └── graph_compute.ex
├── mix.exs
└── test
        ├── graph_compute_test.exs
        └── test_helper.exs
```

Note that the --sup flag has generated an extra directory graph_compute under lib with an application.ex file.

We can declare a dependency on libgraph by adding the:libgraph dependency to the mix.exs file:

apps/graph_compute/mix.exs
```
defp deps do
  [
    # graph_commons
    {:graph_commons, in_umbrella: true},

    # native graphs
    {:libgraph, "~> 0.13"}
  ]
end
```

As usual, use Mix to add in the dependency:

```
$ mix deps.get; mix deps.compile
```

We'll also need to start up our GraphCompute.Application module:

```
def application do
  [
    extra_applications: [:logger],
➤   mod: { GraphCompute.Application, [] }
  ]
end
```

The :mod option specifies the application callback module, followed by any arguments to be passed on application start.

Adding a Supervision Tree (or Two)

We want to build a supervision tree over the process graph. And we'll want to use a dynamic supervision tree with a DynamicSupervisor so that we can stand up new nodes and tear them down on demand.

So that's our supervision tree. But we'll also want to manage a couple of agent processes for caching the node state and storing the graph as a whole. For these, we can set up a static supervision tree with a regular Supervisor.

We can set up both trees with the start/2 function in lib/graph_compute/application.ex. Let's create that module now:

```elixir
defmodule GraphCompute.Application do
  use Application

  # ...

end
```

And let's add in our start/2 function:

apps/graph_compute/lib/graph_compute/application.ex
```elixir
def start(type, args) do
  do_dynamic_supervisor(type, args)
  do_static_supervisor(type, args)
end

defp do_dynamic_supervisor(_type, _args) do
  opts = [
    name: GraphCompute.DynamicSupervisor,
    strategy: :one_for_one
  ]
  DynamicSupervisor.start_link(opts)
end

defp do_static_supervisor(_type, _args) do
  children = [
    {GraphCompute.Graph, %{}},
    {GraphCompute.State, %{}}
  ]
  opts = [
    name: GraphCompute.Supervisor,
    strategy: :one_for_one
  ]
  Supervisor.start_link(children, opts)
end
```

Note that the do_static_supervisor/2 function declares two direct children for the Supervisor process—GraphCompute.Graph for graph management and GraphCompute.State for node state management.

The do_dynamic_supervisor/2 function declares no children for the DynamicSupervisor process—they will be created on demand.

Let's add a genserver/0 function to create a new genserver process on demand for the dynamic supervision tree:

```
apps/graph_compute/lib/graph_compute/application.ex
def genserver() do
  case DynamicSupervisor.start_child(
      GraphCompute.DynamicSupervisor, GraphCompute.Process
    ) do
    {:ok, pid} ->
      pid
    {:error, reason} ->
      IO.puts "! Error: #{inspect reason}"
  end
end
```

Both trees will be created automatically when the application starts.

Agents

We'll also use a couple of agents for managing the state. We'll create a pair of new modules for these.

First, we'll define an agent for managing a copy of the graph state:

```
apps/graph_compute/lib/graph_compute/graph.ex
defmodule GraphCompute.Graph do
  use Agent

  def start_link(initial_value) do
    Agent.start_link(fn -> initial_value end, name: __MODULE__)
  end

  def get() do
    Agent.get(__MODULE__, & &1)
  end

  def update(new_value) do
    Agent.update(__MODULE__, fn _state -> new_value end)
  end

end
```

And we'll also want an agent for managing the state of a terminating process:

apps/graph_compute/lib/graph_compute/state.ex
```elixir
defmodule GraphCompute.State do
  use Agent

  def start_link(initial_value) do
    Agent.start_link(fn -> initial_value end, name: __MODULE__)
  end

  def get() do
    Agent.get(__MODULE__, & &1)
  end

  def update(new_value) do
    Agent.update(__MODULE__, fn _state -> new_value end)
  end

end
```

Nothing fancy there.

Genservers

For the process graph nodes, we'll define a simple genserver interface. Let's create a module for that:

```elixir
defmodule GraphCompute.Process do
  use GenServer

  # ...

end
```

Let's add a constructor:

apps/graph_compute/lib/graph_compute/process.ex
```elixir
def start_link(opts \\ []) do
  case GenServer.start_link(__MODULE__, opts) do
    {:ok, pid} -> {:ok, pid}
    {:error, reason} -> {:error, reason}
  end
end
```

We'll add a minimal client API with a get/1 function and get/2 and put/3 functions to manage our state:

apps/graph_compute/lib/graph_compute/process.ex
```elixir
def get(pid) do
  GenServer.call(pid, {:get})
end

def get(pid, key) do
  GenServer.call(pid, {:get, key})
end
```

```
def put(pid, key, value) do
  GenServer.cast(pid, {:put, key, value})
end
```

We'll also add some callbacks. Let's start first with init/1 and terminate/2—we'll define the process lifecycle handling later:

apps/graph_compute/lib/graph_compute/process.ex
```
@impl true
def init(_), do: do_init()

@impl true
def terminate(_reason, state), do: do_terminate(state)
```

Note that we preface these functions with the @impl attribute and set it as true to signal that these are callbacks.

For the other callbacks we'll need to service the get/1, get/2, and put/3 functions for our client API:

apps/graph_compute/lib/graph_compute/process.ex
```
@impl true
def handle_call({:get}, _from, state) do
  {:reply, state, state}
end

@impl true
def handle_call({:get, key}, _from, state) do
  {:reply, Map.fetch!(state, key), state}
end

@impl true
def handle_cast({:put, key, value}, state) do
  {:noreply, Map.put(state, key, value)}
end
```

We have one more thing to do. We'll also need a callback to handle any other messages received:

apps/graph_compute/lib/graph_compute/process.ex
```
@impl true
def handle_info(_reason, state) do
  {:stop, :normal, state}
end
```

That should be enough to get us started.

Building a Dynamic Process Graph

Now that we've defined some of the machinery for creating and maintaining a supervision tree, we can turn to the process graph itself.

Let's create a new module:

```
defmodule GraphCompute.ProcessGraph do

  # ...

end
```

We should now have a module library tree that looks like this:

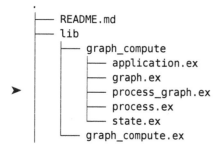

```
.
├── README.md
├── lib
│   ├── graph_compute
│   │   ├── application.ex
│   │   ├── graph.ex
│   │   ├── process_graph.ex
│   │   ├── process.ex
│   │   └── state.ex
│   └── graph_compute.ex
```

We now want to add a simple function—let's call it graph_up/1—that will map any %Graph{} struct to a new %Graph{} struct, where nodes are replaced by supervised processes and the node terms are stored away in the supervised node's process state.

And since we want it to have a generic capability, we will need to use dynamic supervisors for our processes.

So we have a simple four-step plan—map the nodes (or vertices), create a lookup table to link the graph node (or vertex) ID to the process graph node PID, map the edges, and then save a copy of the graph:

apps/graph_compute/lib/graph_compute/process_graph.ex
```
def graph_up(%Graph{} = g) do
  h = Graph.new()
  m = Map.new()

  # vertices
  h =
    g
    |> Graph.vertices()
    |> Enum.reduce(h, fn v, h ->
      p = GraphCompute.Application.genserver()
      GraphCompute.Process.put(p, :id, v)
      Graph.add_vertex(h, p)
    end)

  # map (vertex ID -> PID )
  m =
    h
    |> Graph.vertices()
    |> Enum.reduce(m, fn p, m ->
```

❶ `# vertices`

❷ `# map (vertex ID -> PID )`

```
        v = GraphCompute.Process.get(p, :id)
        Map.put(m, v, p)
      end)
❸   # edges
    h =
      g
      |> Graph.edges()
      |> Enum.reduce(h, fn e, h ->
        %Graph.Edge{label: label, v1: v1, v2: v2, weight: _} = e
        Graph.add_edge(h, Map.get(m, v1), Map.get(m, v2), label: label)
      end)
❹   # graph
    GraphCompute.Graph.update(h)
    h
end
```

Let's go through that in some more detail:

❶ We run through our graph nodes first. For each node (or vertex) we use the GraphCompute.Application.genserver/0 function to create a genserver and add the graph node term to the :id field in the process state map. We then add this process as a node to the process graph.

❷ Next we run again through our graph nodes and build up a map of the graph node ID to process the graph node PID.

❸ We then run through the graph edges. We pattern match over the graph edge, and using our lookup map of ID to PID, we create a new edge for the process graph.

❹ Finally, we save a copy of the new process graph in the GraphCompute.Graph agent.

This gives us our process graph.

We can also define a couple of helper functions:

apps/graph_compute/lib/graph_compute/process_graph.ex
```
def get_state(p) do
  GraphCompute.Process.get(p)
end

def put_state(p, {name, value}) do
  GraphCompute.Process.put(p, name, value)
end
```

These will be helpful to inspect and modify the process graph node state.

Note that we haven't said anything yet about the process graph edge state or the edge properties. Let's consider those now.

Adding Edge Properties

Currently, libgraph has no support for edge properties other than the label and weight. One technique for dealing with this would be to stand up processes for edges and capture the state just as we've done for nodes. We would need to make the following addition (line 6 to line 9) to the edge handling:

```
Line 1  h =
    -     g
    -     |> Graph.edges()
    -     |> Enum.reduce(h, fn e, h ->
    5       %Graph.Edge{label: label, v1: v1, v2: v2, weight: _} = e
    -       p = GraphCompute.Application.genserver()
    -       GraphCompute.Process.put(p, :label, label)
    -       GraphCompute.Process.put(p, :v1, Map.get(m, v1))
    -       GraphCompute.Process.put(p, :v2, Map.get(m, v2))
    10      Graph.add_edge(h, Map.get(m, v1), Map.get(m, v2), label: label)
    -     end)
```

This would create managed processes also for the edges, which have a state map that could be used to capture edge properties.

But for now, let's carry on with our nodes-only process graph.

Restoring the State for a Node

Our process graph nodes are supervised, which means that they will get restarted when they die after erroring—which is a handy thing. But there's a gotcha. They will get reborn as new blank nodes with no previous state. Another process will be set up to take over from the old process.

Obviously, we would like to capture any state from the old process and forward it to the new process—rather like a baton handover in a relay race.

As we saw earlier in Agents, on page 229, we can use an agent to maintain the process state at this handover point. The trick here will be to push any process state onto the agent at the process termination and to fetch that back at the process initiation.

It's time to fill out those do_init/0 and do_terminate/1 private functions that we introduced earlier in the genserver callbacks listed in Genservers, on page 230.

First, we'll deal with the process initiation case. We'll want to handle any process exits by using Process.flag/2 to set the :trap_exit flag to true. And then we'll read any state from our agent and return that:

```
defp do_init() do
  Process.flag(:trap_exit, true)
```

```
  state = GraphCompute.State.get()
  {:ok, state}
end
```

Our processes will be relaunched with a new identity and with the old state.

Then we'll deal with the process termination case. Nothing more is required here than pushing the process state onto the agent:

```
defp do_terminate(state) do
  GraphCompute.State.update(state)
end
```

This should almost be enough. We've recreated the process and the state to go with that process. But there is one more thing we need to take care of—the graph. Our graph has both a node set and an edge set, and any new node will necessarily fall outside both of those sets. That is, it will fall outside the graph. We'll need to fix that.

Recovering the Graph

Let's recap our scenario here. We have a node process terminated for some reason and recreated by the supervisor. We also managed to restore the state to that node process. But the process is now running with a new PID. So the process is under supervision but is outside of our process graph structure.

We need a few things to deal with this. We have to remember the old PID that it was running under before it crashed, and then with the old PID and the new PID, we can use the Graph.replace_vertex/3 function to update the process graph itself as:

```
iex> pg = Graph.replace_vertex(pg, old_pid, new_pid)
```

But we don't want to have to do this by hand. We'll want to do this when a new process is initiated.

Caching Old and New PIDs

The first problem to address is managing the old_pid and the new_pid. We can get hold of the new_pid (or PID) at process create time by calling self/0, and we can store that PID in a :pid field. We can also get hold of the old_pid from the stored process state using the :old_pid field or nil if there is no previous PID, and we then store that PID in the :old_pid field:

```
defp do_init() do
  Process.flag(:trap_exit, true)

  state = GraphCompute.State.get()
  new_pid = self()
```

```
    old_pid = Map.get(state, :pid)
    state = Map.put(state, :pid, new_pid)
    state = Map.put(state, :old_pid, old_pid)

    {:ok, state}
end
```

Good. We've managed the old and new PIDs. We now need to swap them over in the graph. Let's see one way to do that.

Storing the Process Graph

We can use an agent to store the process graph. So we'll set up a new module GraphCompute.Graph as we saw in Agents, on page 229.

We can then call it when we create a new process graph pg by adding this:

```
iex> pg = GraphCompute.Graph.update(pg)
```

And when a process transitions to a new PID, we can call this sequence:

```
iex> pg = Graph.replace_vertex(GraphCompute.Graph.get(), old_pid, new_pid)
GraphCompute.Graph.update(pg)
```

Let's add that now into our do_init/0 function, taking care to pattern match that our agent returns a valid graph structure:

```
apps/graph_compute/lib/graph_compute/process.ex
defp do_init() do
  Process.flag(:trap_exit, true)

  state = GraphCompute.State.get()
  new_pid = self()
  old_pid = Map.get(state, :pid)
  state = Map.put(state, :pid, new_pid)
  state = Map.put(state, :old_pid, old_pid)

➤  with %Graph{} = graph <- GraphCompute.Graph.get() do
      GraphCompute.Graph.update(
          Graph.replace_vertex(graph, old_pid, new_pid)
      )
  end

  {:ok, state}
end
```

So now we've not only restored the process node state but also restored the process node graph.

Simulating a Network

Let's get an example NativeGraph graph.

We previously stored an example of the early ARPANET—see Rendering with OmniGraffle, on page 51. This would make a good candidate.

Although ARPANET may not have been built specifically to survive a nuclear attack, it was still designed to be resilient in the event of network losses and to reroute traffic as required. This small simulation here will aim to demonstrate a similar survivability of a network against inflicted outages.

Let's start off with this small ARPANET graph:

```
iex> arpa = NativeGraph.Examples.Arpa.arpa
#Graph<type: undirected, vertices: [:sri, :ucla, :ucsb, :utah, :sri_h1,
 :ucla_h1, :ucsb_h1, :utah_h1], edges: [:sri <-> :ucla, :sri <-> :ucsb, :sri
 <-> :utah, :sri <-> :sri_h1, :ucla <-> :ucsb, :ucla <-> :ucla_h1, :ucsb <->
 :ucsb_h1, :utah <-> :utah_h1]>
```

This is a simple undirected graph with atoms for nodes. Let's now create a new graph with processes for nodes on the back of this graph. We'll import the GraphCompute.ProcessGraph module to save on typing:

```
iex> import GraphCompute.ProcessGraph
GraphCompute.ProcessGraph
```

We then bring up the process graph as:

```
iex> pg = arpa |> graph_up
#Graph<type: directed, vertices: [#PID<0.513.0>, #PID<0.510.0>,
#PID<0.506.0>, ...], edges: [#PID<0.506.0> -> #PID<0.510.0>,
#PID<0.506.0> -> #PID<0.509.0>, #PID<0.506.0> -> #PID<0.507.0>, ...]>
```

This process graph is a regular graph built using libgraph and can be inspected and manipulated with the standard libgraph library functions:

```
iex> Graph.vertices(pg) |> Enum.sort
[#PID<0.506.0>, #PID<0.507.0>, #PID<0.508.0>, #PID<0.509.0>, #PID<0.510.0>,
 #PID<0.511.0>, #PID<0.512.0>, #PID<0.513.0>]

 iex> Graph.edges(pg) |> Enum.sort
 [
   %Graph.Edge{label: nil, v1: #PID<0.506.0>, v2: #PID<0.507.0>, weight: 1},
   %Graph.Edge{label: nil, v1: #PID<0.506.0>, v2: #PID<0.508.0>, weight: 1},
   %Graph.Edge{label: nil, v1: #PID<0.506.0>, v2: #PID<0.509.0>, weight: 1},
   %Graph.Edge{label: nil, v1: #PID<0.506.0>, v2: #PID<0.510.0>, weight: 1},
   ...
   %Graph.Edge{label: nil, v1: #PID<0.509.0>, v2: #PID<0.513.0>, weight: 1}
 ]
```

All these nodes are processes, and moreover, they are supervised processes. This means we can discover these processes from the supervisor's point of view:

```
iex> Supervisor.which_children(GraphCompute.DynamicSupervisor)
[
  {:undefined, #PID<0.506.0>, :worker, [GraphCompute.Process]},
  {:undefined, #PID<0.507.0>, :worker, [GraphCompute.Process]},
  {:undefined, #PID<0.508.0>, :worker, [GraphCompute.Process]},
  ...
  {:undefined, #PID<0.513.0>, :worker, [GraphCompute.Process]}
]
```

We can also inspect a given process:

```
iex> get_state(pid(0,506,0))
%{id: :sri, old_pid: nil, pid: #PID<0.506.0>}
```

This nil value for old_pid shows that this is a new process and has no history.

Let's exit this process and see what happens. We send an exit signal with the reason :stop, which the process callbacks will handle:

```
iex> Process.exit(pid(0,506,0), :stop)
true

iex> Supervisor.which_children(GraphCompute.DynamicSupervisor)
[
  {:undefined, #PID<0.507.0>, :worker, [GraphCompute.Process]},
  {:undefined, #PID<0.508.0>, :worker, [GraphCompute.Process]},
  {:undefined, #PID<0.509.0>, :worker, [GraphCompute.Process]},
  ...
  {:undefined, #PID<0.523.0>, :worker, [GraphCompute.Process]}
]
```

Here we've exited #PID<0.506.0> which was then recreated as #PID<0.523.0>. If we inspect this process, we can now see that it has captured the previous PID, #PID<0.506.0>:

```
iex> get_state(pid(0,523,0))
%{id: :sri, old_pid: #PID<0.506.0>, pid: #PID<0.523.0>}
```

So, this is good. The supervision tree holds. A new process was created for the stopped process. But what about the graph? Let's fetch our updated graph back from the GraphCompute.Graph agent:

```
iex> pg1 = GraphCompute.Graph.get
#Graph<type: directed, vertices: [#PID<0.513.0>, #PID<0.510.0>,
#PID<0.511.0>, ...], edges: [#PID<0.509.0> -> #PID<0.513.0>,
#PID<0.507.0> -> #PID<0.511.0>, #PID<0.507.0> -> #PID<0.508.0>, ...]>
```

Now let's inspect that graph:

```
iex> Graph.vertices(pg1) |> Enum.sort
[#PID<0.507.0>, #PID<0.508.0>, #PID<0.509.0>, #PID<0.510.0>, #PID<0.511.0>,
 #PID<0.512.0>, #PID<0.513.0>, #PID<0.523.0>]
```

```
iex> Graph.edges(pg1) |> Enum.sort
[
  %Graph.Edge{label: nil, v1: #PID<0.507.0>, v2: #PID<0.508.0>, weight: 1},
  ...
  %Graph.Edge{label: nil, v1: #PID<0.523.0>, v2: #PID<0.507.0>, weight: 1},
  %Graph.Edge{label: nil, v1: #PID<0.523.0>, v2: #PID<0.508.0>, weight: 1},
  %Graph.Edge{label: nil, v1: #PID<0.523.0>, v2: #PID<0.509.0>, weight: 1},
  %Graph.Edge{label: nil, v1: #PID<0.523.0>, v2: #PID<0.510.0>, weight: 1}
]
```

We can see from the vertices/1 listing that the graph now has the new process
#PID<0.523.0> as a graph node and the old node #PID<0.506.0> has been removed.
Also, the edges/1 listing shows that the #PID<0.523.0> node is linked to the same
nodes that the #PID<0.523.0> node was previously linked to. It looks like our
graph is intact.

At this point, it's probably more helpful to view this with the Erlang Observer
tool that ships with Elixir. Let's open that up:

```
iex> :observer.start
```

Go to the Observer window and select the "Applications" tab from the menu
bar. Then from the list of applications displayed on the left-hand side, choose
graph_compute and double-click on that. You should see something like the
screenshot shown in the following figure. (If nothing is displayed, it may be
that you need to force a screen redraw, for example, by altering the window
size or toggling the tabs.)

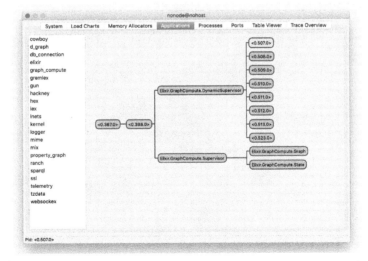

The first thing to note here is that there are two supervision trees: the dynamic
tree for process graph nodes and the static tree for graph and node state.

You can double-click any of the processes shown, and from the "Process Info" pane, you can select the "State" tab from the menu bar to see the state stored in that process. For example, by clicking on the highlighted process, we can inspect the state for that process as shown in this next screenshot.

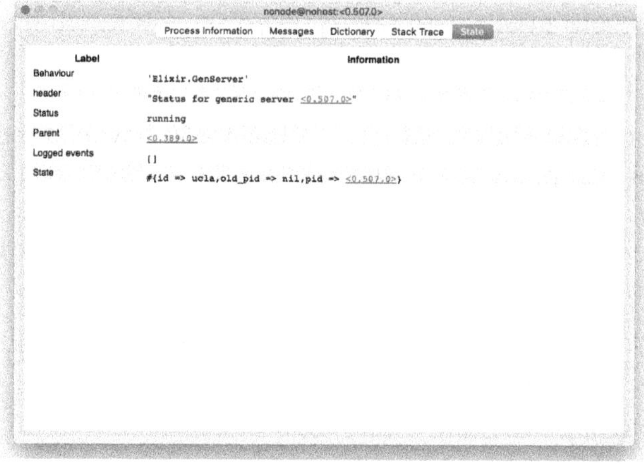

We can see the original values, especially the PIDs with the old_pid showing as nil and the pid showing as <0.507.0>.

To exit a process, close the window to go back to the "Applications" view and right-click over the process name and a menu will pop up. If we select the "Kill process" option, this will bring up an input asking for the reason to terminate.

The default reason is kill, which will bypass the terminate/2 callback. That's not our intention here. Let's try something else—for example, stop. The following screenshot shows the input asking for the reason to terminate and our stop reason.

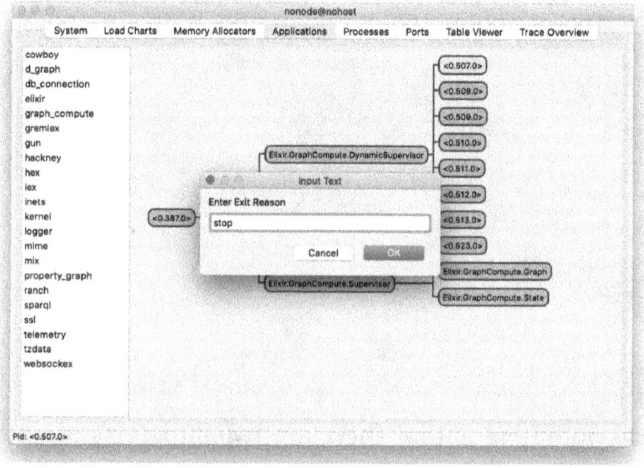

This message is passed on to the terminate/2 callback, which takes care of saving the node process state and its PID value <0.507.0> to the agent process. It then starts a new process with PID <0.1152.0> and assigns the state from the agent process to that new process.

In the next screenshot, we can see a new process <0.1152.0> under the DynamicSupervisor which is named with the new PID.

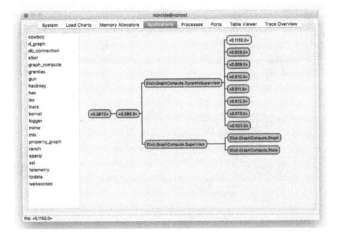

If we now inspect the new process state, as shown in the following screenshot, we can see the updated values, especially the PIDs with the old_pid showing as <0.507.0> and the pid showing as <0.1152.0>.

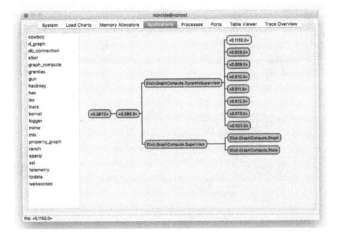

These are the same values we get when using the get_state/0 function:

```
iex> get_state(pid(0,1152,0))
%{old_pid: #PID<0.507.0>, id: :ucla, pid: #PID<0.1152.0>}
```

One other thing to look at in passing is the saved graph state. If you go back to the graph_compute application under the "Applications" view and then double-click the Elixir.GraphCompute.State process button under the static tree, you can see the saved graph state. Not pretty, but it's all in there as this last screenshot shows.

This exercise has shown that a source graph can be mapped to a process graph and its state preserved across the spawning of new processes. The state here is any Elixir term used as the node ID in the source graph and that could carry much more information via a more complex data structure. Note also that we didn't handle labels yet, although these would be simple to map over to the new process graph. And if we wanted to also add in edge attributes, we could bring up some processes for managing edges as discussed earlier.

This is only intended as an example, and we've made no effort to test the viability of this approach for larger graphs. This is a proof of concept—activating the graph by adding processes to the nodes (and to the edges if required), and then putting those under supervision.

But the real thing that we haven't explored here is graph compute capability. That would be fun to play with. We've set up the processes, but haven't specified any action beyond lifecycle support. The next steps here could be to run up some simple applications over this network, for example, message passing and capturing the message in the process node state. But I'm sure you'll all have much better ideas on how to work this up than I do.

Wrapping Up

Well, we've come quite a way in this book. We started off with graphs and ended up with Elixir processes.

We've looked at native libraries (:digraph, and :libgraph) for building graph structures in Elixir. We've interacted with graph databases using a number of packages (:bolt_sips, :sparql_client, :gremlex, and :dlex). And we've tried our hand at a couple of extended applications. We've queried over multiple graph stores and then imported and exported this aggregate graph into and out of different graph databases. We've also run up an OTP supervision tree over some graph structures and played around with that.

There are plenty of things we didn't get to cover in this book—there just wasn't the space. We could have looked at graph algorithms with PropertyGraph models, rules and inference with RDFGraph models, graph visualizations, graph serializations, graph embeddings, and more. We also could have spent more time on the concurrent and distributed side of things.

What we've seen anyway is that graphs are super useful data structures for working with loose sets of data. Graphs excel at providing the joins that typically can be challenging when using relational and other database types. They are also excellent discovery tools as they can literally network data like crazy. And we've also seen that Elixir has a growing number of tools for working with graphs. This can only be a good thing.

So, in closing, only one thing is left to say. Go graphs!

Project Setups

Before setting up a working project, you'll first need to install the graph databases you'll be working with. See Appendix 2, Database Setups, on page 247, for details on where to download the databases from and how to set them up.

The project may be created manually by following along with the descriptions in the book. Code listings are available from the Pragmatic site.[1] Go to their page and follow the instructions or else you can get the download directly from the command line as:

```
$ curl -L -O http://media.pragprog.com/titles/thgraphs/code/thgraphs-code.tgz
$ tar xzf thgraphs-code.tgz
```

There is also a .zip bundle if you prefer that over the .tgz bundle.

Example graphs and queries are included in the bundle.

You'll then cd down into the project directory.

```
$ cd code
```

If you haven't installed all the graph databases, you should take a moment to remove the respective apps.

Right, we've customized our project for the graph databases (if any) we'll be using.

Now you need to install the project dependencies.

```
$ mix deps.get
```

You might also want to configure the IEx startup file .iex.exs:

---

1. https://pragprog.com/titles/thgraphs/source_code

```
import GraphCommons
import GraphCommons.Utils ; alias GraphCommons.Utils

IEx.configure(default_prompt: "%prefix>", alive_prompt: "%prefix>")

GraphCommons.hello()
```

At this point, you should be good to go.

```
$ iex -S mix
Erlang/OTP 24 [erts-12.3.1] ...

Interactive Elixir (1.13.4) - press Ctrl+C to exit (type h() ENTER for help)
This is ExGraphsBook - an Elixir umbrella app:

[:d_graph, :graph_commons, :graph_compute, :native_graph, :property_graph,
 :rdf_graph, :tinker_graph]
iex>
```

Database Setups

This appendix covers download details and some setups for the graph databases we are using in this book.

Here are the databases in order of introduction in this book:

Database	Version	License	Technology
Neo4j Community Edition	4.4.5	GPL v3	Java
GraphDB Free	9.11.1	Ontotext	Java
Gremlin Server	3.6.0	Apache 2.0	Java
Dgraph	20.11.0	Apache 2.0	Go

The version numbers shown here are those used in writing this book.

Installing Neo4j

There are various options for installing a local copy of Neo4j. See the Neo4j Download Center.[1]

You can install native applications with the Neo4j Desktop, which provides its own GUI interface. This may be your preferred solution.

Or you can simply install Neo4j as a standalone server, using either the Community Server or the Enterprise Server edition. In this book, we are using the Community Server for Linux/Mac.

For this, you need to download the Neo4j distribution file and unzip it. You can then execute the startup script which is located in the bin directory of the Neo4j distribution:

```
$ bin/neo4j start
```

---

1. https://neo4j.com/download-center/

The start parameter will run Neo4j as a daemon.

There is also a web browser[2] for interacting with the server. Go to port 7474 on localhost. From here you can query and visualize graphs in the database.

And finally, Neo4j can also be installed as a Docker[3] image. For more details see the Neo4j with Docker[4] page.

Alternate solutions to local installation are to use the Neo4j Sandbox[5] or try out the Neo4j AuraDB[6] cloud service.

Neo4j is free to use but is not open-source software. It's available under a GPL v3 license.

Installing GraphDB

While there are a number of excellent RDF triplestores available, in this book, we've used only one—GraphDB Free from Ontotext.[7]

See the Installation[8] and Quick Start Guide[9] pages for more details. You can download a copy from Ontotext's products page.[10]

The easiest way to set up and run GraphDB is to use one of the native installations provided for the GraphDB Desktop distribution.[11] These come shipped with their own GUI interfaces.

The default way is to install GraphDB as a standalone server. Essentially, you need to download the GraphDB distribution file and unzip it. You can then execute the startup script which is located in the bin directory of the GraphDB distribution:

```
$ bin/graphdb -d
```

The -d flag will run the GraphDB server as a daemon.

2.   http://localhost:7474/
3.   https://www.docker.com/
4.   https://neo4j.com/developer/docker/
5.   https://neo4j.com/sandbox/
6.   https://neo4j.com/cloud/platform/aura-graph-database/
7.   http://graphdb.ontotext.com/documentation/free/
8.   http://graphdb.ontotext.com/documentation/free/installation.html
9.   https://graphdb.ontotext.com/documentation/free/quick-start-guide.html
10. https://www.ontotext.com/products/graphdb/
11. https://graphdb.ontotext.com/documentation/free/run-desktop-installation.html

To admin the server you can bring up the Workbench[12] which is the GraphDB web-based administration tool. This will be at port 7200 on localhost. There are a lot of goodies there, but go to Repositories[13] (under Setup) to create a new repository.

GraphDB can also be installed as a Docker image. For more details see the Docker Hub[14] page.

GraphDB Free is free to use but is not open-source software. It's available under an RDBMS-like free license.

Installing Gremlin Server

Gremlin Server is available from the Apache TinkerPop project.[15]

See the Download Apache TinkerPop[16] page for downloads and the Getting Started[17] page for a walkthrough.

You need to download the Gremlin Server distribution file and unzip it. You can then execute the startup script, which is located in the bin directory of the Gremlin Server distribution:

```
$ bin/gremlin-server.sh start
```

The start parameter will run Gremlin Server as a daemon.

Note that the source code is available if you prefer to build it.

There is also a Gremlin Console distribution for interacting directly with the Gremlin Server. See the Gremlin Console tutorial page[18] for more info.

Gremlin Server is also packaged as a Docker image. And this may be a more convenient option (assuming that you already have Docker installed).

First, get the Docker image:

```
$ docker pull tinkerpop/gremlin-server
```

And then run the Docker image:

```
$ docker run -itd --rm -p 8182:8182 --name gremlin tinkerpop/gremlin-server
```

---

12. http://localhost:7200/
13. http://localhost:7200/repository
14. https://hub.docker.com/r/ontotext/graphdb/
15. http://tinkerpop.apache.org/
16. http://tinkerpop.apache.org/download.html
17. http://tinkerpop.apache.org/docs/current/tutorials/getting-started/
18. https://tinkerpop.apache.org/docs/3.6.0/tutorials/the-gremlin-console/

Gremlin Server is open-source software and is available under an Apache 2.0 license.

Installing Dgraph

Dgraph is available from Dgraph Labs.[19]

For help with installing Dgraph, you should go to the site's Get Started[20] page, or for a tutorial walkthrough, go to the Tour[21] page.

Dgraph no longer supports Windows and Macs directly but instead makes the latest versions of Dgraph available as Docker images. So, you'll need to install Docker first. See the Download page.[22]

Create a folder to store Dgraph data outside of the container:

```
$ mkdir -p ~/dgraph
```

Now get the Docker image:

```
$ docker pull dgraph/standalone
```

And then run the Docker image:

```
$ docker run -itd --rm -p 5080:5080 -p 6080:6080 -p 8080:8080 -p 9080:9080 \
    -p 8000:8000 -v ~/dgraph:/dgraph --name dgraph dgraph/standalone:v21.03.0
```

There is also a standalone server for Linux/Mac which I've installed but it's a bit more cumbersome to use. The Dgraph cluster consists of three different nodes (Zero, Alpha, and Ratel), where each node serves a different purpose. Dgraph Zero controls the Dgraph cluster, Dgraph Alpha hosts predicates and indexes, and Ratel serves the UI for running queries, mutations, and altering the schema.

To access the UI with Dgraph Ratel[23], go to port 8000 on localhost.

An alternative solution to running locally is to use Dgraph Cloud.[24]

Dgraph is open-source software and is available under an Apache 2.0 license.

19. https://dgraph.io/
20. https://dgraph.io/docs/get-started
21. https://dgraph.io/tour/
22. https://dgraph.io/downloads/
23. http://localhost:8000/
24. https://cloud.dgraph.io/

Starting the Databases

It's often easier to have a simple script to restart all services. This is the script I've been using, but you'll need to customize it as appropriate.

apps/graph_commons/priv/scripts/shell/services.sh

```bash
#!/bin/bash

## BOOK

export GRAPHS_HOME=/Users/tony/Projects/graphs

## BOOK - NEO4J

export NEO4J_VERSION=4.4.5
export NEO4J_HOME=${GRAPHS_HOME}/neo4j/neo4j-community-${NEO4J_VERSION}
export NEO4J_CONF=${NEO4J_HOME}/conf
export PATH=${PATH}:$NEO4J_HOME/bin

neo4j restart

## BOOK - GRAPHDB

export GRAPHDB_VERSION=10.0.0
export GRAPHDB_HOME=${GRAPHS_HOME}/graphdb/graphdb-${GRAPHDB_VERSION}
export PATH=${PATH}:$GRAPHDB_HOME/bin

kill -9 `cat ${GRAPHDB_HOME}/pid.txt`
graphdb -d -p ${GRAPHDB_HOME}/pid.txt

## BOOK - GREMLIN

export GREMLIN_VERSION=3.6.0
export GREMLIN_SERVER=apache-tinkerpop-gremlin-server-${GREMLIN_VERSION}
export GREMLIN_SERVER_HOME=${GRAPHS_HOME}/gremlin/${GREMLIN_SERVER}
export PATH=${PATH}:$GREMLIN_SERVER_HOME/bin
gremlin-server.sh restart

## BOOK - DGRAPH

export DGRAPH_HOME=${GRAPHS_HOME}/dgraph

cur_dir=`pwd`
cd $DGRAPH_HOME
dgraph alpha --lru_mb 1024 --graphql_extensions=false &
dgraph zero &
dgraph-ratel &
cd $cur_dir

###
```

Graph Anatomy

Graphs are data models used to manage relationships between things. Or as Wikipedia[1] puts it, graphs are:

> *"... data structures used to model pairwise relations between objects."*

"Objects" here can be any things, or entities if that's a better word for you. And "pairwise relation" simply means some kind of link or connection between a pair of these things (or objects or entities).

Now, in math terms, a *graph* is an ordered pair consisting of a *vertex set* (representing objects) and an *edge set* (representing links between objects), or *G = (V,E)* in the usual math notation, as shown in the following figure.

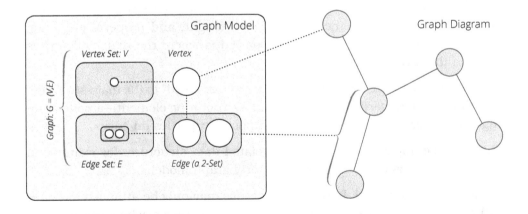

The vertex set is a basic set of vertex objects—vertices. The edge set is a set of edges which themselves are 2-sets, or sets with two members. Each member of an edge is a vertex object. In some cases, the 2-sets are ordered. That is,

---

1. https://en.m.wikipedia.org/wiki/Graph_theory

they form an ordered pair. We then talk about *directed graphs*, or *digraphs*, otherwise, we talk about *undirected graphs*.

Also, while for *simple graphs* the edge set has unique members, in the case of a *multigraph*, the edge set itself is a multiset and allows for duplicate edges. That is, we can have multiple edges between the same vertex pairs.

In the case of *connected graphs*, where each vertex is paired with another, there is a path running through all the vertices. The vertex set may then be unnecessary as all the vertices are contained within the edge set.

Roughly, we can divide the elements of graphs into two main types: structural elements and semantic elements. Let's look at each in turn.

Structural Elements

The graph proper is a set of nodes together with a set of edges relating node pairs and giving rise to paths between any two nodes that are traversable by a sequence of connected edges. The edges may also have an associated directionality depending on whether the graph is directional or not. These elements together constitute the structure or framework of the graph. In a sense, they could be said to define the skeleton on which information elements are added and thus determine the information-bearing capacity.

Semantic Elements

In contrast with the structural elements, the semantic elements provide the information content and include the label, weight, and property elements. How these semantic elements are supported is where the main differences between the various graph models arise.

Semantic elements are typically in some sense "attached" to the main structure. Properties can be regarded as attributes of a structuring element—a node or an edge. Not all graph models, however, support properties on edges.

They may be implemented as an associated data structure, for example, a dictionary. This is the case for the property graph model.

In the RDF graph model, however, properties may only be attached to nodes and are implemented as edge/node spurs on those nodes, where the attached node is a string literal and is a terminus in the graph network and thus not available for onward connections.

So, in a property graph, properties are squirreled away within the graph somehow, while in an RDF graph, properties are represented as an integral part of the graph but are located on the periphery of the graph.

Regardless of the implementation, properties qualify the node (or edge) to which they are attached.

Bibliography

[HN19]   Amy E. Hodler and Mark Needham. *Graph Algorithms*. O'Reilly & Associates, Inc., Sebastopol, CA, 2019.

[IT19]   James Edward Gray, II and Bruce A. Tate. *Designing Elixir Systems with OTP*. The Pragmatic Bookshelf, Raleigh, NC, 2019.

[Tat18]   Ben Marx, José Valim, Bruce Tate. *Adopting Elixir*. The Pragmatic Bookshelf, Raleigh, NC, 2018.

[WW18]   Bruce Williams and Ben Wilson. *Craft GraphQL APIs in Elixir with Absinthe*. The Pragmatic Bookshelf, Raleigh, NC, 2018.

Index

Thank you!

We hope you enjoyed this book and that you're already thinking about what you want to learn next. To help make that decision easier, we're offering you this gift.

Head on over to https://pragprog.com right now, and use the coupon code BUYANOTHER2022 to save 30% on your next ebook. Offer is void where prohibited or restricted. This offer does not apply to any edition of the *The Pragmatic Programmer* ebook.

And if you'd like to share your own expertise with the world, why not propose a writing idea to us? After all, many of our best authors started off as our readers, just like you. With up to a 50% royalty, world-class editorial services, and a name you trust, there's nothing to lose. Visit https://pragprog.com/become-an-author/ today to learn more and to get started.

We thank you for your continued support, and we hope to hear from you again soon!

The Pragmatic Bookshelf

Real-Time Phoenix

Give users the real-time experience they expect, by using Elixir and Phoenix Channels to build applications that instantly react to changes and reflect the application's true state. Learn how Elixir and Phoenix make it easy and enjoyable to create real-time applications that scale to a large number of users. Apply system design and development best practices to create applications that are easy to maintain. Gain confidence by learning how to break your applications before your users do. Deploy applications with minimized resource use and maximized performance.

Stephen Bussey
(326 pages) ISBN: 9781680507195. $45.95
https://pragprog.com/book/sbsockets

Designing Elixir Systems with OTP

You know how to code in Elixir; now learn to think in it. Learn to design libraries with intelligent layers that shape the right data structures, flow from one function into the next, and present the right APIs. Embrace the same OTP that's kept our telephone systems reliable and fast for over 30 years. Move beyond understanding the OTP functions to knowing what's happening under the hood, and why that matters. Using that knowledge, instinctively know how to design systems that deliver fast and resilient services to your users, all with an Elixir focus.

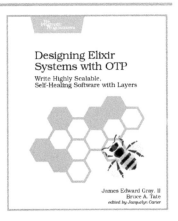

James Edward Gray, II and Bruce A. Tate
(246 pages) ISBN: 9781680506617. $41.95
https://pragprog.com/book/jgotp

Programming Ecto

Languages may come and go, but the relational
database endures. Learn how to use Ecto, the premier
database library for Elixir, to connect your Elixir and
Phoenix apps to databases. Get a firm handle on Ecto
fundamentals with a module-by-module tour of the
critical parts of Ecto. Then move on to more advanced
topics and advice on best practices with a series of
recipes that provide clear, step-by-step instructions
on scenarios commonly encountered by app developers.
Co-authored by the creator of Ecto, this title provides
all the essentials you need to use Ecto effectively.

Darin Wilson and Eric Meadows-Jönsson
(242 pages) ISBN: 9781680502824. $45.95
https://pragprog.com/book/wmecto

Craft GraphQL APIs in Elixir with Absinthe

Your domain is rich and interconnected, and your API
should be too. Upgrade your web API to GraphQL,
leveraging its flexible queries to empower your users,
and its declarative structure to simplify your code.
Absinthe is the GraphQL toolkit for Elixir, a functional
programming language designed to enable massive
concurrency atop robust application architectures.
Written by the creators of Absinthe, this book will help
you take full advantage of these two groundbreaking
technologies. Build your own flexible, high-performance
APIs using step-by-step guidance and expert advice
you won't find anywhere else.

Bruce Williams and Ben Wilson
(302 pages) ISBN: 9781680502558. $47.95
https://pragprog.com/book/wwgraphql

Modern Front-End Development for Rails, Second Edition

Improve the user experience for your Rails app with rich, engaging client-side interactions. Learn to use the Rails 7 tools and simplify the complex JavaScript ecosystem. It's easier than ever to build user interactions with Hotwire, Turbo, and Stimulus. You can add great front-end flair without much extra complication. Use React to build a more complex set of client-side features. Structure your code for different levels of client-side needs with these powerful options. Add to your toolkit today!

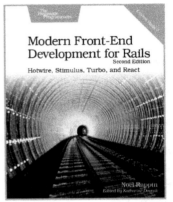

Noel Rappin
(408 pages) ISBN: 9781680509618. $55.95
https://pragprog.com/book/nrclient2

Build a Binary Clock with Elixir and Nerves

Want to get better at coding Elixir? Write a hardware project with Nerves. As you build this binary clock, you'll build in resiliency using OTP, the same libraries powering many commercial phone switches. You'll attack complexity the way the experts do, using a layered approach. You'll sharpen your debugging skills by taking small, easily verified steps toward your goal. When you're done, you'll have a working binary clock and a good appreciation of the work that goes into a hardware system. You'll also be able to apply that understanding to every new line of Elixir you write.

Frank Hunleth and Bruce A. Tate
(106 pages) ISBN: 9781680509236. $29.95
https://pragprog.com/book/thnerves

Program Management for Open Source Projects

Every organization develops a bureaucracy, and open source projects are no exception. When your structure is intentional and serves the project, it can lead to a successful and predictable conclusion. But project management alone won't get you there. Take the next step to full program management. Become an expert at facilitating communication between teams, managing schedules and project lifecycle, coordinating a process for changes, and keeping meetings productive. Make decisions that get buy-in from all concerned. Learn how to guide your community-driven open source project with just the right amount of structure.

Ben Cotton
(190 pages) ISBN: 9781680509243. $35.95
https://pragprog.com/book/bcosp

Build Talking Apps for Alexa

Voice recognition is here at last. Alexa and other voice assistants have now become widespread and mainstream. Is your app ready for voice interaction? Learn how to develop your own voice applications for Amazon Alexa. Start with techniques for building conversational user interfaces and dialog management. Integrate with existing applications and visual interfaces to complement voice-first applications. The future of human-computer interaction is voice, and we'll help you get ready for it.

Craig Walls
(388 pages) ISBN: 9781680507256. $47.95
https://pragprog.com/book/cwalexa

Python Testing with pytest, Second Edition

Test applications, packages, and libraries large and small with pytest, Python's most powerful testing framework. pytest helps you write tests quickly and keep them readable and maintainable. In this fully revised edition, explore pytest's superpowers—simple asserts, fixtures, parametrization, markers, and plugins—while creating simple tests and test suites against a small database application. Using a robust yet simple fixture model, it's just as easy to write small tests with pytest as it is to scale up to complex functional testing. This book shows you how.

Brian Okken
(272 pages) ISBN: 9781680508604. $45.95
https://pragprog.com/book/bopytest2

Pythonic Programming

Make your good Python code even better by following proven and effective pythonic programming tips. Avoid logical errors that usually go undetected by Python linters and code formatters, such as frequent data look-ups in long lists, improper use of local and global variables, and mishandled user input. Discover rare language features, like rational numbers, set comprehensions, counters, and pickling, that may boost your productivity. Discover how to apply general programming patterns, including caching, in your Python code. Become a better-than-average Python programmer, and develop self-documented, maintainable, easy-to-understand programs that are fast to run and hard to break.

Dmitry Zinoviev
(150 pages) ISBN: 9781680508611. $26.95
https://pragprog.com/book/dzpythonic

The Pragmatic Bookshelf

The Pragmatic Bookshelf features books written by professional developers for professional developers. The titles continue the well-known Pragmatic Programmer style and continue to garner awards and rave reviews. As development gets more and more difficult, the Pragmatic Programmers will be there with more titles and products to help you stay on top of your game.

Visit Us Online

This Book's Home Page
https://pragprog.com/book/thgraphs
Source code from this book, errata, and other resources. Come give us feedback, too!

Keep Up to Date
https://pragprog.com
Join our announcement mailing list (low volume) or follow us on twitter @pragprog for new titles, sales, coupons, hot tips, and more.

New and Noteworthy
https://pragprog.com/news
Check out the latest pragmatic developments, new titles and other offerings.

Save on the ebook

Save on the ebook versions of this title. Owning the paper version of this book entitles you to purchase the electronic versions at a terrific discount.

PDFs are great for carrying around on your laptop—they are hyperlinked, have color, and are fully searchable. Most titles are also available for the iPhone and iPod touch, Amazon Kindle, and other popular e-book readers.

Send a copy of your receipt to support@pragprog.com and we'll provide you with a discount coupon.

Contact Us

Online Orders:	*https://pragprog.com/catalog*
Customer Service:	*support@pragprog.com*
International Rights:	*translations@pragprog.com*
Academic Use:	*academic@pragprog.com*
Write for Us:	*http://write-for-us.pragprog.com*
Or Call:	+1 800-699-7764

CPSIA information can be obtained
at www.ICGtesting.com
Printed in the USA
JSHW052357041122
32637JS00002B/6